NARRATING THE OTHER

NARRATING THE OTHER
Australian literary perceptions of Japan

by Megumi Kato

MONASH UNIVERSITY PRESS
CLAYTON

Monash University Press
Building 11
Monash University
Victoria 3800, Australia
www.monash.edu.au/mai

All Monash University Press publications are subject to double blind peer review

© Megumi Kato 2008

National Library of Australia Cataloguing-in-Publication entry:

Author: Kato, Megumi, 1960-
Title: Narrating the other : Australian literary perceptions of Japan / Megumi Kato.
Publisher: Clayton, Vic. : Monash Asia Institute, 2008.
ISBN: 9781876924591 (pbk.)

Notes: Bibliography.
Subjects: Australian literature--History and criticism.
        Japanese in literature.
        Japan--In literature.
        Australia--Relations--Japan.
        Japan--Relations--Australia.
        Japan--Civilization.

Other Authors/Contributors:
        Monash University. Monash Asia Institute.

Dewey Number: A820.93580952

Cover design by Jenny Hall.
Printed by BPA Print Group, Melbourne, Australia - www.bpabooks.com

contents

	Preface	vii
	Introduction	1
Part One	**Early contact and impressions**	11
Chapter one	Contact, Impressions and Premonitions	13
Chapter two	Short Stories, Serials and 'Invasion Novels' of Early Period from the 1880s to the Second World War	33
Part Two	**War-Time Encounters with the Japanese**	51
Chapter three	Fiction of the 1930s and the Pacific War	53
Chapter four	Prisoner-of-War Narratives in the 1940s and 1950s	73
Chapter five	Narratives of the Cowra Breakout and the Occupation Force Experiences	95
Part Three	**Post-Second World War to the 1990s**	117
Chapter six	New Writing on Japan from the 1950s to the 1970s	119
Chapter seven	Reflections on the Pacific War since the 1960s	139
Chapter eight	Writing in a Multicultural Context since the 1980s and the 1990s	165
	Conclusion	189
	Endnotes	199
Appendix	Chronology	205
	Glossary	213
	Bibliography	215

About the Author

Megumi Kato was born in Saitama, Japan. She graduated from Tsuda College, Tokyo, with a Bachelor of Arts, and a Master of Arts in English. In 2005, Megumi received her PhD from the University of New South Wales at the Australian Defence Force Academy in Canberra, where she was also awarded the Ria de Groot Prize for the best female postgraduate research student graduating from UNSW@ADFA. She has published numerous articles, including 'The Scared Who Want to Scare: Fear of a Japanese Invasion in Australian Literature' in *Complicities: Connections and Divisions, Perspectives on Literatures and Cultures of the Asia-Pacific Region* (Peter Lang 2003), and 'Typical Evil?: The Japanese Represented in Australian War Writings' in *Beyond Good And Evil?: Essays on the Literature and Culture of the Asia-Pacific Region* (University of Western Australia Press, 2005). She has translated several books and articles into Japanese, including Sally Morgan's *My Place* published in Japan in 1992. Megumi currently teaches at Meisei University in Tokyo.

preface

This book is based on my PhD thesis, 'Representations of Japan and Japanese People in Australian Literature', which was submitted to the University of New South Wales at the Australian Defence Force Academy, Canberra in 2005.

Until the mid-20th century, Japan and the Japanese were very much alien concepts to most Australians. This book examines how these alien concepts were described and represented in Australian literature. While I have tried to be objective in my approach the reader is asked to bear in mind the following:

First, as an external, non-Australian Japanese researcher, one needs to consider whether my views are fair and balanced. While every effort has been made to examine works with an unbiased and fair attitude, by casting a critical eye on both the writers and their writings and the possible motives for those writings, have I managed to avoid falling into the trap of providing explanations and excuses for the 'Other', in this case the Japanese? Or have I been too critical of 'Orientalist' viewpoints? At the same time, because of my position as a reader of 'Australian literature', have the ways in which I have examined the various works contained too much understanding and acceptance of the Australian/Western discourse in describing the Japanese, and not enough dispassionate analysis? While I have tried to minimize such possibilities, as in the works themselves, either of these biases is possible.

Second, is it meaningful to single out the Japanese, rather than more inclusive groupings such as Asians in general, for such detailed consideration? When the world is considered (by some) to have become a borderless and diverse place, is there any real meaning or significance in giving Japan the role of a unique subject in Australian literature?

Third, and related to the second point above, is the problem of 'nationhood'. Unlike China and Chinese people, Japan and the Japanese are often thought of (and described) as a monolithic entity, of being one and the same. The mobility of Chinese people and their flexibility in interacting with the outer world has meant the nation and the people are not always seen as one and the same. In this sense, Chinese people may have been portrayed on a more individual basis, more often given names and faces by Australians than the Japanese. While it is beyond the scope of this book to explore the differences between Australian perceptions of Japan and of other nations such as China, comparative research would provide valuable insights into such cultural contacts and interactions.

Fourth, and finally, reciprocal studies of Japanese images of Australia and Australians would add a very important dimension to what has been attempted in this book. A comparison between the two countries and their respective images would be valuable to our understanding of the history of contact and interaction between Japan and Australia. By clarifying the similarities and differences in such descriptions, we would be able to have better views of the present and perhaps future relationship between these two countries.

Acknowledgments

As an external, part-time, international student with fulltime teaching and administrative responsibilities in Japan, writing a doctoral thesis and transforming that thesis into a book, was only possible with the help, support, kindness and generosity of many people.

First and foremost I am deeply grateful to my supervisor Professor Bruce Bennett at ADFA@UNSW, for his guidance, intellectual supervision, encouragement and patience. Bruce and his wife Trish's warm hospitality during my twice-a-year stays in Canberra often extended to include my family, and I am grateful for their kindness and moral support. I also wish to express my gratitude to Dr Adrian Caesar, for his advice and assistance while he was my co-supervisor between 1996 and 2002.

To Dr Mark Radford, I am grateful for his patience and guidance in reading all my draft chapters and giving many helpful comments and suggestions. I obtained the original idea for this thesis when Mark gave me a copy of *Slaves of the Samurai* by W Kent Hughes, his great uncle. Since my first visit to Australia in 1982, Professor Anthony and Robin Radford and the Radford family helped me understand Australia and its people in a very special way that guided much of my subsequent thinking and interaction with my research subject.

My gratitude also goes to Associate Professor Robin Gerster for his advice since his time in Japan as a visiting professor of Australian Studies at Tokyo University. It was Robin who suggested I send my manuscript to Monash University Press, for which I am deeply grateful.

I also wish to express my gratitude to the following people: to the academic and administrative staff of both the Australian Defence Force Academy and Meisei University; to the library staff at the University of New South Wales, Australian Defence Force Academy, the National Library of Australia (including the Asian Collection), La Trobe University and Meisei University; to the staff at the Australia–Japan Foundation and its library; to Professor Dennis Haskell for inviting me to the conferences at the University of Western Australia, and his generous and insightful comments on my thesis; to Professor Peter Pierce for his kind and helpful comments; to Dr Roger Bourke who generously gave me open access to his PhD thesis; to Dr Ouyang Yu for giving me permission to read his PhD thesis; to Dr Lyn Jacobs, who was my tutor at Flinders University from 1982 to 1983, for showing me her detailed bibliography; to Professor Kateryna Longley for giving me access to Dr Dai Yin's PhD thesis; to the members of the Australia–New Zealand Literary Society of Japan and the Australian Studies Association of Japan for their encouragement and intellectual guidance; to my colleagues in the Faculty of Japanese Culture and General Education (Meisei University) for their intellectual stimulation, friendship and support; to Professor Aiko Utsumi, Dr Mayumi Kamada, Dr Keiko Tamura and Dr Sayoko Iizasa for including me in their research circle and encouraging me all the way; to Emma Hegarty and Jenny Hall, my editors, for their confidence, help and support in transforming my manuscript into a book; to the many people whom I met at conferences and on other occasions for their generous comments and encouragement.

Finally, I would like to thank my parents, Motohiko and Yoshiko Toyoizumi, and my parents-in-law, Fumiaki and Michi Kato, for their understanding and support; and my family, Shigeaki and Sali, for their sacrifice, patience and support over the years I have spent following my research dreams.

During the course of this research I was supported by a number of grants. In particular I would like to acknowledge the following: Grant-in-Aid for Young Scientists, Ministry of Education of Japan, 1997–1998; Grant-in-Aid for Exploratory Research, Ministry of Education, Culture, Sports, Science and Technology of Japan, 2000–2001;

Suntory Foundation Research Grant, 2001–2002; Grant-in-Aid for Scientific Research, Japan Society for the Promotion of Science, 2004–2005; and the Risona Asia-Oceania Foundation Research Grant, 2005.

Introduction

As early as 1831, more than 20 years before Japan opened its doors to the world, Australia and Japan experienced their first cross-cultural contact, an encounter full of mutual misunderstandings, trials and errors. When the Australian whaler, *Lady Rowena,* was badly damaged during a storm in the North of Japan under the command of Captain Bourn Russell, its crew evacuated and landed on the east coast of the northern island of Hokkaido. For the first recorded time, Australians encountered the Japanese on Japanese soil.[1] It was a time when Australia, together with many other European countries, looked at the Pacific as a region of opportunity. But it was also a time when Japan was still closed to outside contact. Japan's isolationist policy kept it apart from its neighbours and the international community. Heavy punishment was inflicted on both Japanese and non-Japanese alike who broke this isolationist policy. In such an environment of stress and mistrust and without formal communication channels, both parties tried to push their own ideas and ways on the other by means of gestures, bartering and finally force.

Eventually, after managing to finish its repairs, the *Lady Rowena* was able to depart from the coast of Hokkaido and Japan, leaving both sides no better off in their knowledge of each other and probably a good deal more frustrated and distrustful.

Before he left Japan, Captain Russell sent a letter to the Emperor of Japan asking him to recognise the potential power and advancement of Europe and to open the nation to them. There is no record that this letter actually was read, or that it even reached the Emperor, or the Shogun, who was the effective military ruler of the time. This incident shows how difficult it is to display tolerance and reach an understanding when encountering a 'different other' for the first time.[2] It also provides a glimpse of what was to become one of the patterns of interactions between Australians and Japanese over the next 150 years.

Since that first contact by Captain Russell and his crew, how have Australians perceived Japan and the Japanese? Historically, the relationship between Australia and Japan has been one of drama and extremes. The two countries were virtually unknown to each other in the 19th century. By the beginning of the 20th century these countries had become 'hesitant' allies. In the 1940s, they had moved from 'hesitant allies' to 'true enemies'. After their real clash as 'true enemies', they became 'best' business partners, albeit with some degree of woe and misfortune underlying an otherwise smooth relationship.

A complication in the Australia–Japan relationship has been the definition of Australia itself. Captain Russell was an Englishman. Since that time Australia's own identity has been elusive and changing. Its history of colonisation, federation and a possible future as a republic, combined with its own internal demographic changes and its political, diplomatic, military and economic orientations, have formed the basis of how Australians look at the other countries and people. This way of 'looking' has often been closely related to a shift in Australian society during each phase of its history. As Spivak suggests, it would:

> not be possible to read 19th century British literature without remembering that imperialism, understood as England's social mission, was a crucial part of the cultural representation of England to the English...[t]he role of literature in the production of cultural representation should not be ignored (Spivak 1995:269).

Australia, on the periphery of the British Empire, identified itself as part of the empire for a long time and many sought to base their cultural heritage there. Naturally, literature of the time reflects aspects of this mentality from the 19th century and earlier. However, because of its own status as a colony and its actual location in the Asia–Pacific region, far from Europe, Australia's position in regard to the 'Other' is different from that of Britain and other European countries. This difference is illustrated to some extent by Dai's comment on how Europe saw the Australian Chinese—'Australia is not absolutely viewed according to the European map...[and] Chinese people seen as an exotic element, are represented in some writings as part of the Australian exoticism' (Dai 1994). This perception of Australia itself seems to have had an influence on Australians' own views of people from other countries, especially Asians.

Since the Second World War, and especially since the 1970s, the boundaries between nations have become less of a barrier, with people crossing frontiers in greater numbers for a greater number of reasons. Meeting those who are different and 'other' is no longer unusual. But with greater cross-national and cross-cultural contact has come the need to understand what happens as a result of this contact: how people interpret and react to the strange and foreign elements they see in other nations and people, both real and virtual, and how this contact reflects upon self-perceptions.

Are people's views of the 'Other' influenced by whether contact is 'friendly' or 'antagonistic', whether the 'Other' is to be 'admired' or 'overcome'? For Australians, as Broinowski points out, 'European history remained a much more important component of their national identity than their Asia–Pacific geography had ever been', and 'all of Asia was more distant and exotic than Europe'. This presents a kind of neo-orientalist framework that Broinowski calls the 'Far East Fallacy', although Asia was strictly speaking Australia's near north (Broinowski 1992:15). It was in these early years of contrast—especially in the late 19th century and the first half of the 20th century—that some of the Japanese stereotypes, true or false, were formed in literature and these stereotypes have persisted through Australian literary history. This is the power of 'repetition', as Said (1985:122) has suggested, by which the 'observed' are reconstructed and repeated within the 'observer's' context. Only occasional literary works, by writers of great insight or humanity, tend to diverge from the stereotypes.

This book traces some of the ways Japan and the Japanese people are described within an Australian literary context. Japan and the Japanese seem obviously 'other', in the sense that Australians regard themselves as fundamentally different to the Japanese historically, traditionally, racially and culturally. Castro (1995:3–4) sees Australia as a nation which is 'constantly in the grip of its own fear and loathing', which 'has had to define itself against others'. Less dramatically, Morris-Suzuki (1998:5) points out that the 'creation of nationhood involves not only the drawing of political frontiers but the development of an image of the nation as a single natural environment or habitat'. Australians perceived and perhaps some may still perceive, a need to guard the coastline of the continent as its frontiers and to keep Asians at bay—physically, psychologically and culturally. In the Australian landscape, Asian characters were not welcomed. The land was guarded in such a manner as to make clear that it did not want them.

The '"yellow peril' myth is the monotonous product of racism', asserts Dai (1994:2) and because of this 'there is not much left for people to say about how Australian literature described Chinese people'. However, by contrast with such a seemingly partial and unbalanced presentation of the 'Other', when examined closely in the case of Australian literature about Japan, there are more complex and contradictory descriptions of the Japanese in the writings of various authors. Even if the creation of unknown Japanese characters is only an imaginative invention, the works included in this book show a versatility of views and literary techniques.

Unlike the visible 'Other' in Australia, especially the Chinese who came during the gold rush years of the mid-19th century, the Japanese as the 'Other' were not so much real as imagined in 19th century Australian writings. They are vividly visible only in imagination. Japanese contract pearl divers and plantation labourers in northern Australia were almost entirely absent from the immediate horizon of most Australians and were seen as less of a threat to the livelihood of Australians than the Chinese on the goldfields. They therefore represented a different kind of exoticism. Such products of imagination are often used in ways that suit the user's purpose. If, as Said (1985:203) suggests, Orientalism is a system or 'a product of certain political forces and activities… [and i]ts objective discoveries…are and always have been conditioned by the fact that its truths, like any truths delivered by language, are embodied in language…', the ways Australians use their 'objective discoveries' of Japan as their 'knowledge' signify their desire or determination about how they want to see, form and represent Japan and her people. Their imagination, concepts, notions and definitions interact with one another, to create a version of a nation called Japan, Japanese culture, Japanese society and Japanese ethnicity within an Australian literary and social context. Thus, to examine how Australians have created their own images of the Japanese and how they have represented such images is not to define the true nature of an 'Other' but to identify the ideas and images of Australians themselves. In other words, by looking at how Australians have differentiated themselves from Japan and the Japanese in their writings, it may be possible to capture glimpses of the transient meanings of 'identity', 'culture' and 'nation' for Australians.

During the first epoch of the Australia–Japan relationship, approximately from the 1880s to the 1920s, there emerged certain stereotypes of the Japanese in Australian writings based on little if any actual physical contact. Japan changed from a young and vulnerable '*mousume*' (girl) to a massive and masculine possible enemy. The composite picture coincides in part with Said's (1985:207) and Dai's (1994:33) observations of orientalism as conceptualised by the West as a mixture of male and female elements. Morris-Suzuki (1998:111) defines these types as: female Japan: 'submissive, delicate and exotic, young and unmarried'; and male Japan: 'modernising, militaristic and menacing'. Because of the different political, diplomatic and economic relationships between Australia and Japan in these early days and such historical events as the formation of the White Australia policy, the Anglo–Japanese Alliance, Japan's military expansion and eventually the First World War, these two quite distinct images and impressions of Japan are projected in many Australian writings.

Although many early visitors from Australia to Japan were not entirely free from Orientalist stereotypes, authors such as James Murdoch, a Scottish-

Australian resident in Japan, and Rosa Praed, one of the few female visiting writers of this early period, managed to break through some of the standard stereotypes of European Australians, thus giving a new dimension in writing about Asian people. While texts are often regarded as products of the time in which they were written and should not be attributed only to the author him/herself, an author's political and ideological stance, sex, and background are sometimes taken into account in the assessment of the texts, as in the cases of Murdoch and Praed. Whether, for example, the author is male or female, military or civilian, democratic or socialist, often seem to have an influence on the way the 'Other' is portrayed.

Besides a few stereotypical Japanese characters, there are certain words and phrases that constantly appear and re-appear in descriptions of Japan and the Japanese in Australian writings. As Broinowski (1992:13) points out, Japan is often regarded as having a 'paradoxical' existence. Kipling, as Broinowski reminds us, was not sure about Japan: 'the Chinaman's a native...but the Jap isn't a native, and he isn't a sahib either'. Japan is 'child or monster, enemy or ally' and in the title of Meaney's (1996a) book, Japan is a 'problem' containing Australian fears and phobias. Japan clearly belongs to Asia, the Orient, the 'Other' which should be observed, manipulated and somehow overcome. However, because of its own imperialism and ambitions to expand and become dominant in the Asia–Pacific—desires that became evident after Japan ceased its policy of seclusion in the mid-19th century—Japan is not an easy 'Other' that could be tamed or subjugated. Moreover, Japan showed its eagerness in introducing European ideas and influences in its own development. It chose to westernise without resistance, a decision different from the normal East–West context of colonised nations and peoples. In Said's (1985:204) formulation, 'Orientalism is fundamentally a political doctrine willed over the Orient because the Orient was *weaker* than the West, which elided the Orient's difference with its *weakness*' [my italics]; however, Japan was not weak enough to be confined in this orientalist basket. Japan took the initiative and westernised itself under its own terms.

Because of the attitudes and behaviour displayed by the Japanese, adjectives like 'arrogant' and 'proud' are often used about them by Australian writers. It seems intolerable for the stereotypical Westerner that the 'Other' should be arrogant. However, from the time of its early military expansion to the present, 'arrogant Japan boasting of its supremacy', is described by authors ranging from Murdoch at the beginning of the 20th century, to the war memoirists during the Second World War in the 1940s and 1950s, to Hal Porter after the war. Japan's apparent self-image of supremacy seems to 'irritate' many Australian authors who believe in their own notion of white supremacy. Thus the bitterness of prisonerhood during the Pacific War is described most vividly, when white men became enslaved by the 'Other', which is perhaps one of the very rare cases in history when the West was enslaved by the East. It is interesting to note that despite its long history of genetic mixing, Japan's early propaganda about its 'racial purity', coincides with Australia's own racialist policy of a 'White Australia'. Such juxtapositions may reveal a strange similarity between a British colony on the periphery of the Empire and a developing non-white nation's yearning to be equal to the world's dominant powers.

'Ignorance' is another word that often appears in describing Japan and the Japanese and this also raises an interesting juxtaposition between Australia and Japan. Especially through the eyes of foreigners visiting Japan in the late 19th and the beginning of the 20th century, it is often emphasised that the Japanese were ignorant, if not indifferent, to world concerns. It is also noted that the Japanese themselves admit their own ignorance, especially about Australia as a part of the West, in their writings (Frei 1991:214). This ignorance of each other seems to be mutual, as both countries have long looked at each other not through direct and practical contact and communication, but rather often through third-party European discourse.

Another characteristic of the representations of Japan and the Japanese in Australian literature has been the concept of 'ambiguity'. Words such as 'ambiguous', 'vague', 'obscure', 'two-edged' and so on are used quite often in the writings. Even the simple 'yes-no' response can be ambiguous in this cross-cultural context and misunderstood as the opposite to what was intended (it has often been noted by visitors to Japan that the Japanese give the affirmative response directly both to the content of the question itself and because the word 'no' sometimes sounds too harsh to utter, especially to seniors). Gerster (1999:92–95) suggests that Japan, as the subject of research and writing, seems to be 'lost' to some authors, because of its two very different positions: one a contemporary first world, business-oriented nation and the other a culturally authentic self. Nobel Laureate Kenzaburo Oe (1995) also points out this ambiguity about Japan, attributing it to Japan's modernisation under Western influence, as well as its simultaneous determination to keep its tradition and culture. The titles of publications on Japan, such as *The emptiness of Japanese affluence* (McCormack 1996) and *Japan swings* (McGregor 1996), also show this perception of a fundamental 'contradiction' in the idea of Japan by present Australian authors.

A number of contemporary books written by foreign authors, in fact, have referred to Japan as 'lost'—for example Alex Kerr's *Lost Japan* (1996) and Alan Booth's *Looking for the lost: journeys through a vanishing Japan* (1996).[3] This state of being 'lost' has applied, in turn, to some Australian authors, who look at Japan with eyes full of romantic illusion, only to be disillusioned by the Japan they actually see. This disillusionment leads to the apparent 'incomprehensibility' of the Japanese, as when a Japanese wife's smile is 'vague' and can not be tolerated by her English husband in Dawe's story at the end of the 19th century; or their depiction as 'obstinate' people after the Pacific War, who did not fit into the conquerors' expectations of the conquered, as can be seen in Porter's novels and stories. During direct contact under the extraordinary and harsh circumstances of war and captivity, many cases of puzzlement or confusion about the enemy or captor are evident and are expressed in writings of the time.

One example of typical Australian treatment of the 'Other' in writings about Asia is shown in the way they put an end to their attraction or affair with the country and her people. Broinowski calls this the 'solution to the complications of "the East"', which most Australians are said to regard as being 'as simple as an air ticket home'. Also according to Broinowski (1992:184), it was only in 1987 that, for the first time in a novel (*Julia Paradise*), an Australian man chose 'the happy ever after' ending with his Asian woman.

However, besides the usual stereotypes and patterns, there were more daring writers, who wrote within, but were not constricted by, the ordinary social contexts, who delved into the 'deviant' or 'unique' 'Other'. Although it is easy to slip into standard forms, such authors refused to conform to the usual archetypes or formulae, but instead developed their own original concepts that allowed new cross-cultural discoveries. This suggests that such authors were able to look at themselves not as powerful and distant spectators but rather as part of the 'Other'. They assumed the ambivalent position of both coloniser and colonised, a historical Australian legacy as part of the Empire, and also as a colony, both geographically and mentally. Such Australians do not remain trapped in a closed standard of European canonical evaluation, but possess more balanced and open views. This is especially so in regard to gender issues, examples of which occur in works of fiction by Rosa Praed, Elizabeth Kata and Ann Nakano, as well as other topics such as class-consciousness and other biases within Australia. One example of such writing is that of Ross Davy, who introduces male homosexual affairs in Japan in his 1985 novel. This may well have been possible because the relationships occurred somewhere other than Australia, somewhere in which the 'normal' constraints of a home society are felt not to apply (Broinowski 1997:184).

The relationship between authors and readers seems to be complicit in creating Japanese images in Australian writings. Authors' choice of topics regarding the 'Other' is influenced by the implied demand of their readers. Such dominant icons as 'Cho-Cho-San'—Madame Butterfly—may have endured because the stereotypes of such stories regarding the 'Other' reinforce popular views and offer order, safety and stability to readers. Despite the fact that he was one of the early Japanologists in the Meiji Era who had direct contact with the Japanese and had much influence on positive Australian thinking on Japan[4], even Murdoch could not resist the temptation of writing novels with a typical western Don Juan theme, or that of Cho-Cho-San, (like 'mousume') who is redeemed by a Western saviour. By placing the Japanese into familiar patterns and categories—doll-like figures in fantasy, or enemies in a possible invasion plot, or 'economic animals' and so on—it becomes easier for authors to appeal to the 'mass' understanding of the 'Other'.

At the same time, the reading audience is given certain images and information about the Japanese, which suit the purposes of some writers. For example, journalist-writers' stories of invasion plots by the Japanese have helped to form an Australian sense of crisis, thus encouraging military conscription and establishment of the National Guard, which in turn has helped to encourage a sense of defensive nationalism.

In other types of writings, authors become mediators between different cultures. They act as an agent, introducer, middleman or interpreter of Japanese culture for an Australian readership. As the one who mediates between the cultures and at times 'crosses over' them, such authors observe or imagine, comprehend or misunderstand, lead or mislead their readers in their journey towards the unknown 'Other', the Japanese. As the title of Anna Broinowski's play *The gap* (1995) reveals, authors can guide their readers (or viewers in a play) to look at and perhaps to cross the 'gap' of ideas, concepts and communication.

Some writers adopt a 'cultural espionage' type of character in their stories. Kencho, a Japanese husband estranged from his Australian wife in Rosa Praed's *Madame Izàn* (1899), is one such character. In *Stepper* (1997), Brian Castro depicts a polyglot character, Stepper, a Russo-German spy acting in war-time Japan, as a freer, more trans-national person who is able to move between cultures for his own (and Russia's) purposes. It is interesting to note that Murdoch, a scholar and writer, also acted as a clandestine agent for Australia, with a mission to visit Japan and meet with diplomats and officials after he became the first Professor of Oriental Studies at the University of Sydney.

The ambiguity and duality of the Japanese people are often compared with their 'true'-selves behind the 'masks', as Porter's collection of essays on postwar Japan, *The Actors*, shows. This work reveals an Australian uncertainty about the Japanese 'Other'; thus the role of 'interpreter' or 'translator' becomes essential.

It becomes especially important in such extreme circumstances as war and captivity, when the middleman or mediator's performance is directly related to the life and death of other people. A middleman—a cultural-go-between—bears the burden of trying to please both sides, often ending up satisfying neither. This may also apply to some authors who try to overcome the confinement of prototypes and break through the ambiguity of the 'Other'. One extreme solution to the problem presented by such middlemen was to annihilate both sides and put an end to the unbearable conflict by killing oneself, as shown in Roger Pulvers' novel, *General Yamashita's treasure* (Japanese translation, 1981; English version, 1994).

By examining the neglected category of Australian literature about Japan and the Japanese, this book tries to see how the mental attitudes towards the 'Other' can also influence Australia's own society. In examining Hage's criticism of multiculturalism in Australia, Foong (1999:10) points out that 'public space is about *affect*' (my emphasis), and that 'words and images have a huge capacity to perform and to wound, and nowhere is this clearer than in the race-based utterances that have been used as a form of incitement'. By examining how images and stereotypes of the Japanese changed, or did not change, as Australian society took its course, how literature contributed to the formation of such images and stereotypes, and how they are influenced by historical incidents and events, certain human tendencies may be uncovered. At the same time, the literature studied may indicate something about what Raymond Williams (1959; 1961) called the 'structures of feeling' in a society—in this case—Australian society at different times.

Commenting on time and literature, David Malouf (1999) says that authors may not survive but the images they created do persist. Kim Scott (1999) points out that imaginative fiction can portray a range and manner of things that merely descriptive social realism cannot. By examining Australian literary works on Japan and the Japanese, this book may play a role in identifying a new dimension of Australian writings. There have been few similar attempts, except in relation to the Chinese (see Ouyang 1994; Dai 1994), in which Australian literary history is examined from a different, 'foreign' perspective. In Cleary's war novel, *The Long Pursuit* (1967), his Australian protagonists came to realise that 'history was just the propaganda of the victors'; if so, it is necessary for us to reconstruct history from many points of view, not only the winner's version.

This book refers mainly to Australian novels and short stories. Prose fiction provides perhaps most scope to explore character, situation and behaviour in cross-cultural relations. However, Castro (1995:27–36) suggests that autobiographies and memoirs may also challenge 'authority and critics', thus giving new dimensions in literature, and so in this light, some war and captivity memoirs are also included. In order to give a reasonably comprehensive picture, some works from popular genres such as thriller and formula romance are also examined in this study, as are occasional plays and poems of significance.

Has the Australian notion of Japan and the Japanese changed over time, or has it remained the same since that first encounter of the *Lady Rowena*? Have the increased opportunities over the last 50 years for both parties to be closer—through air travel and communication technologies—dramatically influenced ideas of the 'Other' and generated broader and more pluralistic views? Has the official policy of multiculturalism worked towards an erasure of typical biases against the 'Other'? Is Orientalist discourse giving way to a more cosmopolitan discourse? There are many voices from Australia's past and present, some loud, some more muted, telling us about the 'other', revealing aspects of both themselves and their society. These voices are both a reflection of the times in which they occur and the individual voices of the authors. They provide us with a historical, geographical and psychological snapshot of a country's changing view of itself and its world.

Part One

Early contact and impressions

chapter one

Contact, impressions and premonitions

In 1853, Commodore Perry forced open the door to Japan. After more than 200 years of self-imposed isolation, Japan became host to an influx of European visitors. An influx long awaited perhaps, by both sides. Diplomatic officers, soldiers and sailors, merchants, academics, teachers, explorers and travellers all went to Japan for many different reasons. They observed, recognised and explored. They sought experiences, opportunities and possibilities. This unknown and exotic 'Far-Eastern' nation became a focus for 'conquest'— economic, educational, political and sexual. This form of Western colonisation had occurred in other Asian countries; however, this time it was different as Japan itself eagerly sought and absorbed the European influence.

At the time, the Japanese government was changing its direction, adjusting the nation to the new reality under such mottoes as 'Fukoku Kyohei' (national prosperity and defence), 'Bunmei Kaika' (civilisation and enlightenment) and 'Datsua Nyu'ow' (de-Asianisation and Westernisation). In order to fulfil its aims, Japan invited many European 'experts' from various fields to provide an introduction to Western scholarship and refinement. Some of these early visitors included the German advisor, Roesler, who prepared the enactment of the Constitution, the French advisor, Boissonade, who helped codify laws, and academics and artists such as J Hepburn, WS Clark and Ernest Fenollosa.[5] These Western specialists stayed not only in the major metropolitan areas but also in other less urban parts of the country. The number of such foreigners soon equalled several thousand. The eagerness of the Japanese to acquire knowledge from the West is revealed in a short article called 'Selling Books' which appeared anonymously in *The Bulletin* in 1904, which described Japan's 'large orders of educational books—history, geography, science—no fiction...[f]acts and figures—dictionaries, encyclopaedias, arithmetics [*sic*]'.

This increase in the number of visitors was soon followed by official records, documents, articles, travel accounts, essays, impressions, notes, sketches, journals and fictional works based on Japan written by Europeans.

Unlike Jonathan Swift and his fictitious episode of Gulliver drifting ashore on an imaginary Japan in 1709, these new writers recreated Japan as a real place for Western readers through their own encounters and experiences. Each piece of writing represented their discoveries; each interestingly coloured with their own backgrounds, personality, prejudices, ideologies, flexibility, capacities and adjustability. Without the need to reflect reality responsibly or accurately in the same manner as newspapermen and diplomats were required to, literary people were free to represent Japan to European readers in any way they wanted. They employed Japanese settings to dramatise their stories and enhance the exotic atmosphere, sometimes by exaggerating or even distorting reality.

One such writer was Pierre Loti from France, who after his salacious voyages to Tahiti and Istanbul, disembarked on the shores of Nagasaki with the expectation of a brief and convenient liaison with a Japanese 'mousumee' (or 'musume', 'musme').[6] Loti's intention was to write another story of the West's adventure in the sensual East—a man's possession of a woman because of her difference, a typical form of dominance in the West–East dichotomy. This form of dominating the 'Other' is clearly seen in Loti's work *Madame Chrysanthème*, which has been the subject of much criticism since the 1970s by Edward Said and other post-colonial critics. Loti's approach to Japan was typical of Western writers during this period, and gave rise to the 'Butterfly Phenomenon' (Broinowski 1992:106), named after *Madame Butterfly* by JL Long (1889). This phenomenon became popular through Puccini's opera (1904) and was associated with being melodramatic, chauvinistic, stereotyped, conventional, tragic, and in some cases vulgar.

Other writers took quite different approaches towards Japan: they observed its people and society from a less condescending and more sympathetic point of view. One such writer was Lafcadio Hearn, who was of Irish-Greek parentage and educated in England. He came to Japan as a journalist in 1890, became an English professor, married a Japanese woman and eventually assumed a Japanese name and became a naturalised citizen. His unprejudiced nature and interest in native cultures had already been observed during his days as a newspaperman in America, when he wrote many articles on the myths and superstitions of Afro-Americans and Creoles. Unlike other writers, Hearn did not write as the 'powerful, ruling one', who boasted his knowledge over the powerless, but rather as the one who tried to observe, learn and even absorb differences between the West and the East. His aim in Japan was to discover what motivated the Japanese as well as their thoughts, ideas, values and religion.[7]

Wenceslau de Moraes (1854–1929), a Portuguese writer who was the first consular representative of his country in Kobe, was also one of the pathfinders of the present so-called 'Japanologists'. During his service from 1898, and even after his discharge from his position because of the revolution in Portugal in 1910, he kept sending his articles, essays and stories on Japan and the Japanese to Portuguese readers. A contemporary of Hearn, Moraes also chose to settle in Japan permanently. Other Westerners stayed in such colonised places as Egypt, India, or Macau—a domain of their own countries where they were able to take full control of almost anything for a certain period for their career or research. However, by staying in Japan, people like Hearn and Moraes were regarded as eccentrics or oddities, and their activities were seen as 'absurd', 'inadmissible', and almost 'suicidal'.[8] Writers like Hearn or Moraes have since been described as suffering from what Broinowski (1892:103) calls the 'Hearn syndrome', where Europeans who were tired of the materialism and corruption of the Western world expected unrealistically to gain inspiration and excitement in Japan.

At this time in history, (late 19th and early 20th century), there were very few Japanese living in Australia, except for places like Broome, Darwin and Thursday Island where plantation workers and pearl divers worked under contract. There were few clear images of the Japanese in Australian writing, unlike the Chinese who had already established their own place in Australian history and society by the end of 19th century. The first consulate of Japan was opened not in Sydney or Melbourne but in Townsville in 1886, for the purpose of protecting the contract workers in the area. By then, about 2,000 such temporary migrants had come to work, mainly in Queensland. Although some interactions did occur during such occasions as the Sydney International Exhibition in 1879 and the Melbourne International Exhibition in 1880, or through business and diplomacy, the Japanese figures in literary works with Australian settings remained limited. Most Australians had never seen a Japanese and would probably not have been able to distinguish a Japanese from a Chinese, just as most Japanese of that time had never seen foreigners and would not have been able to tell the difference between Australians, the British and the Americans. At this time, the Japanese in Australia tended to live far from urbanised Australian locales. They lived in marginal environments, like AB Paterson's (1902) pearl diver Kanzo Makame, who

> was king of his lugger, master and diver in one,
> Diving wherever it pleased him, taking instructions from none,
> Hither and thither he wandered, steering by stars...

and who eventually became a victim of a fellow Japanese diver who abandoned him, and lay dead in the depths of the sea, 'helmeted, ghastly, and swollen'.

By the end of the 19th century, some Australian writers had visited Japan in the course of their travels in Asia. One of the earliest Australian writers was James

Hingston, who decided to include Japan in his world travel to see the wonders of the newly-opened country. After 25 years as a journalist in Melbourne, Hingston took a long vacation and sailed around the world. The outcome of his visit to the major countries of the five continents was *The Australian abroad: branches from the main routes round the world* (1879), published in two volumes. Hingston's visit to Japan seems to have been around 1870, soon after the Meiji Restoration, when he might have witnessed the introduction of telegraphy to Japan, when 'commoners' were allowed to adopt family names, the first girl-students travelled to the United States to study and ex-samurai still carried their swords.

In his published observations of this newly 'discovered' country and its people by the West, Hingston wrote about their diet, physical characteristics and clothes as well as both their fine and popular arts. He also commented upon their differences from other Asians. Hingston was said to have publicly stated that he wrote on any subject, 'not insisting on exactness, so long as he was sure of a reader's attention...People don't want to be instructed and won't be bothered about the truth' (McCrae 1930). How much he exaggerated and dramatised his observations in Japan is not known, yet his writings are filled with first-hand surprises and impressions provided by an unknown people and their society. The 'surprises' he observed included the 'cleanliness' and the 'strength and endurance' of the Japanese and the 'mildness' in everything, from tobacco and food to religion. Such reactions may reflect the biases generally held by contemporary Europeans of the time. As he points out, it was a time when 'educated Englishmen are utilised by the Japs', thus showing the beginning of the cultural, material and emotional interactions between the Japanese and foreigners (McCrae 1930).

Nineteen years after Hingston, Douglas Sladen also visited Japan as a tourist. He stayed there for about seven months and published a book called *The Japs at home* (1892), which he (wrongly) claimed to be the 'first travel book about Japan ever published in England', as well as using the word 'Japs' for the first time in the title of a book (Sladen 1892:preface; 1939:348).[9] Sladen went to Australia after graduating in History from Oxford University. He graduated in Law from Melbourne University and was married in Melbourne. Although he was appointed as the first lecturer in Modern History at Sydney University in 1883, he decided to return to England the next year. He later travelled around the world, visiting countries including Japan. Sladen's direct impressions and thoughts on Japan were first serialised in *The San Francisco Chronicle* before being made into a travel book. It also formed the basis of a novel called *A Japanese Marriage* (1904). Sladen's observations of the Japanese also show the interactions between the Japanese and Western outsiders at the dawn of this relationship, including the painstaking efforts of the Japanese to speak English as a means of Westernisation.

Later, as Romance became fashionable in Australia in the 1880s and 1890s (Dutton 1982:170), and the number of expatriate fiction writers who travelled overseas from Australia increased, more was written about Japan and its people, although for most of these writers, the end destination was England and Europe, not Japan. Some of these writers chose to view Japan in a similar way to their British and European predecessors, with a strong Occidental preconception about how this far-East country should be described and presented. Many saw little difference between the countries in Asia; even those who actually visited them often gave only a hasty summary of what they saw. It was enough for many of them to state that the East was different from the West, and often to simply make a sweeping generalisation about Asia as a whole.

A typical example of a contemporary writer with a strong preconception about the approach of the West to the East was Carlton Dawe. Born in Adelaide, Dawe spent some of his life travelling in Asia before settling in Britain in 1892. Among his prolific publications (more than 70 works over forty years), he wrote stories based on the meeting between West and East in Japanese settings in a number of novels and collections of short stories; examples include *Yellow and White* (1895), *Kakemonos: tales of the Far East* (1897), *A bride of Japan* (1898) and *Rose and chrysanthemum* (1900). Frequently using the first person in his stories, Dawe seems to position himself as a Western writer in the East. He sees himself as an observer of the strange and incomprehensible; an explorer, adventurer and sometimes intruder upon Oriental mysteries. He is an informant of the differences between West and East, and his position as well as his Western characters' is that of a transient one in this Oriental world. The East in Dawe's stories serves only as a background for his narrative; his Occidental characters never really belong there. Dawe's writing also reveals certain types of Western figures, which recur in later literature: the saviour, the dilettante and the depraved. Alongside these Western characters are the native Japanese, often male stereotypes who are described as dirty, cunning, greedy, backward, sensual, and ludicrously comical. Dawe's stereotypical stories also show a sexual power relationship between the European male and Japanese female.

Some stories from Dawe's collection *Yellow and White*, *Kakemonos: Tales of the Far East* and *Rose and Chrysanthemum* represent these stereotypes rather baldly, with the plot simplified because of their short story form. In 'His Japanese Wife' from *Kakemonos*, an Englishman, Cuthberton, marries a native Japanese woman and keeps it a secret for a while from the Western community. However, as the days pass by, he begins to question what he has done and realises he has made a mistake as he becomes ostracised by his Western circle. Although he used to be a character who was admired by his friends for 'his pathetic eyes and a thoughtful dark face', they now think he has committed the most thoughtless thing possible. They are surprised at first, then disgusted and finally punish him as an outcast. Cuthberton faces the criticism bravely, believing what he has done is an act of 'clean-living'. However, their Western ethical code has another version in the East, where it seems to be more appropriate for Westerners to apply the double standard—he should have taken her as a mistress, not as a spouse. Clearly from the story, if a Westerner wishes to 'retain the favour of the world', that is of the West, 'a state of immorality is preferable to one of clean-living.' When his Western circle of friends first find out that Cuthberton is living with a native woman, they take it for granted that she is a housekeeper-mistress. The Western community may approve of keeping a mistress, but if one deviates from the code and 'descends' to the level of the native woman (or 'raises' her to one's level), it is 'a fearful mistake' in the East. To this Western response, Cuthberton disgustedly says, '[w]e may degrade a thousand of these women, but we must not raise one...Such is our Western morality here among these simple folks, these folks whom we hope to impress with our great principles'.

Cuthberton's confidence starts to waver, however, when he begins to suspect his wife's infidelity. Cuthberton may have been trapped by the woman's charm, for her coquettishness is emphasised to the point where she flirts with her husband's friend, the narrator of this story. In the story, however, there is no explanation why Cuthberton chose to take her as his wife. There is no description of whether she is an ex-housekeeper or geisha, of her family, or what kind of background she came from. This lack of personal information from the woman's side makes it difficult to see why Cuthberton has been caught between the two worlds—East and West, between true emotions and rationality, or indeed why he should suffer such deep agony. When a son is born to him, 'a little ugly, pig-eyed Jap which he could scarcely look upon without loathing', he sees 'the enormity of the crime he [has] committed.' He has degraded himself by marrying a native woman and fathering a half-breed child and laments what he has done...In the end, Cuthberton lives 'as a native', a depraved man, drunk and forgotten, until one day his dead body is found floating in the sea. As a morality tale, Dawe's narrative does not encourage inter-racial marriages between the Europeans and the Japanese.

There are several such stories, in which a Western man becomes seriously involved in a relationship with a Japanese woman, and in which such a relationship has to be punished, often with death of either or both of them. Another such story that affirms this idea is 'The Musume' in *Rose and Chrysanthemum*, where a married Westerner kills his redeemed Japanese wife because of the ostracism he faces. The husband becomes desperate, not only because of his isolation from the Western community, but also because of the gap between him and his wife—she was 'a native...and nothing could alter that' (Dawe 1900:52).

Racial prejudice at the time underlies this story, as it does in most other contemporary stories. In an article in *The Bulletin* (Anon 1910), a Colonel Onslow praised the Japanese because, despite their different civilisation, 'they were just as good as [the Australians] were'. However, on being asked if he would like one for a brother-in-law, he would not deny that this was impossible, which seems to be a less aggressive and indirect expression of the widely-held racism at that time. Like Cyril Fielding or Adela Quested in EM Forster's *A Passage to India* (1924), or those early Japanologists like Moraes or Hearn, when visiting Westerners try to be close to the natives, they lose in two ways: Western society regards them as an unusual dilettante, often abnormal and eccentric or sometimes corrupt. Furthermore, to the natives in the Eastern cultures where they choose to live, Westerners are regarded as only visitors (or intruders, as Aziz says) and do not fully fit there either. There is also a double standard in the male-female relationship, as Dawe (1900:119) himself states, 'No one blames the man...in the East, as in the West...it's always the woman who suffers...who pays'.

'Sayonara' from Dawe's *Kakemonos* collection is also a typical 'Butterfly' melodrama. An Englishman called Vershiel takes a fancy to securing a *mousumee*, Hina-san, from a 'cha-ya'—a tea-house where drink and food are served while watching girls perform—for six months, which was a common practice for both transient Western men as well as for Japanese men themselves. The name *Hina* means a chick or baby bird, as well as a Japanese traditional doll. As the name indicates, she is small, lovely, childish and ignorant. She is 'a pure woman' and once devoted, she adores Vershiel as 'a god-like personage', a saviour figure, and 'her breast [is] full of love for him'. Vershiel, however, is 'coldly calculating and extremely punctilious', taking no regard of Hina-san's feelings, for 'everybody knew that sentiment and the native women were as widely separated as the poles'. When the term is over and Vershiel is to return to England, he says 'sayonara' (farewell) and goes away, thinking that 'by emptying his purse in her lap he discharged all obligations'. Hina-san is left pregnant with his child, believing his half-promise to come back, which 'he had no real intention of fulfilling'. Eventually the money is spent by her family and they become angry with her and her baby—'her white shame'—and she leaves in a vain search for Vershiel. Like Madame Butterfly, when her last hope is shattered, she commits suicide by drowning herself and the child in the sea.

This 'Madame Butterfly' pattern repeats itself in various forms in Dawe's stories. In 'Oshima' from *Yellow and White*, Oshima, a married woman in

Nagasaki, meets 'the Stranger', and after seeing him secretly for a while, is discovered and banished as a labourer to a mine owned by her old and ugly husband. 'The Stranger' and his ship then sail away, calm and undisturbed by what has happened. In 'Lotus-San' from *Rose and Chrysanthemum*, the girl meets a young Englishman in her father's orchard, and as the man's father's smug comments reveal, the Englishman 'makes love and rides away', leaving the pregnant girl with promises and hopes. Although the man tries to compensate her financially, she eventually realises her fate and commits suicide. All these variations on the same theme compose the major part of most of these stories, and reveal a pattern that offers a comfortable solution for both the writer and the (Western) reader.

As Broinowski (1992:35) points out, Dawe is one of many European male writers who do not hide nor are hesitant about their double standards. 'The native woman doesn't count. Heaven knows, her own men think little enough of her: we think less' (Dawe 1897). A 'native' woman is a 'piece of tinselled heathenism' who knows nothing of Christ (Dawe 1898). They are hence, outside the realm of Christianity and the moral codes of the West. To make it more appropriate and conceivable, Dawe gives his female Japanese characters sensual elements by describing their physical beauty rather than their thoughts, or by suggesting an inclination to infidelity. As was the case with harems and female slaves repeatedly mentioned in European writing about the Islamic world or Gauguin's half-naked natives in the paradisal South Pacific islands, stories coloured with Oriental eroticism and exoticism seem to be a useful motif that authors include to attract readers to their stories of the East. Japan was somewhere they could employ the double standard, break the Western code and free themselves from a European structure, for it was the Far East, far from home. This situation is reinforced by the apparent power relationship inequities, with Westerners typically exceeding the Japanese in wealth. These stories show that when people are eager to escape poverty, they can be easily exploited.

A Bride of Japan (Dawe 1898) is another novel bearing the 'Butterfly' theme. It was published in the same year as Long's *Madame Butterfly* (1898), and is based on the stories from *Kakemonos* and written again from the Western masculine point of view. The story presents a more serious perspective on the incompatibility of West and East. The protagonist, Henry Tresilian, marries a *mousumee* called Sasa-san, in whom he sees 'a delicately dainty morsel of orientalism [who] just stepped out of a silk *kakemono* (scroll-painting)' with her clean olive skin and the coral pin in her hair. It is an act of brave sacrifice, for he thinks he is saving her from her arranged marriage to a rich, old tycoon. While he hesitates, he finally decides that it is because of his pure Christian faith that he does what he does, despite the apparent possibility of criticism and alienation from the circle of Westerners living there. However, as time passes, he starts to question, as Cuthberton did—'Have I done wrong?' The once sweet, graceful and pleasant Japanese wife, previously compared with the scented plum-blossom, eventually becomes an irritating presence for him, 'in the barbarous dress, chanting her barbarous songs' playing a 'samisen' (or *shamisen*, a Japanese string instrument). The way she obeys or sympathises with him, the way she calls him 'her lord' and not 'husband,'[10] the way she smiles vaguely when he is furious, all serve to disturb his mind. 'That was it—how could he be her husband?' This sense of agitation finally leads him to snatch and break her *samisen*, leaving the 'heathen' woman with an 'idiotic smile', frightened and confused, and himself with the despair of a white man 'who sold his birthright, a creature without race or caste, in every place an alien'.

For such characters, when the first curiosity and passion of the West are satisfied and the novelty of the East loses its impact and effect, only disappointment and regret remain. For people like Tresilian, the gap between East and West is far greater than he first thought: like oil and vinegar, or oil and water, however close they come, they never blend into one. What seems at first to be the charm of the East turns out to be a spell, which is broken when the fundamental dissimilarity between the races becomes overwhelming. Tresilian could not stand his Japanese wife bearing the same name—Mrs Tresilian—as his mother. It seemed easier for Western men to carry Loti-like attitudes, flamboyant, playful and at the same time practical, than to fully commit themselves to accepting the difference of cultures between the West and the East.

Eventually Tresillian loses interest in life and business and thus also becomes an outcast figure. He 'who ruled once' wants to rule again. However, it is impossible now that he has become equal to the 'natives'. Sasa-san, now frightened of him and after being informed that he was seeking sympathy from a lady-friend of his own race, is then attracted to a more attentive and flamboyant man and elopes with him. She leaves behind their son whom Tresilian has detested since the moment he was born. Realising his harshness towards her and understanding the consequence, Tresilian decides to wait for her, raising their child alone. His act of compensation is to recognise the child as his own son and fulfil his paternal duty. However, even when he becomes fond of his son, who starts to become more English and less Japanese, the child's presence is not fully accepted as in the short story. In the end the child dies from a disease and when Sasa-san finally returns, she too dies, stricken by shock, remorse, and shame. By letting these two perish, Dawe completed this marriage of the West and the East. He successfully avoided breaking the Western God's bond of marriage, in other words, a Christian contract, and at the same time terminated an 'impossible' relationship.

Contrary to the short story about Cuthberton where the motivation for marriage is not fully described and the agony of the protagonist remains unconvincing, Tresilian's reason for marrying a native woman is very clear. It was not merely for a momentary affection, or 'illusion of affection' for her youth, beauty and novelty, but also because of his strong sense of duty as a Christian. He is a saviour, liberator of the native woman from Japan's barbaric society as well as from her own entangled relationships. In a sense, she deserves to be saved more than other natives, for she is neither geisha nor *mousumee*; she is young and innocent. While her father is only a market gardener, his ancestry was once of the Samurai clan. For Tresilian it is unnatural, absurd and irksome to actually become affectionate towards an ignorant native woman, who 'possesses no thought with [sic] him'. However, swaying irresolutely between 'I will or I will not', he eventually follows the gospel of his life: 'Do unto others as ye would they should do unto you'. Within its context, it is an act of heroism, a self-sacrificing deed, and by marrying her Tresilian believes his influence will be such that it will erase from her all the unfavourable elements about Japan. At a critical moment, however, Tresilian is driven to despair when he witnesses Sasa-san squatting and eating smelly, rotten fish using chopsticks with her old family. He, who thought he would overcome philistinism by the noble act of marrying her, is now trapped by his own narrow evaluation of the traditions, customs and social system of the 'Other.'

As Menikoff suggests, a woman's position in the Orient is very much emphasised by Dawe as 'obeisant if not subjugated in society', and infidelity often becomes a form of rebellion against the patriarchal system. Perhaps women's affairs with, or marriages to, Europeans are meant to be one such form of rebellion, thus allowing the European male character to become a saviour figure. However, these women are also often exploited and eventually destroyed by the Westerners (Menikoff 1988:97). Employing simple, Eurocentric plots typical of the time, Dawe presented in his short stories and novels contemporary ideas of race, gender and power relations between the West and the East in the late 19th century.

Western communities in Japan during the early period of interaction are described in Sladen's *A Japanese marriage*. They were places where Westerners were able to escape what they saw as the restrictive social standards of their own countries, as shown in Dawe's novels and stories. The protagonists and other main characters of Sladen's novel are all Westerners; as the author states, it is 'an attempt to present the life of the English in Japan' (Sladen 1904:vii). Japan provides not only the location but also the opportunity for the male protagonist and his sister-in-law when, despite the church's prohibition of 'not taking one's sister-in-law to wife', they become married. Notwithstanding some negative reaction in the Westerners' community, the protagonists wed in a 'Japanese marriage'. According to the author, the time is one when 'analysing your passion is the modern form of scandal', thus showing that unconventional and informal things can happen. Because it is in Japan where Western standards may not be applied as strictly as at home, and where it does not involve 'natives' in the relationship, the author allows his characters to marry outside their own religious system.

Another novel of Western adventure in the East based on this Orientalistic pattern is AG Hales's *Little Blue Pigeon* (1905). Hales, being a war correspondent from Australia in the Boer and Russo–Japanese Wars, set many novels in places other than Australia. *Little Blue Pigeon* is a rather simplistic romantic adventure novel, perhaps written to cater for younger readers. It is to a modern reader, an archetypal James Bond story, and half the characters are spies from England, Russia and China. All are engaged in secret manoeuvres in Japan for their respective countries and there is a threat of possible war between Russia and Japan. Clifford, an English agent, tries to prevent his Russian counterpart, Boris Metchkin, from obtaining intelligence about a shipment of arms from England to her ally Japan and passing it on to the Russian government.

Some points in Hales's story characterise it as a typical Western discourse similar to Dawe's, while others show it to be distinctive from other contemporary Australian works. First, the way Hales uses female characters: it is again *cha-ya* girls who represent Japan (although Little Blue Pigeon is depicted, like Sasa-san, as a daughter of a ruined 'samurai' family in order to meet the criterion of being a heroine), and their love-hate relationships with the foreigners affect the course of events. The only female European character is a British agent, who in contrast with the 'ignorant' Japanese, shows independence, intelligence and capability. Hales, however, also gives the Japanese heroine more latitude to think, act and perform than Dawe's Japanese 'mousumees'. Of course, Little Blue Pigeon is a mere *cha-ya* girl, a commodity, who, at a critical point, is secured for money by her lover, the enemy of Clifford. Again what captures the imagination first is her physical attractiveness—her smallness and prettiness 'in an old-world fashion', and her feminine voice 'full of low, cooing notes', with 'sensuous tones'. What she has in addition to her physical gifts, however, is her cunning, ambition and yearning for power. It is as though she is compared with the hidden ambitions of Japan at that time and its imperialistic intentions towards the West and South—in her veins runs the 'blood that was rich in tradition, glorious with the deeds of brave men'.[11] What she accomplishes by helping Clifford turns out to be beneficial for her own country, although she is not aware of it. The hero Clifford is again the saviour of the girl, and then becomes the educator for her to achieve her own ambitions.

With his rich experiences and insights as a correspondent, Hales gives journalistic touches to the story, offering warnings about Japan to his readers as seen in other novels and stories by Australian journalists. At one stage, when Russian and Chinese agents in the story talk about the possible China-Japan tide about to sweep the South Pacific and overrun Australia, which 'hate[s] the yellow man worse than the Americans hate the black man,' the Chinese sneers at Australia's naïveté in entrusting everything to the British, and its lack of self-reliance in arms and ammunition. He goes on to criticise Australia's want of self-reliance under the over-burdensome British administration, and predicts the ruin of the British Empire as a result of 'yellow' expansion in the South Pacific, the movements in Canada and South Africa to become republics (Hales 1905:175–9), and a possible Japanese invasion of Australia itself.

Like Dawe, Hales often makes clear his ideas of the relationship between the West and the East, which perhaps reflect those of the majority at that time. 'The Anglo-Saxon hand will never fit in the Japanese glove, though diplomats make treaties and missionaries preach peace', and 'the yellow blood runs counter to the blood of the white races' and never mingles, as 'a rivulet of oil touching the waves never becomes part of the ocean'. However, with more balanced attitudes than some other writers, Hales allows criticism of Western nations in the story by letting a cosmopolitan Chinese spy Quong Foy speak. Quong Foy:

> had not a wondrous opinion of either British or Russian diplomacy, which, in his estimation of things, had only produced an eternity of wire-pulling and few practical results beyond a few almost needless wars and the filching of weaker neighbours' territory (Hales 1905).

The Russian agent, Metchkin, wanting to 'tame the brown men' in order to conquer them all, fails to fulfil his wish because he underestimates Japan, just as he overestimates Russian superiority. Corruption and deterioration of the Russian army and Russia's political instability are targeted by Quong Foy (Hales 1905:233). Hales also mounts criticism against British imperialism by way of his Russian character who says that 'there is no morality in statecraft, only expediency…and if you steal another country's territory to benefit your own nation you cannot defend the theft upon moral grounds' (Hales 1905:160). Although as a novel it leads to an easy conclusion with the villain's death and no further comment on the destiny of the rest of the characters or nations involved, Hales, with a broader view of the world as a well-travelled journalist, is able to give his novel a less typically Orientalistic structure than other authors like Dawe.

Ono, in his *Pygmalion complex: genealogy of Pretty Woman* (1997), looks at the Occidental desire to dominate Oriental women so often repeated in literary works, as a version of man's hope of creating the ideal woman, just as Pygmalion created Galatea. As in Shaw's Higgins–Eliza or Webster's Daddy Long Legs–Judy relationships, there has been a pattern in literature of men possessing, idealising and educating women, which can still be found in Hollywood films as well as in various forms of literature. Ono argues that eroticism and exoticism both focus their interest in the 'difference of the features of the body' and it is always the interest shown by man in woman, the civilised in the uncivilised, the powerful in the powerless. This desire, as Said (1985:110) insists in his influential book *Orientalism*, is disguised as a form of scientific analysis or research in medicine or anthropology, thus giving it authority. It remains embedded in the genealogy of Orientalist literature. Furthermore, in the novels and stories we have discussed, Japanese women are described not as they are but as their male authors think they should be. They are sensuous, sweet, tender, affectionate, easily approachable, helpful, useful and convenient to discard in many cases. However, these characteristics only apply to the heroines. Other women—older women, very young girls, and women of lower class—are given only indifferent and biased descriptions as presented by Dawe or Hales.

James Murdoch had a different approach in writing stories about Japan. While retaining some typical Western views, he used Japanese settings more interestingly than the former writers, without making the stories banal versions of Orientalist discourse. After his education at Aberdeen and Oxford universities and a brief position as the master of a school in Australia, Murdoch, like Hales, started as a journalist for English newspapers in Japan, and both taught and published there. In later years, he became the first professor of Oriental Studies at Sydney University, as well as the lecturer of Japanese at Duntroon (1918). He influenced politicians such as WM Hughes and EL Piesse, with his opinions and comments on Japan being sought in both politics and diplomacy.[12]

It seems male visitor-authors of the late 19th century could not but succumb to the temptation to write typical 'fantasy' type stories, and Murdoch was no exception. Before tackling Japan seriously, he wrote his first story in verse on Japan called *Don Juan's grandson in Japan: with notes for the globe-trotters' benefit* under the pseudonym A Miall. It was published in Tokyo in 1890 and invited critical comments from some university colleagues including Kanzo Uchimura.[13] As the author himself states, it was *non virginibus puerisque canto*—not the verse for boys and girls. This verse, which is chanted by 'a vagabond bard from the parched plains of Australia', is nothing but a frivolous adventure of an English youth travelling around Japan, including such episodes as a missionary's vain attempt to convert geisha-girls to Christianity. Although the story is insubstantial, Murdoch tries to introduce and explain places and things Japanese in the footnotes, thus showing signs of being a 'Japanologist'.

In Murdoch's stories in the volume *From Australia and Japan*, a young man, either British or Australian, quite often a journalist, typically falls into unusual circumstances that happen because of the exotic and extraordinary background in which he finds himself. The young man serves as an observer who participates in what he sees and hears, thus introducing cultural differences. He acts at times as a mediator between the West and the East. In 'A Yoshiwara Episode', a young journalist named Whitmore challenges a Japanese man in Yoshiwara, a 'huge Japanese Vanity Fair', to a series of contests in order to buy out a young geisha-girl, so she could go back to her family. Whitmore wins three contests—drinking *sake*, a tournament of *go* (a Japanese board game), and a match of *kendo* (Japanese fencing). In the latter game, he gains help from an older woman whom he had helped escape from a Japanese drunkard. The longest of the stories found in *From Australia and Japan*, this episode shows not only the author's effort to try and supply information and introduce a sense of the novelty of Japanese culture and society to his audience, but also introduces cross-cultural connections between West and East.

Compared to such contemporary short stories as Leontine Cooper's 'Another Mysterious Disappearance' (1890), Whitmore's adventures, although very much exaggerated, seem to be more realistic and accurate in terms of time and location. 'Another Mysterious Disappearance' was written two years before Murdoch's stories and is referred to by the author as 'a fairy tale'. It's about a miraculous reunion of a Queensland couple who had once separated when the husband fled to Japan for a change of scenery. In this story, Japan features in the background, offering the tale a little more romanticism, mysticism and Oriental exoticism than perhaps a story about a disappearance in the Australian bushland. In the 1890s Japan was a most unlikely meeting place for Australians. In the story it merely becomes a convenient setting in which the author does not try to hide his ignorance of Japan, but rather takes advantage of it as the Japanese location adds peculiarity and mystery to the story as well as emphasising the Australian nostalgia for home.

'A Tosa Monogatari of Modern Times' from *From Australia and Japan* (Murdoch 1892b) is another story of an improbable encounter between Australians in Japan. When an Australian, Webster, visits the border of Tosa and Awa (in Shikoku), up among the mountains, and recites a stanza of Adam Lindsay Gordon's 'The Sick Stock Rider', he hears an echo reciting the following stanzas. Eventually it is discovered that it came from an ex-socialist called Morrison who had fled Australia because of his failure both in politics and in a love affair. He became a Buddhist monk in the temple of Tosa. On his deathbed Morrison hears the melancholic Australian verse and chants it to himself, then passes away. Discouraged by the failure of socialism in Australia, Morrison had chosen Japan as a place to practise Buddhism, a situation similar to the one of Harold Stewart in much later years.[14] Murdoch also uses Japanese settings to describe the relationships of Europeans in other stories. For example, in 'The Bear Hunt on Fuji-san', Mt Fuji is employed as the stage for a comical story in which a young Australian woos an English woman.

Published in the same year as *From Australia and Japan*, Murdoch's *Ayame-san: A Japanese Romance* (1892a) is a novel which despite its similar plot development to that of the writings of Dawe and Hales, features some originality in its use of Japan and the Japanese. It is again a story of the liberator-Westerner (this time a pair of Westerners) saving a young, pretty Japanese woman caught in a predicament. One of the pair, O'Rafferty, is half-Irish and half-Japanese and has visited and stayed in many countries in and out of the army, including the Australian gold mines. Gifford, 'a Scotchman by birth, an American by adoption, an artist by profession', also travels around the world as an illustrator-correspondent for an American journal. It is his artistic inclination that allows him to appreciate what is artistic—regardless of whether it is Western or Eastern. By giving the main characters cosmopolitan backgrounds and broader views on life, the author has tried to approach the story in as much of an unbiased way as possible. The girl they are to save, Ayame-san, whose late father was again of the samurai class and who is raised by her artist-uncle, retains the pride and nobility of her class.

The author, Murdoch, acts as the mediator-introducer. He tries to explain Japanese systems and manners, often regarded as incomprehensible by many Western writers. Unlike the easily approachable girls in the stories of Dawe and Hales, Gifford takes pains to obtain access to Ayame-san, through convenient 'accidents' and finally through a proper formal introduction. He understands that young girls are not to be addressed casually, and when talking with her, pays great attention not to place 'either her or himself on a level with a tea-house girl by launching into compliments on her linguistic ability'. The 'Butterfly' theme is repeated when Gifford has to leave Ayame-san and she descends to poverty. She moves to another place with her family but longs to see him again. She keeps her dignity, however, and struggles to help her uncle save face.

The villain in this story, a Chinese man called Ishida, who reduces Ayame-san to poverty in order to force her to marry his son, resembles very much Daidai in Dawe's *A Bride of Japan*. Ishida displays anger and vindictiveness at losing the heroine to a Westerner, much like Murdoch's Tajima in 'A Yoshiwara Episode,' who challenges the Westerner for the destiny of a *cha-ya* girl. These 'native' villains are often presented by their Australian authors as cunning, greedy, and comical. As Ouyang (1995b) has shown, Chinese characters are also often depicted in a biased, stereotypical manner in late 19th century Australian texts.[15] Ishida in *Ayame-san* is a quack-doctor, land-owner, fishmonger, money-lender and politician, who squeezes money out of others. Although his ways are not illegal, in many respects he is a stereotypical image of the rich, bad Japanese of those days. As Menikoff (1988:97) points out, in Dawe's Japanese stories, it is often suggested that money is earned in some illegitimate, dishonest way, 'by exploiting works, selling daughters into bondage as wives or as geishas' and the same pattern repeats itself here in Murdoch's story. Ishida is a gentlemanly villain, who, with his fortune made from the narrow living of peasants and fishermen, buys votes and sends his son into the newly formed parliament. He tries to entrap Ayame-san and force her to marry his son. With extraordinary tricks, disguises and cheating, Ayame-san is saved in the end from her near depraved circumstances and reunited with Gifford. This contrivance offers an easy solution to the plot and makes the novel typical of Western narratives on the East. However, despite the simplicity of its plot and the typification of its characters, there seems to be an effort by the author throughout the text to present things with unbiased description and comment. This may be due to his own position as a 'Japanologist', a researcher, educator and introducer-mediator himself. Set in 1890, the novel faithfully reflects the tendency of the time and includes many actual incidents of that year in Japan, such as the preparation of the Imperial Constitution, the murder of a minister and the first election for the Lower Chamber. The author also mentions Japanese customs, conventions and manners, including the match-making systems and the etiquette of not speaking for oneself but letting others do it instead. With this novel, which is abundantly filled with photographs by his fellow professor at the Imperial University of Tokyo, WK Burton, Murdoch seems to try to convey more accurate images of Japan and the Japanese.

Murdoch's observation and knowledge of Japan over a period of nearly 30 years not only as a novelist and journalist but also as a scholar, enabled him to produce three volumes on the history of Japan. From an early age his memory retention was uncommon, and he had a remarkable knowledge of many languages including Latin, Greek, Sanskrit, French and German.[16] In order to write a history of Japan, he studied archaic Japanese, research which would have definitely been helpful in furthering his knowledge and understanding of Japan's historical background. Perhaps he was the first writer from Australia (although originally from Scotland) among his contemporaries who quoted Japanese names of things and places in most of his works.

In his lecture for the School of Oriental Studies at Sydney University, Murdoch (1919) he clarified the difference in meaning of the phrase 'Oriental Studies' for British (or other Europeans) and Australians. For Australia, he argues, the places that Europeans called the Orient are not East but actually North, physically closer than they want to admit. He insists that especially China and Japan, due to their proximity and resources, and future possible relationship to Australia, cannot be ignored (Murdoch 1919:15). Again, Murdoch is perhaps one of the first who, based on first-hand experiences, warned of Japan's ability to borrow, modify and reproduce Western materials both physical and mental (Murdoch 1919:16).

> It cannot be too strongly emphasized that the true explanation of the recent rapid rise of Japan to power and reputation is to be found, not in the external trappings of her civilization, but rather in the inherited mental and temperamental characteristics of the nation responding to and reacting on the new and stimulating environment, and working along the lines of true evolution (Murdoch 1919:28).

Having seen the Russo–Japanese War that resulted in the first Oriental victory in modern war over the Occidental, he was convinced that Japan would evolve its Occidento-Oriental civilisation further, so that in terms of industry and armaments it would become one of the leading nations of Asia. Thus both Murdoch's scholastic and journalistic approaches to responding and reacting to Japan made him a most acute observer of Japan and this is often reflected in his fiction.[17]

As we have seen, expatriate Australian authors writing on Japan during this early period were generally male. Rosa Praed was one of the few notable Australian female writers of her time, along with such authors as Ada Cambridge, Jessie Couvreur ('Tasma'), Barbara Baynton and Miles Franklin. Moreover, she was one of the very few travel writers who took an interest in Japan as a setting for her work. As Pesman (1996:4) points out, travel has many meanings: 'migration, diaspora, exploration, adventure, pilgrimage, recreation, escape, quest, and desire'. Especially for women, to be away from their normal social codes and domestic obligations and to divert and transgress the ordinary and common life, gave them the opportunity, perhaps far more than it does now, to spark their imagination.

Although she was brought up on cattle stations in Queensland, Praed spent the majority of her time in England from 1875, returning to Australia only once after she left, three years after her marriage. The characters and settings of most of her novels were either from 'Home' (Britain) or from Australia, with her themes being the contrast and contradiction between the two. Her novel *Madame Izàn* (1899) was written after Praed's second voyage from Australia to England via Asia in 1895, when she visited Nagasaki and Kyoto. The way Praed presented Japan and the Japanese, and their relationships with Westerners in this novel was quite different from the works of her contemporary male authors. The development and conclusion of *Madame Izàn* challenged current taboos, when xenophobic articles by male authors like William Lane were widely circulated in Australia.

Madame Izàn is a 'tourist' story and indeed, it is a story of a very unusual tour. As we have seen in the works of Dawe, Hales and Murdoch, when the Orient/ Asia/Japan is the setting, it allows for the extraordinary to happen, especially for and to males. In terms of the 'sexual encounter', men are freed from their moral, religious and social codes and obligations. As a woman, Praed was perhaps more conscious of her audience and of her reputation, a consciousness as Pesman (1996:15) points out, that was common in the 19th century. At the same time Praed also tried to meet the expectations of her readers for the 'exotic'.

While Praed's novel presents a mystery, of finding the heroine's alienated husband, it is also a story of self-discovery. The heroine Izo (Isobel) Izàn, a beautiful Australian woman, was blind before an eye operation. Regaining her sight after nearly twenty years, she starts to look at herself again in a new way, taking advantage of travel as a chance to free, rediscover, and reconstruct herself. Izo, for both physical and circumstantial reasons, tries to see everything in a new way—almost with a small child's eagerness and innocence. When Japan is regarded through her unbiased and unprejudiced eyes, it is not described as 'a country of barbarians' as recorded by some other European tourists. Neither has she any illusions or preconceptions. Izo, who knows what it is like to be 'oppressed and looked down upon' (Praed 1899:135) and marginalised, is able to sympathise with the 'natives'. This is in contrast with her English chaperone-friend Herminia, whose sympathy goes only to the people, systems, and traditions of England.

Praed's reputation as a writer 'of women's formula romantic fiction' (Wilde, Hooton & Andrews 1994:569), is reflected in the fact that the novel is a melodrama. Izo's motivation behind marrying a Japanese man in England is to escape her miserable situation as a blind orphan. While her Japanese husband returns to Japan for urgent matters, a rich uncle suddenly appears from Australia and enables her to undergo surgery to regain her eyesight. Izo then travels to Japan in search of her husband. The guide on their tours in Japan is actually her disguised husband Kencho Izàn/Shirakawa, who has successfully deceived even Herminia who had seen him in England.[18] This is also a kind of Cinderella story, although the situation of a European woman marrying an Oriental is taboo in the eyes of the then majority of both Western and Eastern cultures. If we borrow Dawe's word, it is 'degrading' for the West to be linked so intimately with the East. In order to compensate for this unusual situation, the Japanese character has to be both physically and materially considerably better than the ordinary Japanese. Indeed, Izàn/Shirakawa is a Viscount, rich and educated in England, who knows well both European and Asian histories and art. He has the gentleness and subtleties of the East and the elegance and manners of the West, and importantly 'eats like an Englishman', thus having more than enough reasons to be counted as a suitor or to meet Western criteria. Because of these characteristics, Izàn/Shirakawa is able to compete in the wooing of Izo with his rival Australian suitor, Windeatt, a man from the bush, who has 'an autocratic way of speaking to those he considered beneath him, the result, probably, of dealing with obdurate black-boys and shearers in branding-yards and wool-sheds, and obtuse Mongolians'. This is perhaps another device by the author to justify the promotion of the Japanese character to such an 'elevated' role. If the 'Beast' wants to woo the 'Beauty', he has to have at least a title and a tender heart, just as the *cha-ya* girls have to be of an ex-samurai clan to be saved.

While Praed is often considered a writer who 'succumbed to 'cultural cringe' in her writing' (Wilde, Hooton & Andrews 1994:569), in this story it is the English and American tourists who are criticised for their carelessness and ignorance towards the country they are visiting. Apart from Izo, the only European person in the story who has an observer role is Windeatt's novelist sister, Mrs Eugarde. Other characters just dismiss Japan as a 'country of heathens' in a similar way to the characters from Dawe's stories. They form tourist groups co-ordinated by Thomas Cook, with guidebooks by Murray or Dresser in hand. These people only complain about the inconveniences they encounter and look negatively at the superficial differences. They do not try to understand Japanese history, religion, tradition, customs and manners. On the other hand, Izo and a few more sensitive ones are able to 'realise the necessity for reconstructing preconceived notions of things and persons Japanese' (Praed 1899:125). Praed's observations of Japan are often more detailed than those of contemporary male writers and often bear the characteristics of a journalistic viewpoint. Like many other writers on Japan, she uses typical adjectives such as 'subtle,' 'delicate,' 'exotic,' 'mysterious', but she also lets her characters speak of Japan in different words and phrases. In disguise, the husband-guide, when talking with Izo about Japan's future, says it is Japan's mission among nations to 'complete the circuit' by marrying Eastern tradition and Western progression (Praed 1899:160). Rickshaw runner Yamasaki, who laments the neglect of old traditions because of the government's policy of modernisation, shows unusual enthusiasm for military action (Praed 1899:173). Speaking for the rest of the nation, he reflects Japan's soaring morale during this period and the future possibility of wars and imperialism.

Murdoch (1919:30) also mentions, as Praed did, that 'in Japan even the lowest coolie is something of a patriot'. Those who visited and stayed in Japan saw the danger of the rising military and imperial might. Back in Australia, those who had not visited Japan had enough stories to create an imaginary foe. Upon learning the possibility of Japan's southward movement, they chose Japan as their potential enemy in their novels and stories. This gave rise to a new category in Australian literature of that time, which can still be traced to the present day.

chapter two

Short stories, serials and 'invasion novels' of the early period from the 1880s to the Second World War

At the same time as such peripatetic writers as Dawe, Hales, Murdoch and Praed, many other writers appeared on the Australian literary scene who wrote about Japan and the Japanese, or used Japan as the setting of their stories. These writers published their work in several magazines that began publication from the 1870s. Among the most influential examples of these magazines were the weekly *The Bulletin*, (established in 1880), *The Town and Country Journal* or *Australian Town and Country Journal* (established in 1870), *The Boomerang* (established in 1887), *The Centennial Magazine* (established in 1888), *The Clarion* (established in 1896), and *Smith's Weekly* (established in 1919).

The development of fictional narratives, especially short stories, increased dramatically from the end of the 1880s, and 'reaches its greatest vigour and range throughout the nineties and into the early years of the twentieth century' (Levis 1950). This was also a period when the quantity of fiction published dramatically outnumbered verse for the first time—publication of verse in Australia had, until this time, exceeded fiction.[19] Relatively established writers like Dawe, Hales, Murdoch and Praed were able to publish their books both in Australia and overseas, mainly in England and America. Other writers were able to publish by having their novels and stories serialised in magazines and journals. As the literary editor of *The Bulletin* AG Stephens (1895) optimistically stated, this was the period when 'native' Australian literature started to flourish, and novels and short stories began to appear.

Many writers were very much affected by the ethos of the time—the excitement of federation, nationalistic ideas, the union movement, and the increasing Australian awareness of their own physical location, which was actually closer to 'the East' (or 'the North') and farther from 'the West,' something suggested by Murdoch during his inaugural lecture of the first Oriental Studies Program at the University of Sydney. Geoffrey Blainey (1966) argues that this distance from Europe has played a significant role in shaping Australia as a nation. As a result, the themes and topics of the stories concerned with Japan also varied from romance to political writing. Unlike the well-travelled writers discussed in Chapter One, some of the 'local' authors had never visited Japan. In Australia, resident Japanese were scarce in number, their existence limited mainly to the pearling industry and the sugar plantations in the north.[20] This number was also declining as the Japanese government started to encourage expatriate Japanese to return, expressing concerns that working conditions in Australia were not good for them (Henry Frei 1991). Thus Japan and the Japanese came to be described not as real figures, but rather as metaphors. Although the number of such stories about Japan is too limited to make specific categorisations, it is possible to make some classifications according to their respective themes. In doing so, the reason Japan and the Japanese appeared in the Australian periodicals in those early days becomes clear. My tentative classifications of the themes of short stories from the 1880s to the First World War (discussed in detail below) can be summarised as follows:

- the Japanese as seen in Australian society (pearl divers, prostitutes, and so on)
- Japan as a source of romance
- Japanese 'invasion novels'.

The Japanese as seen in Australian society

The way in which the Japanese were described in Australian stories from the late 19th century was affected by the social atmosphere of the latter half of the century. The year 1888 celebrated the centenary of Australia's European founding. It created a surge of nationalism, and a move to establish a white nation. During this time, anti-Chinese and anti-Japanese movements became very strong. Australian fear and hostility toward the 'yellow peril' was increasingly expressed, with the help of visual effects produced by many cartoonists, politicians, journalists and literary authors, most of whom were contributors to contemporary magazines and more or less were the opinion-makers. Indeed, both those on the political right and left agreed, without question, that Australia should be a 'white' country and Asians and other coloured races should be excluded. Unlike the Chinese, the Japanese were very few in number and were hardly seen by the majority of people living in urban towns. There were some minor frictions between Australians and Japanese, such as unemployment problems arising from the depression in Queensland and the Australian fear of Japanese ownership of pearling ships in Darwin (Frei 1991:74–75). However, they were not everyday problems for the majority of Australians. Thus the negative feelings of Australians against the Japanese tended to be aimed at the 'faceless' Asians as a group.

'The Mates of Torres', written by George Randolph Bedford in 1911, was a serialised novel in *The Lone Hand,* to which the author was a frequent contributor.[21] Bedford himself launched the mining and literary journal, *The Clarion,* in Melbourne in 1896, and throughout his varied career he remained a regular contributor to these periodicals. As 'a militant Australian nationalist', Bedford advocated 'republicanism, White Australia, vigilance against the Japanese, a parochial form of socialism, and a military alliance with the United States of America' (Nairn & Serle 1979). These beliefs were also apparent in 'The Mates of Torres.' Among the five episodes of the series, two are about Japanese divers working for Australians, with similar plots, describing how the Japanese divers try to cheat their employers and how the Australians discover the plan, prevent it, and punish them. In both stories the cunning and shrewdness of the Japanese divers are emphasised, and their stupidity and real weaknesses exposed at the last minute, thus offering 'poetic justice'. They are didactic stories. Excluding the fourth episode about the discovery of treasure under the sea, the other two episodes are also about the punishment of villains: the first is about a crafty captain of an Australian Custom's vessel who smuggles opium, making 'a little dirty money with the niggers' (Bedford 1911a:305), and the second is about a sly Malay trepang hunter who avoids paying the tax charged by the Australians. The Japanese characters in Bedford's stories are very close to the Chinese characters insofar as both races are depicted as villains. Their greed and craftiness are emphasised in stories such as 'A Golden Shanty' which appeared in *The Bulletin* in 1887 and 'Ah Ling's Religion' also in *The Bulletin* in 1901. In reality, Japanese divers were often regarded as hardworking and skilful. However, Australians were led to see this 'virtue' as a manifestation of their real intention—the desire to take over Australia (Frei 1991:81).

In the two episodes about the Japanese pearl divers, there are some passages that reveal the typical contemporary relationship between Australians and the Japanese. For example, when the Japanese, the Australians' 'natural enemy' (Bedford 1911a:393) are laid off, they embrace Christianity as preached by the local missionaries, which, 'they [are] ready to learn with the English language and to forget as soon as they [can] speak it commercially' (Bedford 1911a:393). Such negative attitudes are emphasised so as to arouse the suspicion, disgust and antipathy of Australians, and this alleged underlying pragmatism was described as a common trait of the Japanese in these stories.

Moreover, although the names of the Japanese crew are given and they speak individually in the stories, they are not given their own voices. They are always in a team or in a group and are not fully depicted as individuals, a courtesy often granted in stories about other nationals. Their deception, theft and attack on Australians are not portrayed as individual acts, but rather as representative of Japanese malice as a whole. As Ouyang (1995) points out, this non-individualised description of Asian people, including the Japanese, may be a stereotypical representation of the yellow race 'en masse', 'as a faceless mass in enormous numbers' and very different from the representation of such authors as Praed and Murdoch. Since Japanese contract pearlers started working on Thursday Island, Broome and elsewhere in northern Australia in the late 1870s, Australia was, for them, an El Dorado where they were able to make enough money to build a mansion back home. But it was also a place of exile where, amongst other things, they suffered at the hands of Australian employers who were 'unfeeling and lacking in humanity', and lived with unsatisfactory medical facilities (Frei 1991:48). Ignorance and insufficient communication on both sides caused misunderstanding and mistrust, with stories like 'The Mates of Torres' providing a typical negative tone in describing the Japanese.

Bedford was highly motivated toward the making and protecting of Australia, as his later career in politics indicates. His writings 'reflect his adventurous spirit, romantic idealism and passionate love of Australia' (Nairn & Serle 1979:242) and in 'The Mates of Torres,' he presents the friction between the Australians and the Japanese, less serious than that of a feared Japanese invasion but enough to arouse disgust and hatred.

The uniqueness of the industry-based life and the diversity of race in the pearling town of Broome in Western Australia was atypical of contemporary Australian society. Unlike other cities, Broome seemed to entertain a 'high degree of inter-racial harmony'; however, it was also occasionally disturbed by conflicts among different racial groups, notable examples include the Japanese race-riot in 1920.[22] As the industry depended heavily 'on coloured labour for both its skilled and unskilled labour', European masters 'deliberately structured the pearling workforce along ethnic lines in an attempt to divide and rule' (Schaper 1995:112;114). Thus from both sides grouping by race and ethnicity was encouraged and helped to create the image of non-white groups as 'en masse'.

Among the very few exceptions to this mass-treatment is Ion Idriess's depiction of the Japanese in the pearling industry in Broome in *Forty Fathoms Deep: Pearl Divers and Sea Rovers in Australian Sea*, published much later in 1937. Idriess who became a popular author, wrote both fiction and non-fiction based on his observations during his wanderings from the east to the west coast of northern Australia. In *Forty Fathoms Deep* (1937) he describes the Japanese divers, both good and bad, as members of the society in Broome. Although not main characters, his Japanese cast includes Old Sakai, one of the best divers in Broome, whose death as a result of an underwater collision with a whale is lamented by the whole society. Although the Japanese tend to separate themselves as a group, there are some occasions when they share their events with others. For example, during the lantern festival, when the Japanese console the spirits of the dead with dances, dinners and sailing miniature luggers out to the ocean, other racial groups (mainly whites) are invited to join in.

Like Aboriginal, Malay and Koepanger people, Japanese divers are still occasionally dimissed in sweeping generalisations or classified collectively as a group (a typical recurrent phrase is 'with the all-conquering fatalism of his race'). Yet, because Idriess attempts to become an observer not from the outside but from the inside, the observed are depicted more vividly and individually than in many other stories. At the end of the book, Idriess (1937:278) writes: '[l]et us give and take with the East: supply it as the demand grows and work in harmony with the Eastern nations to our mutual benefit.' Such a statement seems to come from those who actually interact with the East, someone who has seen the reality and thus knows there is no need to have fear of the 'Other'.[23]

Like Idriess in *Forty fathoms deep*, Henrietta Drake-Brockman, in her novel *Sheba Lane* (1936), depicts the exotic town of Broome in the 1930s, where the local community is made up of many ethnic groups, including the Japanese. Although the main characters are all Europeans and the plot is about their entangled relationships, Japanese characters, some with names and distinct characters, contribute to the multicultural atmosphere of the pearling town. The presence of the Japanese acts as a foil, and helps one of the main characters, Chris from England, to realise his bias against the different groups. He has too much 'caste prejudice' and 'never [seeks] to cultivate the Jap's society even for entertainment' (Drake-Brockman 1936:106). He becomes indignant when a wealthy Japanese buys good seats and sits among Europeans at the theatre (Drake-Brockman 1936:96). However, during time spent on a pearling boat, he watches how the Japanese work and witnesses the paralysis and eventual death of a good diver called Hashimoto. It is then that he realises the Japanese man is also a human and his own narrow views are expanded. Monty, an old man, nostalgically recalls the 'old days' in Broome when there were more Japanese people: 'There were…a lot of Japanese women. Pretty little things they were. Any amount of 'em here. House-boys and all sorts before the White Australia Business' (Drake-Brockman 1936:72). Compared with mainstream Australian society in the 1930s, stories set in Broome offered different views about the Japanese, even if they were indirect views about particular subtypes of people.

Another early account about the Japanese in Australia, which was published in 1902 in *The Bulletin* by the anonymous (apparently male) author 'CN', is about *cha-ya* girls in a mining town, entitled 'The Vigilance at Coolaba.'[24] This brief narrative tells from an ordinary miner's point of view, how the 'upper-class people' of the town hold double standards. With their mining town's recent prosperity, the richer people decide to expel the *cha-ya* girls, and send for their 'respectable' wives instead. The cha-ya girls had given comfort to both the rich and the younger, poorer miners who could afford only to look at their faces through the windows. The expulsion was decided upon in order to 'refine the moral atmosphere' of the town. Although, like 'The Mates of Torres,' this story is about the Japanese in Australia, the situation is similar to that described in Dawe's stories: Western men, 'respectable' western women and degraded native foreign women like the Japanese. However, the author's sympathy is clearly with the courtesans in this story. In terms of gender and power, they are not to be verbally attacked but pitied as sacrifices or scapegoats. By contrast, the owner of the *cha-ya*, Kumasura, is depicted as a cold-hearted employer of the girls—he is despised for his profession and despite the fact that he is also dismissed, he gains no sympathy. The same stereotype has been given to the Chinese depicted in short stories in contemporary periodicals—that of a greedy, cunning man who exploits others for profit. This figure is clearly contrasted with the typical view of an admired masculinity held by diggers or mates in the bush, who praise solidarity and egalitarianism (among themselves) and despise self-centred avarice.

For some male authors, as in 'The Vigilance at Coolaba', sympathy is more easily given to women of other races (and perhaps vice versa, as we have seen in Praed's case). A contributor to *The Bulletin*, Efari (1913), in his memoir 'These I have known' talks of his experiences overseas and fondly recalls his encounter with O Tsusuke-san, who was a housekeeper for him in Kobe. Although, with her expressionless face, 'that inscrutable mask', she remains mysterious to him, he knows that she defends him 'from the rapacity of her countrymen' and always waits for him. The author's other amorous experiences include a dancing girl in England and a Samoan girl who stayed with him—all novel and exotic women in unusual situations. As this story and other stories like Dawe's or Hales's show, it seems that women of different races, in so far as they amuse the man and remain under his control, do not provoke negative comments in Western masculine writings. More broadly, as Spivak argues, women of different races are 'made to carry all that is hidden and denied in white women'.[25] As Broinowski (1992) puts it, the Asian or Middle Eastern woman is very often seen as a victim in Western discourse, and the worlds of East and West are divided—one as female, emotional, instinctive, subservient and exploitable, the other as male, pragmatic, rational and dominant.

However, when Western power is threatened and the situation seems dangerous, anxiety and harshness seem to appear in the writing. 'The Shell Fighters', which was published in *The Bulletin* in 1909, shows the potential hostility held by Australians toward the Japanese in the form of an adventure romance of the sea. Japanese shell hunters, who are interested in the profitable northern seas of Australia, are trying to move into the area, when they meet a ship sailed by the 'Dangoes'. Here, Australians are not the direct enemy of the Japanese but rather are observers and they act as umpires in a fight between the Italians and the Japanese. In the end, the Japanese lose in the 'rastle', pay respect and give a peerless pearl to the Italians. In this story, unlike accounts by Idriess who knew the reality, the author again puts the Japanese in the category of typical villains who are destined to be defeated. However, he does not describe the Japanese as extremely wicked either, for the Australians are not directly threatened by them. There is a tone of alertness, perhaps suspicion, but it is not as strong as in some other stories that warn of the future possibility of a Japanese southbound movement. More political stories that propagandise the necessity of active vigilance against Japan had already appeared by this time in many other writings. These will be discussed later in this chapter.

Japan as a source of romance

In some Australian short stories published from the late-19th century, Japan provided a romantic and exotic background to a plot—as seen in 'Another Mysterious Disappearance' in the previous chapter—and was more obviously scrutinised in some women's writings. For example, in *The Australian Town and Country Journal*, two short stories in *The Children's Corner*' edited by Ethel Turner, 'Roses and Grey Mist' and 'Purple Wisteria', used Japan as their settings. They are about a love affair between a Western man and an Eastern woman, in a simpler and more compact narrative than Praed's *Madame Izàn* (though in *Madame Izàn* the relationship is reversed). It may be because these 'authoresses' had not had enough knowledge of Japan, (although whether they had visited Japan or not is not known) and thus chose to adopt a more conventional and comfortable pattern for their main characters than create a more audacious relationship between an Eastern man and a Western woman, like Praed. Also because of the restriction of the short story form, characters have to fit into certain limitations, unlike novels, which can expand and introduce many turns in the plot.

'Roses and grey mist' by Edith Graham, a prize-winning story for *The Australian Town and Country Journal* and serialised over four issues in 1910, is about a young girl called Mizpah, whose mother is English and father Japanese. She speaks fluent English and falls in love with a young American lieutenant and eventually helps him by leaking military secrets stolen from her father. However, when she discovers that the lieutenant is betrothed to his English cousin, she regards this bond as more sacred and important than their verbal promise and refuses to go to the United States with him. The heroine is depicted, although she is half-English, as being very Japanese in nature. She constantly expresses her admiration for 'Mt Fuji, the land of rice fields and flowers', her feelings for her kin and 'the faith of her ancestors'. The story ends with the disclosure of her conspiracy and she is arrested, (possibly to be executed) as a traitor to her country. The development of the plot is very similar to the triangle of Pinkerton—Cho-Cho-San—Mrs Pinkerton, thus showing another variation on the 'Butterfly Phenomenon'.

'Purple Wisteria,' written by an author called 'A Gipsy Girl' and published in 1911, is also a story of the eternal triangle, but it develops differently (*The Australian Town and Country Journal* 14.6.1911:36). The story seems to be written in a more hasty and simplified manner than 'Roses and grey mist' and tells of a young girl, Saya, whose mother was English and father Japanese. Because of her beauty she serves as a model in the Japanese landscape for foreign tourists and painters. A young Australian artist instantly falls for her and they become engaged. However, he is to go back to Australia and leaves her with a promise to return. In Australia, the artist suffers from a disease and almost loses his eyesight. An Australian woman, Carmen, saves the artist and takes care of him. Yet knowing the promise given to Saya in Japan, she sorrowfully backs out of the triangular relationship, brings him back to Japan and sails away. Here, we see a variation on the usual 'Madame Butterfly' solution in which the Oriental woman is abandoned by the Occidental man and dies in sorrow. The last half of the story tells of how Carmen bravely deals with the situation for others' sake. If the author had further developed the inner emotions and conflicts of Carmen, this story could have established a new type of feminine writing in Australia.

The way these two authors represent the heroines of mixed race, letting them keep their English heritage while remaining conscious of their 'Japaneseness', may be regarded as a similar technique of integrating Japanese characters as in Praed's *Madame Izàn*. In this tale, Kencho, the Japanese husband of the Australian heroine, is not of mixed race; however, he is educated in England, has the 'manners and refinement of an English gentleman' and speaks the language perfectly. The heroines here have not lost their Oriental beauty and exoticism, but at the same time, are able to speak fluent English and retain an element of Occidental culture as well. It is a kind of 'promotion' for the Japanese, as we have seen in the case of *cha-ya* girls of ex-samurai clan in the previous chapter. This 'promotion' is probably needed by the authors in order for the women to conform with the codes of contemporary society in Australia. By setting the heroines in this way, the authors may feel that it is easier for them to be wooed by European men. At the same time, by making the girls half-English and thus more accessible, the writers' uneasiness in depicting a totally unknown group of people—the Japanese—may have been lightened. They are able to write not about the 'Other' but rather another story about 'themselves'. Interestingly, these heroines of mixed-races obviously need to have been products of interracial marriages; however, not much explanation about this social contract is given in either story. This may suggest that the authors were not very familiar with such situations and these parent-characters were there only to serve as background. These mixed-race or hybrid figures, those who are in-between cultures or 'cultural-go-betweens', keep recurring in later works as interpreters, translators and spies, thus providing Australian readers with a more accessible means to legitimately accept Japanese characters as real people.

On the other hand, although these stories are written from a moral perspective and always end in 'legitimate' relationships as in *Madame Izàn*, they also seem to offer a means by which women writers are able to express their dreams or desires. As the setting of the story, Japan may provide the author with more freedom to move, and as seen in Cooper's 'Another mysterious disappearance,' (1890) a place in which 'a fairy tale' can safely unfold. The stories from these women writers are not as ambitious or fantastic as the stories of some male authors; however, within the scope allowed to them by society, it was easier for them to further romanticise their stories in the Japanese context than in the familiar Australian one. This category of 'romance', which is based on fantasy and the unknown, which is part Oriental and part Occidental, may be a unique form of English writing in Australia during this period. After the two world wars, more accurate and real information about the 'Other' permeated among the general population and more and more authors started to tell of their first-hand experiences; stories based on fantasies were replaced by stories based on real events and experiences.

Japanese 'invasion novels'

At the end of the 19th century, a young English actress staged a series of dramatic 'shockers' at the Brisbane Royal Theatre. One of these stage plays dealt with a Japanese invasion of Australia. At the end of the drama, a Japanese man-of-war is attacked by an Australian submarine torpedo and sinks, with the sea 'becoming full of drowned Japanese'. The final scene was welcomed by the audience with 'wild applause, and the singing of local patriotic melody' (*The Bulletin* 23.10.1897).

This was a period when both romantic and hostile approaches to Japan can be observed side by side in Australian literary works. The hostility derives from a general fear at the time of the 'yellow peril', Asian invasions of Australia and from the actual culture shock and friction caused by contact between white settlers, Asian immigrants and temporary workers in Australia.

While both socialists and nationalists were trying to establish a 'utopia' for white colonists, other races were not included as part of their scheme. Social Darwinism, as Meaney and many others have pointed out, 'lent a pseudo-scientific authority' to the Australian self-consciousness of 'nation' or 'race' and supported the idea of the Aborigines being a 'dying race' and the inferiority of other non-white races (Meaney 1996). Richard White (1987) also argues how Darwin's theory was misapplied and used to justify the social order, while explaining away the racial conflict of those days. Examples include the article 'White, yellow and brown', in which Randolph Bedford justifies using the Aborigines and the natives of Australian Papua in the defence of Australia from Asian invasions, for they are 'born soldiers'. Although he admits the white settlers have treated them in degrading and cruel ways, he sees no contradiction in their fighting for 'White Australia', for 'they are Australia's own black men' and '[i]t is their protection, too' (Bedford 1911b).

Unlike the fear of a Chinese invasion of Australia, which was heightened because of the increasing number of Chinese present in Australian society, a fear of a Japanese invasion was based on international politics. As Frei calls it, this phenomenon was the 'Japan syndrome'. Australia seemed to react to Japan's every move. On seeing Japan's victory over China in 1895, Australia made Japan the major target of an Australian immigration restriction bill the following year. After Japan's victory over Russia in 1905, Australia founded a league for national defence and eventually federal decisions were made to allow for the introduction of compulsory military service in 1911 (Frei 1991). Japan's capture of Formosa was regarded as part of its southward advance, one step closer to Australia. More patriotic and nationalistic concepts of Japan such as 'Dai Nippon Shugi' (Great Japanism), 'Hakko Ichiu' (Eight Corners of the World under One Roof) and 'Kodo Shugi' (the Imperial Way Policy), suggested Japan's future course of imperialism and expansionism and resonated ominously in Australia. The British–Japanese alliance in 1902 did not quieten Australia's uneasiness although it was meant to prevent Russia's movement in Manchuria and in the Balkans and was in the interests of the two countries concerned. The treaty did not necessarily mean a non-aggression pact between Australia and Japan. Like Bedford, many journalists and writers expressed their suspicion about Japan and were not reassured by the treaty.

The self-image of many Australians at that time as seen in various writings and drawings, was that of a naïve and unprotected young country. As citizens of a country made up of six British colonies, Australians had just celebrated their nation's centenary and with nationalism at an all time high, they were about to be born again as a new federal nation. Words that are often associated with 'young' include 'immature', 'inexperienced' and 'innocent' and indeed these were the images that Australians used for themselves. Australia's potential enemy was seen as 'old', 'cunning', 'shrewd and 'experienced' (although at the same time Japan was often seen as inexperienced in terms of international politics) and a non-Occidental country. Despite the lack of experience with Japan as a real, rather than imaginary, enemy, Australians' fears were dramatically increased. Many cartoons and illustrations that appeared in periodicals of the day clearly show how Australians saw themselves; they frequently depicted Australia as a young, vulnerable boy or woman, who was about to be harassed or captured by malevolent monsters from the East.

With the nationalistic movement and the recent British–Japanese alliance, some Australians strongly advocated independence from their mother country. Some socialists, like William Lane, announced the necessity of establishing a 'utopia-like' society for workers, posing the idea of 'a closed continent, of building up a free community apart from the world', which, in his case, suggested an impossible community in Paraguay (Wilde, Hooton & Andrews 1994:445). Although such ideas may have been unrealistic and mostly failed, they involved many intellectual, as well as political figures. Examples included James Murdoch, who was influenced by Lane's ideas and left Japan for a year to join him in Paraguay. Nationalists were keen to educate the majority who still regarded themselves as being part of the Empire. Part of the argument for the necessity for independence from Britain, included Australia's position in the Pacific and its defencelessness in the wake of war. As Meaney points out, Britain's indifference towards Australia was often criticised in Australian writings. The lack of enthusiasm from Britain in protecting Australians from their potential enemies was disappointing and Australians eventually started to express their determination for independence and self-protection. As seen in Mackay's (1908:11) verse of that time, although they were 'sons of the Empire' and 'whene'er she calls, then on land and sea - / Our swords from their sheaths will leap', they would 'fight not as dependents—but equal peers'.

Thus, what Meaney calls 'invasion scare novels' (1996) became a category of its own and developed its own uniquely Australian tone. Invasion novels were also published in Britain, including George Chesney's *The Battle of Dorking* (1871) and William Le Queux's *The invasion of 1910* (1916). However, their subject was Britain versus Germany or France and it was about wars between 'equals' in the West. In the case of Australia, the race issue was the dominant part of the theme. Chinese invasion novels were published earlier, which seem to have been an Australian response towards a number of incidents, such as the Chinese commissioners' visit to Queensland in 1887. Although the commissioners came to investigate the condition of the Chinese colony, it was generally suspected that the real purpose of the visit was to prepare for the future occupation of that area (Ouyang 1994). Another influence was the negativity directed towards the Chinese presence observed in Australian mines, plantations, on the coasts and eventually in urban towns and cities. After the publication of such Chinese invasion novels as 'White or yellow? A story of the race war of AD 1908' written by 'Sketcher' (William Lane), published in the *Boomerang* in 1888 and *The Yellow Wave* by Kenneth Mackay in 1895, Japanese invasion novels and stories started to appear. Examples include 'The day the big shells came' by Arthur Adams for *The Bulletin* in 1908 and 'The Commonwealth crisis' by CH Kirmess, which was serialised in *The Lone Hand* from 1908 to 1909 and then turned into a book with a new title, *The Australian Crisis* (1909).

Australians' publicly expressed fear of Japan gradually became distinct from their fear of China, and articles and comments that targeted Japan started to appear. For example, in *The Bulletin* (31.8.1895), a column was written to show how the Japanese government was concerned when Japanese coolies in Fiji 'fell sick of an epidemic, [and that it] sent a doctor all the way from Japan to enquire into the circumstances'. The columnist concludes that Japan is 'imbued with a keen spirit of patriotism' and is thus different from China and that the Japanese seem to be 'determined that intruders in Asia shall know that Japan must be reckoned with'. As mentioned in the previous chapter, the same observation of Japanese individual patriotism was made by Murdoch and Praed. The writer of an article on the Japanese expedition to Antarctica emphasises that 'the Japanese must need to have every glory.' The writer quotes a lieutenant, the leader of the expedition:

> [w]e are doing this for the honour of our Sovereign. Whilst the means at our disposal are inferior to those of our rivals, by succeeding we shall show to the world that we are the equals and the superiors of races better endowed than we are (*The Australian Town and Country Journal* 4.1.1911).

More and more articles expressing caution about Japanese movements started to appear in journals and magazines.[26] Such scholars as Murdoch and HB Montgomery in their 'expert' books on Japan expressed optimism and viewed Japan in a positive way. After staying in Japan and learning about its politics, society, culture and people, British-born Montgomery welcomed Japan's alliance with Britain, declaring that Japan's 'strength will never be put forward for any selfish aims or from any improper motives' (1908). Such political figures as Senator Edward Pulsford and EH Foxall, a private English secretary, were among those few who voiced their pro-Japan opinions (Frei 1991). However such positive bias was rather rare and most articles carried an anti-Japan tone.

In 'The sham of our defence: our toy army and our tiny fleet' which advocates 'the need for Real Military Training and the Provision of Super-Dreadnoughts', Arthur asserts that '[i]f Japan is not the enemy, then there is no enemy' (1911). Bedford declares that the alliance is 'a bad example' and such folly will give Japan 'a jumping-off place for an Australian invasion afterwards' (1911b). He continues that '[t]he Australian's first duty is to Australia, his second to the people of his blood; first, loyalty to country, and then loyalty to race' (Bedford 1911b:225). He tried to stir Australian patriotism with colour-consciousness. It was typical wartime writing, as revealed in Tolstoy's contemporary condemnation of journalists and writers and their articles and stories during wartime, which aimed to arouse fear and anxiety among the readership with their patriotic phrases and hyperbole. These articles exposed weaknesses within the nation and exaggerated the possible enemy's power and malice (Tolstoy 1961 [1904]:211, 220).

'The day the big shells came' and 'The Commonwealth Crisis' were written in such an atmosphere. It was after the Russo–Japanese war, with the proposed Japanese southward movement becoming more and more aggressive and Japan's confidence in fighting in a world war becoming obvious. It was the period when in Japan, 'Southward-ho!' protagonists started to show their strong interest in the South, with such protagonists as Yosaburo Takekoshi using a slogan 'To the South! To the South!' (Frei 1991) which must have stirred further fear and anxiety in Australia (Meaney 1996:228–263).

In 'The day the big shells came' (Adams 1909), an ordinary Sydneysider, who is called 'Didn't Think Australian', is the protagonist. He 'didn't think' Australia should be independent, nor should Australia build up the defence forces and prepare for a possible invasion. He 'didn't think' that 'Asia had already discovered Australia, and was doing some hard thinking about ways and means of how to take possession of it from a nation of Didn't-Thinkers'. He works in the city, goes back to his house in the suburbs, spends a quiet evening, and presumes that tomorrow will be the same ordinary day. However, 'the big shells come,' and the Japanese start to attack Sydney. Without even a rifle the 'Didn't Think Australian' is unable to protect himself and his family, and eventually the Japanese march on and invade his house. Strangely, the first Japanese to break into the house is 'a quiet little Jap gentleman whom he had often seen in the streets of Sydney—a merchant or something—smoking a little black pipe and wearing a hard black hat'. But now the Japanese merchant is wearing his military uniform; under his gentle disguise he is a fierce, wicked soldier who intends to take over the house, that is, Australia. It is the camouflage of the Japanese that Australians should have seen through. The 'Didn't Think Australian's' unprepared resistance against the Japanese has no effect and his voice of struggle echoes in vain. As a journalist-novelist-playwright whose 'forte was urban social comedy' (Nairn & Serle, 1966:9), Adams introduced an ordinary man into the invasion story and let him represent Australians as a whole. This tragic-comical story clearly embodies the aim of the author to warn against ignorant and indifferent Australians; and with the protagonist's death, it comes to a bleak end.

The other Japanese invasion scare novel, 'The Commonwealth crisis' (serialised 1908-9) employs a more political approach. In the preface, the author states decisively that the idea of the story is a warning of 'a coloured invasion of Australian territory' and that his intention is to inform people of the dangers 'to which the neighbourhood of overcrowded Asia exposes the thinly populated Commonwealth of Australia'. Although the author's identity is not clear, the style is both journalistic and political; the author affirms that it 'deals exclusively with realities,' and the occasional interpolation of the author's facts and figures to the novel provide it with a realistic and urgent tone.[27]

The form of this novel is retrospective from the year 1922 upon events supposed to have happened in 1912. In that year, the Japanese military of 6,000, already trained in Formosa to adjust to the Australian climate and start a colonial life, secretly land on the shores of the Northern Territory for the 'peaceful invasion'. It is explained by the Japanese government as an unofficial migration without the authority of the 'Mikado', the emperor; however, it is a well planned colonisation provoked by Japan's constant famine and the increase in its population. Thus Australia starts its resistance against the invasion and in the development of the story, some particular defensive strategies may be identified. First, as is mentioned, the author's strong warning of the need for preparation against the invasion. When a Thomas Burt discovers the invasion, he is not believed by anybody—his neighbours and the local bureaucrats—and this delays the action which Australia should have taken, thus ending in the Japanese landing and the consequent armed clash. Here the contemporary Australians' negative attitude towards, or tendency of avoiding reality or a crisis, is emphasised.

Second, Britain's indifference and lack of support for Australia becomes an issue. Considering the alliance with Japan to be valuable in Asia, Britian does not want to show its objection too quickly. The English wonder 'how far they should commit themselves in defence of the principles of racial exclusiveness which were not shared by the masses in the United Kingdom,' (Kirmess 1909:73) and are unconcerned about 'the significance of race contrasts' in Australia (Kirmess 1909:187). Eventually, in other British self-governing dominions, 'Maoriland, Canada, South Africa, and the United States,' the Defence League of All the Whites is organised; however, Britain's reaction to this is to threaten these dominions by creating financial sanctions against them. Australian stocks are 'knocked out' in the London market, causing further economical turmoil in Australia.

Vexed by the slowness of the government, 'the White Guard' is formed by 'a more aggressive type of Australian'—'the shearers, skin-hunters, drovers, station-hands, prospectors and many adventurous vagrants'—'for revenge and retribution' (Kirmess 1909:548). This is a voluntary campaign carried out by mates in the bush fueled by their eagerness and ambition, as well as their romantic yearning for adventure. In spirit at least, they seem to be similar to the 'diggers' who volunteered during the Boer War and the Great War. The inactivity and slow reaction on the part of the government/politicians, as expressed in 'The Commonwealth Crisis', are exaggerated and extrapolated to also mean the ignorance of the ordinary citizens. The episode of the White Guard reflects the author's message to Australians to stand up and take action; just as Fox, the editor and presumably the author of this novel and others did when they established the National Defence League in 1906. The battle is fierce, the beloved commander-in-chief falls and the White Guard, although heroic, is exterminated. The novel ends with the Japanese colony still remaining in the Northern Territory with Britain's mediation and the author concludes on a bitter note of propaganda, telling Australians to beware of the Asian invasion and to promote white settlement in the North. In the final part of the story, the internal conflicts among the Australians, as well as the external friction with Britain, are depicted more seriously than the colonisation of the North by the Japanese themselves, thus showing the political shakiness and instability of contemporary Australia (Dixon 1995:152).

The novel reflects current events; it was serialised in 1908, the same year the Japanese consulate in Townsville was closed and the movement to expel Japanese from Australia reached its height. In the story, when the Imperial Government takes economic sanctions against Australia's Act to compel Asians in Australia to register, Australia becomes a 'wounded giant groping blindly round...for something he might wreak vengeance on—for some victim' (Kirmess 1909:421). Australians boycott and eventually assault Asians in towns and in the country. The author believes that Australians are usually generous and because of this they have avoided 'the infliction of personal revenge on private individuals for failings of the race to which [the Asians belong]'; however, there is no way to prevent this 'anti-colour riot' now and 'the unfortunate coloured aliens still residing in the country' are targeted (Kirmess 1909:422).

Most authors of these invasion scare narratives were journalists who were able to obtain first-hand information of Australia and its surroundings and they wrote not only to inform readers but also to 'educate' them. Consequently, as Ouyang and Meaney insist, these invasion novels are more political than 'scientific' or 'dystopian' (Meaney 1996b; Albinski & Ikin 1995a:74). As a result, there is again scarcely any description of the Japanese as individuals in these novels. The Japanese are mostly treated as a 'mass', thus forming a threatening and uncanny composite figure who harasses the Australian people. These novels are not meant to convey human nature and characteristics, or to depict dramas which would occur in personal contacts and relationships, but rather to give strong messages to 'enlighten', (perhaps to brainwash) the general public. For that purpose, there is no need to describe the enemy personally. In fact, this also applies to the Australian characters. 'The Didn't Think' Australian is presented as nobody of particular distinction but an ordinary Australian man, an allegorical figure. In 'The Commonwealth crisis,' the first character Thomas Burt, does not play an important role except to be a member of the White Guard. Many other Australians are also not fully individualised. In 'The Commonwealth crisis,' it is not the individuals but the nations that are the chief characters.

Indeed one significant role of such journals as *The Lone Hand* was in establishing and promoting images of Japan as a possible enemy. When Australia was trying to form a 'nation', thus creating a boundary for its own identity from the alien 'other', the 'loss of boundaries...[which may be considered as] a particularly masculine anxiety', occurs when a Japanese invasion is made the topic of such journals, and becomes a serious issue (Dixon 1995:135). When American President Theodore Roosevelt warned Australians to 'beware of the 'unmanned' North' and of the 'rape by the Japanese', this engendered fear became an important topic for many male authors.

In *The Lone Hand* itself, articles on Japan and its expansion were frequently published, especially around the time of 'The Commonwealth crisis'. Examples include Louis Esson's sequential articles on Japan under such titles as 'Japan's *Jiu-Jitsu* Diplomacy', (August 1908) which talks about Japan's 'tricky' diplomatic attitude towards China, 'Japan the Gamester' (September 1908) which criticises Japan's despotic Meiji Constitution and 'Japanese Imperialism' (October 1908) which warns against Japan's aggressive foreign policy. Short stories of actual battles between Australia and Japan often appeared too and in many such stories the problem of how to outwit and defeat the more numerous and more heavily armed Japanese becomes the main topic.[28]

One of the very few examples of articles which present a Japanese point of view is a comical letter to the 'Most Honorable and Highly Perfumed Editor of the Lonely Handcuff', written supposedly by a Japanese (1.9.1909). With many errata, this 'Japanese' letter writer tells how he is astounded by such Australian habits of beach bathing, Chinese gambling and croquet playing, as well as the country's weakness as a nation. The writer proposes that Australia be 'policed by polite Jap[sic]', governed 'from paternal Tokio'. This article is an example of contemporary thoughts about how ludicrous it is for an ordinary Japanese, with such different lifestyles, to have such an ambition as to take over Australia.

Authors of other contemporary magazine articles include such political figures as William M Hughes, then a Member of Parliament and GF Pearce, then Minister of State for Defence, as well as critics on military subjects such as Arnold White ('Vanoc'). Hughes argues for the importance of military training for all male subjects in the country, citing the example of Switzerland in 'Defence' (1.1.1909), while Pearce warns that Australia can be a very rich prize for nations 'alien in ideals as well as in race' and proposes arming on a gigantic scale ('Democracy and Defence' 1.3.1913). White condemns Britain for being a 'bad European' by signing a treaty with Japan, thus contravening 'the unwritten law that white men should stand together against all combinations of coloured men' ('The Defence of Australia' 1.11.1911). The juxtaposition of such political articles next to the short stories in a single issue has the effect of strengthening the persuasive or propagandistic intention of the authors of the fictitious works.

Alfred Deakin, who diverted public funds to assist in the foundation of the magazine, was a close friend of Frank Fox, the second editor of *The Lone Hand*. Deakin, a prominent figure of the time, was the 'chief architect of Australia's defence and foreign policy', especially from 1903 to 1910. Deakin is said to have 'believed his immediate task was to awaken public opinion to the possibility of an Asiatic invasion' (Dixon 1995:136). Naturally many of the contributors to the magazine were 'people who saw themselves as leaders of public opinion and sought to enlighten the 'popular mind' (Dixon 1995:139). In order to heighten awareness of the recently federated Australian nation and achieve the power to do what they needed to do, Japan became one of the Asiatic enemies that provided an effective 'evil' symbol for politicians, journalists and novelists, and it became a natural target in *The Lone Hand* and other publications.

When different authors approach Japan and try to describe its people, there are, as we have already seen in early Australian writing, various ways in which they do so and how the Japanese figures appear depend on the author's gender, power, position and his/her own ideas and ideologies in the Australian context.

When the Japanese are represented as a potential enemy, they are faceless and dubious figures; in terms of Australia's fear of Japan and indeed of Asia as a whole, they become a composite 'mass'. Louis Esson used this technique in an article for *The Lone Hand*: '[Japan, led by] a handful of clever despots...can act quickly and "en masse", and this may have echoed in the consciousness of Australians as a fearful image of the invading "Other"' (Esson 1908). It should be remembered that Japan itself took measures, especially in the pre-Second World War years, to present itself as an unanimous entity so that it could heighten its nationalism as well as show a united front to the outside. It employed such propagandistic slogans as 'Ichioku Isshin' (a hundred million hearts beating as one) or 'Ichioku Hinotama' (a hundred million people as one bullet) (Dower 1986:30–32). Thus it was a reciprocal gesture to stereotype and represent Japan as a 'mass'. It was a time when Japanese nationalism was expressed aggressively outward and Australian nationalism was expressed inward. Japan's southward imperialism was countered by Australia's desire to remain intact, though it felt vulnerable as an isolated and endangered part of European imperialism—in particular the British Empire. International politics of the time was very much reflected in the Australian literary scene, which resulted in the new category of invasion novels. However, when Australia finally faced Japan as a real enemy during the Second World War, their description changed again. This is discussed in the next chapter, the 'War Experience'.

Part Two

War-Time Encounters with the Japanese

chapter three

Fiction of the 1930s and the Pacific War

What was the Australian literary reaction when the imagined fear of a Japanese invasion of Australia became a reality? A possible attack by a strange enemy, the action and ensuing reaction and battle, escape and refuge, and for some, captivity, were no longer merely the products of the imagination of anxious, nationalistic writers, but had become a real possibility at the outbreak of the Second World War. Japan, before and during the First World War, was not really a fully-trusted ally, but at the same time it was not yet a potential enemy. In fact, the British–Japanese alliance of 1902 was renewed in 1911 for a further ten years until the Washington Conference in 1921. Macmahon Ball, one of the Commonwealth representatives of the Allied Council to Japan in 1946–47, commented that some Australians even reacted to the Russo–Japanese War in 1905 with a favourable view towards Japan, for its 'heroic resistance to Russian encroachment on the Asian mainland' (Ball 1969:21). While there was 'anxiety lest the conclusion of the Alliance might be used as a lever by Japan to extract concessions from Australia in terms of Japanese immigration and settlement', (Ball 1969:20) and suspicion on the part of Prime Minister William Hughes that Japan might use the alliance to gain access to Australia and suddenly betray her to Germany, Japan as an invader was still imaginary for most Australians before and, for a short time, after the First World War.[29]

However, as the First World War proceeded and as Britain concentrated its activities in Europe, Japanese naval activities in the Pacific became more conspicuous to Australians. Japanese ambitions were already obvious before and during the war, with such examples as the annexation of Korea in 1910, the occupation of Tsingtao, the 'Twenty-one Demands' to the Chinese Premier in 1915 and the dispatch of troops to Siberia in 1918. At the time of the First World War Armistice, Australia and Japan had already crossed swords on the issue of race. In drafting the Covenant of the League of Nations, Japan's suggestion to incorporate the principle of racial equality met strong opposition from Hughes, the Australian delegate, and was not adopted in the final draft.

Although there were more composed observations of Japan made by others at the same time—examples include the Director of Military Intelligence EL Piesse (1919–23) (Meaney1996:45–47; Frei 1991:93)—this opposition arose out of a fear of Japanese meddling with Australia's immigration policy, which in turn might have undermined the White Australia policy. There was also the threat of Japan's possible southward movement to Australia that led Hughes to demand full rights to control immigration and trade in the German part of New Guinea in order to prevent Japanese from settling there (Ball 1969:26–27).

After the Washington Conference in 1921, at which the treaties that enabled Japan to retain naval fortification in the Northwest Pacific were established, there was 'comparative tranquillity in the Pacific for nearly ten years' (Ball 1969:28). Japan was a lesser problem although it remained a nuisance, and during this period even 'yellow-peril phobic' Hughes could afford to reduce his government's defence budget (Meaney 1996:27). However, in the interwar years of the 1920s and 1930s, Australian nationalism grew and '[t]he conservatism of the Anzac myth was then in concert with dominant ideologies'. As 'part of an Imperial Culture', Australians, whether conservatives or socialists, were often indistinguishable from Britons in their outlook (Caesar 1998:156). National defence was always a major concern and newspaper articles in Australia showed a constant interest in Japan; its postbellum development in industry and trade, its social changes and the internal movement toward democratisation and external military movement around the periphery. Prominent examples include *The Lone Hand* correspondent Dr J Ingram Bryan and his articles on Japan from 1918.

Japanese invasion scare in the 1930s

Japan's seizure of Mukden in 1931 ended the seeming tranquillity in the Pacific. The series of Japanese military movements in the 1930s, beginning with the Manchurian Incident in 1931 started to shake not only Australians' composure but also that of many others in the Asia–Pacific region. At the beginning of this decade, Japan was a good trading partner of Australia, which was still in the throes of the Great Depression. Japan's imports of wool and wheat from Australia almost doubled during this period, which suggests that Australia's reaction to Japan's diplomatic and military initiatives was not as quick as it could have been. However, as Japan's expansion proceeded, Britain remained more preoccupied with an immediate threat from Italy and Nazi Germany in Europe in the late 1930s. The Australian government was nervous about Britain's Eurocentric imperial defence policy as the mainstay for its own security and so Australia's uncertainty and caution increased in the Asia–Pacific.

Fools' Harvest, written by Erle Cox and published in 1938, was one invasion novel that reflected a fear of a Japanese invasion held by many Australians at the time. Cox, like the authors of earlier invasion novels, was a journalist and first serialised the story in *The Argus*, to which he often contributed. He then published it in book form in 1939. In a comment on its introduction on the cover, the novel was called a 'possibly prophetic novel' on 'the war of the future'. It depicts how Australia could easily be invaded by some Asian power, seized and controlled for a long period before it could free itself and start to rebuild itself as a nation. With a story inside the main narrative, the novel focuses on a retrospective of the hero whose manuscript on the invasion in 1939 and its aftermath in Australia is found and published in the 1960s. The narrative is occasionally interpolated with 'editors' notes' and facts and figures, which leaves a realistic and quasi-scientific impression upon the reader, much like 'The Commonwealth Crisis', discussed in Chapter Two.

According to Cox's story, on 'Bloody Saturday' 23 September 1939, Australia becomes the victim of a surprise raid by an unknown enemy, whose flag mark is the 'red diamond on a black square'. The unprepared Australians are scattered in chaos and their disordered and misdirected scratch troops and guerilas yield to the methodical and systematic attack of the enemy. In three weeks the whole of Australia is held in captivity under the control of 'the Paramount Power' and Australia's socio-political state becomes like that described in George Orwell's *Nineteen Eighty-Four*, where strict regulation of information, speech and commodities are put into practice. However, unlike *Nineteen Eighty-Four*, the situation described here was brought about not by politics but by the racial 'Other'. The fear of totalitarianism is exaggerated in order to remind contemporary readers of Fascism, Nazism and Japanese militaristic imperialism and of the possible consequences should Australia be conquered by such a force.

The enemy's identity is revealed as 'Cambasia,' which states the necessity for military 'action' (not war) against Australia due to their 'unavoidable protest against repeated acts of harsh trade discrimination against Cambasia and to secure similar rights of migration to those afforded to European countries' (Cox 1939:141). As in 'The Commonwealth Crisis,' the enemy is depicted as a whole, and its 'overwhelming number' is emphasised. 'Destroyers' or 'invaders' are the names given to the enemy without individual personality. Each of them is given only a military title like 'a soldier' or 'a sergeant,' or described as groups such as 'a team,' 'a squadron' or 'military police.' The only 'Cambasian' personality who speaks out is the Brigadier General; however, he does so as a symbol of the malice of the whole enemy (Cox 1939:183). The enemy, faceless and arriving 'en masse,' brings similar terror as in other invasion stories, and against their cunning raids each of the amateur Australian soldiers fights as a 'man'.

In another contemporary invasion novel, GD Mitchell's *The Awakening* (1937), the enemy, possibly one of the Axis Powers, surges also en masse to Australian shores, lands and invades, again always as a group and without individual faces. Australians' individual manliness, and heroic and self-sacrificing bravery inherited from their predecessors, is very much valued in Mitchell's novel, expressing the idea of individual heroism inherited from the 'Anzac myth'. The Australians could have had well organised forces but for the leftists, 'the "parlor pinks" and all their tribe [who] arranged themselves with every form of pacifism...to oppose all attempts at adequate defence measures' (Mitchell 1937:24), or 'the altruists, sentimentalists and other well-meaning but thrice accursed visionaries' (Mitchell 1937:180). Regardless of how courageously the Diggers' sons fight against the enemy, their naïveté at having believed 'that there would be no more wars' only leads them to reap a fools' harvest (Mitchell 1937:149).

The invasion has such urgency and provides such a tense atmosphere, that while the enemy itself is invisible, the disorderliness of the Australians in a situation of panic is conspicuous throughout the story. At the first attack in Sydney, people lose their sense of restraint and order, and show their ugly sides by starting to loot and setting off riots. On the run from the cities, fugitives fall into a state of panic, and their rage, fear, raving, lawlessness and demoralisation are contrasted with their previous decency and ordinary life. The principal fear is the fall of their 'white' country into alien hands. The escapees are all white people, and there is no mention of Aboriginal inhabitants in this novel. 'Cambasia', or perhaps Japan (and its people) is presented as vicious and malignant. Being an imaginary enemy, they are the medium through which the author attempts to bring out Australia's ignorance of the danger and possible consequences of war. In the fictional battle, Japan and the Japanese are created as a group 'enemy', as in other invasion novels, which pretend to offer realism but seem to lack reality. These invasion novels thus offer a strong means to warn unprepared Australians. WM Hughes, in his foreword to *The Awakening* (dated 15 July 1937), argues the necessity of the 'force', insisting it is 'compatible with pacifism and essential to the future safety of Australia and the white race'.[30] In such novels, the fear of an imaginary foe was used to arouse a feeling that a great threat may debase or undermine Australians' 'mateship' or manliness, which had often been regarded as intact in the Australian context.

Into a real battle with the Japanese

In the two years after the publication of *Fools' Harvest*, the anxiety manifested in journalistic sensationalism was intensified with the announcement in 1941 that Australia was at war with Japan. The outbreak of the Pacific War was the event 'about which there had been recurrent discussion in Australia for more than half a century' and now it had finally come true (Ball 1969:66). However, unlike the previous wars in which Australia fought with much sympathy and allegiance towards Great Britain, this was a war which Australians had to fight in close proximity to their own land and against a long-time and yet totally unknown enemy in a strange theatre with much more modern arms and strategy than previous wars. Australians were going to experience a very different war out of which a unique literary experience, different both from the First World War literature and from the invasion novels, was to be born.

Like some literary works from the First World War, many novels and stories from the Second World War were written by authors who themselves had served in the military, thus forming part of the memoirs genre. Many novels about the First World War took years to appear because there was 'a period of shocked silence before potential soldier-writers could become articulate' (Barnard 1987:95). Besides, silence was sometimes chosen by 'revenants who returned from the dead', and who were 'discouraged from talking of the strange and estranging aspects of their experience, except to each other' (Pierce 1996:15–16). According to Bingham, writers need time 'to mature in their thinking, to develop rich and useful insights concerning those terrible and yet wonderful days', in order to present war novels and books on prison-camp life (Bingham 1985:x). In this chapter, war novels written in the 1950s, comparatively soon after the war, are examined to gauge the authors' reactions to the enemy and to war.

There do not seem to be the optimistic and glorious elements in Second World War writing that mythologised the soldier figure in the same way as literature arising from the First World War. However, while it may have taken time, writers did want to tell their stories of the war with the Japanese. As publication figures show, over 400 pieces of Australian war fiction were written as 'the Australian response to the conflict' (Hosking 1985:234). If the aim of the invasion novelists was to frighten and agitate their readers using imaginary and unreal battles, the aim of Second World War literature authors may include convincing their readers of their extraordinarily devastating and destructive experiences which were real and constant in the war theatre.

As is often pointed out, many literary works after the First World War articulate a brand of Australian heroism, mixed with elements of the bush myth, 'Pride o' Race' (such as that of Ginger Mick), nationalism and loyalty to the British Empire. As Gerster (1992:ix) points out, Australian writers on war were often the 'publicity agents for the "Digger" as an exemplar of heroic racial characteristics'. It was said to be a kind of 'test-match' for Australia, and as with the great sacrifice in Gallipoli, the Australian myth of masculinity and the maturity of the nation was to be proved in the battlefield. As Ginger Mick, the protagonist of *The Moods of Ginger Mick* (1916) sees it, it was 'the struggle of Australians' purgative coming of age, which would lay the foundation for future vigorous growth' (Gerster 1992:35). There is this 'glory syndrome' (Gerster 1992:2) which is found in the First World War literature, and it presents Australian soldiers as the 'twentieth-century embodiment of classical heroic virtue' (Gerster 1992:5), which in turn might have served as a means to create an Australian mythological figure, which embodies a general, almost homogeneous, image of ANZAC soldiers, typically 'tall, lean and bronze'.

However, the Second World War gave Australian war literature, especially the battle narratives with the Japanese, a very different perspective not only on war itself but also on their own soldiers, the nation and the enemy. Unlike the almost 'quixotic' enthusiasm often observed in the Great War writings, many of the 'sons of Anzacs' went into action with 'an attitude of cynical realism', without any expectation of 'martial glamour and glory' (Heseltine 1964:221). This time, unlike the foreign travel to the Middle East, Africa and Europe, which 'seduced many young Australians into enlisting during the Great War' (Gerster 1995:192), it was jungle and rain forests, in which enemies were hiding and waiting for them, that characterised this Asia–Pacific war. Although back in Australia, such poems as Mary Gilmore's 'No Foe Shall Gather Our Harvest' became a kind of battle hymn and helped to boost nationalistic sentiment against the Japanese and their possible invasion, outside in the real war theatre was an alien atmosphere, an atmosphere in which soldiers found themselves in a sphere separated from the world to which they belonged. In Eric Lambert's *The Veterans* (1954:94), when the soldiers are sent to New Guinea after a three-week leave, they know as 'the veterans' that they are going back to 'the maddening, stupefying, soul-killing monotony; the endless repetition; the slow bemusing torture of regulations, once again the hateful authority of fools, careerists, and brutes'.

Jungle and the Japanese—double 'Otherness'

In 1941 Japan for the first time became Australia's official enemy and the two nations were to face each other directly after so many imaginary battles over almost half a century. Australian soldiers, before fighting against the Japanese, had to fight against a new setting: the 'jungle'. As Krauth puts it, each of them had to fight their 'private war against the jungle'. They were 'cocooned' by the jungle, thus being subject to physical confinement, as well as subject to the psychological restrictions of war (Krauth 1983:16). Unlike the open battlefields in the Middle East, this was Australians' first experience of jungle warfare. Their uniform was changed from khaki to dark green and they were tormented by both the enemy and this adverse green battleground. Jungle or 'the green hell' and its 'crowding suffocation and disorientating alienation' (Krauth 1983:17) was a theatre where many things devastated and discouraged Australian soldiers. Its miasma, rotting fungus and tangled lianas made them sick and slow in their movements; mosquitoes kept pestering them in the steamy heat; 'mud covered their boots above the ankles and thick leaf mould floated as a slippery trap' (Cleary 1954:268). TAG Hungerford's *The Ridge and the River* (1952) begins with a description of the 'humidity and wetness' of the New Guinea jungle. For those who came from dry, temperate weather and open fields, the enclosing jungle was always chokingly 'wet', 'soaked', 'sodden', 'damp', 'moist', 'dank' and 'soppy'. Rain did 'all the damage' possible in the battle (Forrest 1985:77). In this unbearable climate and condition, soldiers 'rotted slowly, insidiously, and the heat sapped [them]' (Forrest 1985:221). Jungle and ranges were always 'ancient and without end' for the Australian soldiers, young and old, infantrymen and officers alike. It was a rotting forest and here the 'offensive required intense internal cohesion between groups and between individuals,' and 'without that cohesion, the jungle absorbed and dissipated an attack like a sponge absorbs water' (Forrest 1985:77). This was where the traditional 'mateship' of the Australians was tested; it also often led to harsh conflicts among them.

As Gerster puts it, Australian soldiers had to fight against 'the twin terrors of the jungle and the Japanese', (Gerster 1992:220) and sometimes the two became identical. When a section went on a jungle patrol, they were 'walking towards Japan' (Forrest 1985). Jungle and Japan became synonymous with a fearful existence and thus came to mean a total 'Otherness' for them. The Japanese were invisible among the jungle, 'where there were eyes...everywhere behind the leaves,' which eventually drove the soldiers into mental despair (Forrest 1985:112). Fighting against this invisible enemy in the rainforests of New Guinea was such a strain on their nerves that the platoon members in *The Climate of Courage* even expressed their wish to withdraw and wait for the enemy back on the mainland so that they could at least see them (Cleary 1955:223). Without knowledge of, or direct encounter with the Japanese, their fear of this unknown enemy was increased in this atmosphere.

The 'sound effects' of the jungle were also dramatic in these novels. The voices of the Japanese soldiers in the jungle, 'shrill and mocking', pestered the hiding Australian soldiers and echoed 'sometimes distant, sometimes close at hand, continuing for hours and hours like a nightmare' (Lambert 1954:212–223). The night-birds' eerie sounds were thought to be 'Japs signalling in the deep jungle' (Hungerford 1971:50). Later, Russell Braddon commented baboons' voices were high-pitched and 'sufficiently human to sound demented' to prisoners-of-war's ears in the Malayan jungle in *The Naked Island* (1961:184). It was crucial to 'listen to the jungle' in ambush or on patrol so that they could have the jungle on their side and did not have to fight the two enemies together. 'Jungle smell' is often a topic as seen in Norman Bartlett's *Island Victory* (1955:16) where 'the thick, jungle, and the heavy tropical smell of rotting vegetation' is compared with 'the home smell, the good, dry, earthy, gummy, Australian smell'. It also features in *The Veterans* (Lambert 1954:175), where 'the flat, hot, earthy smell of the jungle' is emphasised.

The jungle has sometimes been described as a greater enemy than the Japanese, and not just for Australians. Norman Mailer described the jungle in *The Naked and the Dead* (1948), as the 'worst opponent' to the allied Americans on Anopopei island[31] in which 'a choked assortment of vegetation was sucking for air and food like snakes at the bottom of a pit' and '[e]verything was damp and rife and hot as though the jungle were an immense collection of oily rags growing hotter and hotter under the dark stifling vaults of a huge warehouse' (Mailer 1948:45). With its limitlessness, the jungle 'absorbed the sound of war, all their wounds inflicted by the hand of man' (Forrest 1985:15). The Japanese even became 'no more destructive than the jungle', when the Australian battalion in New Guinea continued to be in action for three weeks and 50% of the soldiers were suffering from malaria, dysentery or scrub typhus (Cleary 1955:221). For the fugitives in *The Long Pursuit*, the enemy were the Japanese, the native nationalists and 'the wild country' which eventually added the worst of all enemies, 'despair' (Cleary 1967:166). Jungle, which often becomes metaphorically synonymous with the Japanese, also overawed the Australians with its scale, 'too large for the eye to comprehend', like 'the fourth dimension'. It obstructed the Australian section which was heading for the blue sea, and becomes the symbol of victory, freedom and liberation from 'the enemy' (Forrest 1985:100–101). In jungle warfare, 'life was suspended'; deprived of nerve or feeling, soldiers were cut off both from their past and from their future, and only the moment that they had to survive existed (Forrest 1985:55).

To the Japanese presented in some novels, however, the jungle was no less alien than to the Australians. It seemed to be an 'Otherness', by which they were also affected. In Hungerford's 'Last Entry in Red' (1950), the Japanese central figure, Ayashi, sees the jungle as a place where 'the ceaseless drip of water on to the ageless mould might slowly send a man mad', and his every move is also watched 'in the eerie, lifeless green twilight of the great swamps, with a million unwinking phosphorous eyes' (Hungerford 1989:81). When he is killed in combat, his body is quickly 'claimed by the jungle...a green beetle walked over his lips and disappeared into his nostrils, and a waving tendril of kau-kau...swayed over him and fell across his chest' (Hungerford 1989:88). Hostility and the destructive power of the Burmese jungle on Australians and the Japanese alike is emphasised in Russell Braddon's 'Song of War' (1958). The jungle which conceals both parties seeks to 'silently...destroy them both,' and it was 'no man's ally, not even neutral' (Braddon 1958:8).

In *Fires on the Plain*, (1967), a Pacific War novel, Japanese author Shohei Ooka reveals how Private Tamura, a sensitive and intelligent man wandering in the jungles of the Philippines starving, swings like a pendulum between madness caused by sheer hunger and his sense of being a civilised man; he is finally driven to cannibalism.[32] George Johnston (1943:193) notices that the jungle claims its destructive and demoralising power over their enemy the Japanese, too. Jungle warfare thus added hardship for both sides in the battle against the enemy.

Japanese as enemy

Fighting against the Japanese was a new experience. War against the Japanese 'produced nationalism's other side, xenophobia', and 'learning to hate the Japanese enemy through propaganda gave new impetus to Australian racism' (Alomes & Jones 1991:269). Australian soldiers may have been lectured about 'Japanese mentality and morale' before the real combat; however, much of what was told to them was propaganda, which made them more wary of Army Intelligence (Lambert 1954:94). Now the Japanese had become 'the enemy', which brought them on to the same stage, the 'war theatre', as the Australians. In terms of race relations, many Australians were convinced by such advocates as Hughes who insisted that racial inequality showed up in their enemy's capability. Their enemy, of a different race, had to be weaker and could not rival Australians at war. In order to confirm the superiority and dominance of the white race, as Said (1978:204) points out, the difference—that is the 'weakness' of the Orient which is to be conquered and controlled by the Occident—has to be emphasised. As such, the part that the Japanese play has to be that of 'the inferior'. In order to prove this inequality in racial difference, or to cling to the belief in their racial superiority, some of the Australian characters were given prejudiced attitudes. Polo, an Australian private and one of the fugitives in Sumatra in *The Long Pursuit*, is shown to need prejudices as his 'crutch': 'if he didn't have 'em, his inferiority complex would bowl him over' (Cleary 1967:135). For the other fugitive Maynard, 'most men's nationality was part of their personality, they wore it like a second skin', and like Polo, he admits his bias not only towards the Japanese and the Sumatrans but also towards other Europeans, thus showing an Australian exclusiveness which reveals the extreme contrast between a sense of self and the 'Other' (Cleary 1967:105). When people of other races become their allies some of the Australians show their reluctance to welcome them as such. In Eric Lambert's *The Dark Backward* (1958), however, the protagonist Anthony Harding holds a more balanced view of the native guerillas in Malaya with whom he co-operates in the fight against the Japanese. In this novel, the Japanese military is described as the symbol of imperialism; thus a force which in the author's socialistic view has to be destroyed. It is ironic that later the allied force becomes the next symbol of imperialism, which extinguishes the Malayan guerilla force including the protagonist's Chinese lover.

Racial difference gives a kind of permission to be hostile and cruel toward the enemy of another race, and sometimes this dehumanisation makes it easier to kill. According to Norman Bartlett in his novel *Island Victory* (1955), the enemy was 'enormously more a stranger than a German or an Italian, fellow products of Christendom, could ever be' (Gerster 1995:194). For Ron Fisher, a nineteen-year-old Bren gunner, the ten 'live' Japanese that he first sees are 'something less than men'. He would punch the enemy into the mud with his Bren, and then sit down and write a tender letter to his mother telling her he is fine and asking about domestic matters (Forrest 1985:102–104). In *The Climate of Courage*, the Australian army, after fighting in the Middle East and now in New Guinea, 'were suspicious of the new enemy, expecting the Japanese, because they were Oriental, to be more diabolical than the Germans, were preparing for...killing by gas' (Cleary 1955:169). However, it may not be appropriate to cite only this sentence here for in the following sentence the author mentions that 'such Occidental diabolisms as the napalm and atomic bombs' were 'still secret and did not yet worry the conscience, if any, of the Army'.

Racial difference was, of course, used as war propaganda in Japan also, and Japanese soldiers and civilians were all told that, as one, they were to fight against the cruel white invaders of the Asia–Pacific, 'Kichiku-BeiEi' (Demon Beast the British and American). When the Japanese enemy was not yet directly known, and was still seen collectively, their description was also collective. 'The Japanese look all the same...act the same, like puppets' (Lambert 1958:29) to the Australians, and they are again often described 'en masse' as in the invasion novels. Jon Cleary's later novel *The Long Pursuit* (1967:20–21) begins with a scene in which a group of Japanese soldiers on bicycles singing martial songs, ride into a British–Australian ambush and are wiped out by machine-gun. When shot, 'they fell lavishly, like Indians in cowboy films'. This 'mass' or group depiction which Ron Fisher called 'the pagan avalanche' was sometimes incredible and 'the ranks formed again and charged forward' (Forrest 1985:150–156).

However, when one recognises the human being in the enemy, despite the racial differences, and when the soldiers happen to have direct contact there are moments when they hesitate to kill another human being. In *The Long Pursuit*, the fugitive group in Sumatra encounters four Japanese. Some are younger than the youngest member of the fugitives, and they look confused at this unexpected encounter, for '[w]ar for each of them was still a brand new experience, and amazement at their own involvement was as much part of their feeling as enmity' (Cleary 1967:72–73). The fugitives argue but decide not to kill the Japanese and leave them there. Later, Maynard, one of the fugitives, when trying to steal valves for the radio from the Japanese store, observes Japanese soldiers who are strolling by the stalls of the natives and sitting outside some bars and cafes without guns; and then he realises they are exactly like relaxed English soldiers in Kuala Lumpur or in Singapore which in turn gives him a kind of shock (Cleary 1967:185). When an enemy is without his gun, without the symbol of war, he can look more human despite the racial difference. While hiding in the Japanese base, Maynard realises the Japanese guards turned a blind eye to beggars, the native flotsam, who stayed inside the Japanese base to avoid the heavy rain. He is again surprised to see that the Japanese could also have pity even while his hatred of them is reaching its peak. There are, then, epiphanic moments of truth, when one is able to recognise humanity in one's enemy. However, these moments are not strong enough to prevent the present military action and Maynard has to kill one of the same guards soon after this episode (Cleary 1967:235). In chasing a Japanese on the run in New Guinea, the protagonist in 'Back from Gangaya' (Lambert 1953:159) just cannot pull the trigger when he looks into his cornered game's eyes 'a long, hopeless, far-away look already seeing death' so captures him as a prisoner instead .

The shock that one receives in witnessing the human side of the enemy unarmed is perhaps best described in *The Ridge and the River (*Hungerford 1971). Two Australian soldiers, Malise and Evans, when on their patrol accidentally see Japanese bathing in the river. About a dozen Japanese, all naked and exposed, are splashing water, playing with and teasing each other, and eating bananas. Their gestures and actions are exactly the same as any Australians in similar circumstances. For Evans, it is the first time he has seen a Japanese 'unarmed, undressed, helpless, playing', which makes him afraid with 'a strange new fear'. Previously the Japanese were always:

> cruel, foreign—a remote face and a shapeless figure half screened by the cover of an ambush position, or a waddling, armed ape who might have raped

European women in Hong Kong and would like to do the same in Perth or Sydney (Hungerford 1971).

As he watches them from behind, he sees similarities in each of the Japanese to his own platoon members and realises they are the same as any other men. It frightens him because now he knows it will be impossible for him to kill them as he used to kill the 'curious Japanese things', as he had killed animals. On the other hand, Malise, whose mother is a half-caste Aborigine, does not share the same shock or thoughts as Evans; he knows what being the 'Other' means and is not shocked to see the enemy's human side. Later that afternoon, however, when they are attacked Evans shows no hesitation in throwing grenades in the middle of the enemy and he returns without any doubts to the instinctive nature of fighting in order to survive (Hungerford 1971:92–94).

It is easier for one to kill his enemy without sympathy. Again, similar responses towards the Japanese enemy can be observed in American war writings such as Mailer's *The Naked and the Dead*. In the novel, when Sergeant Croft is about to throw a grenade he sees one of the Japanese soldiers who '[has] a pleasant bland face with wide temples and a heavy jaw' looking cow-like with sturdy and calloused thick hands, and he cannot believe this Japanese soldier is going to die in a second (Mailer 1948:189).[33] Ridges, who believes he is killing only heathens, is flustered when he learns there are over a hundred thousand Christians in Japan and that he might have killed some of those in the previous battle (Mailer 1948:218). In *The Ridge and the River*, young Manetta's reaction is of the same kind as Ridges' when he finds out that Wallace and others have killed twenty Japanese instantly in an ambush. They may have been '[f]ive fathers, a school-teacher, four fishermen, five farmers, two clerks, two university students, and a professional gambler' (Hungerford 1971). It is enough to Manetta's tired, tensed body and soul to cry out: 'Oh, God, won't I ever get used to it? Twenty of them, and not birds or fish or rabbits. Men, men, *men*!' (Hungerford 1971:135). In *Island Victory*, too, Australian soldiers try to forget that the Japanese solders are first human before they are 'soldiers for the Emperor', otherwise they cannot bear the actions of killing other human beings (Bartlett 1955a:88).

These feelings would not have been experienced except in hand-to-hand battle, within close physical proximity. For the RAAF in *Island Victory*, when they were in the air the enemy was not only the Japanese but 'the weather, misjudgments, some mechanical eccentricity or other' (Bartlett 1955a:17). For them the Japanese are 'abstract enemy, slant-eyed bastards in semi-human guise'. However, on the land, although the enemy become more fearful for their closeness, they are 'more ordinary, men who sighed and laughed, slept and groaned' and they themselves feared Australians as Australians feared them (Bartlett 1955a:116). In David Campbell's short memoir 'Recco over Rabaul'

(1942) the emphasis was not only on the enemy in the Zero pilot's plane, but on the air battle, the mechanical problems and navigation skills needed to endure the long flight in a damaged plane. It was the era of a highly mechanical and technological war, which in turn had altered the notion of such wars when 'height detaches the bomber pilot from actual violence' and the distance from the actual battle scene makes him wonder if 'there [is] a war on this soft spring morning.' Campbell flies over an enemy ship to attack, slides small 'darts' from his aircraft, sees a plume of smoke start from the stricken ship and 'congratulates himself on his good bombing' without actually witnessing his enemy. Only when he is counter-attacked does he realise there is an enemy who has the intention of killing him (Campbell 1955:179–188).

Besides seeing the enemy at a close distance, there seem to be other important factors involved in recognising one's enemy of a different race as another human being. Photos of the family and letters kept in pockets, a familiar tune, or common religious beliefs often give pause for one to change one's views of 'the other' even when their outlook, language, custom and manners are very different. Examples include the Japanese junior officer in the novel (and film) *Blood Oath* (Williams 1990). The senior officers make him the scapegoat for murdering Australian prisoners on the island of Ambon, but he gains sympathy from an Australian soldier when the soldier recognises in the Japanese a humble belief in Christianity and love for his family.

'Cause' for the Australians

Was there, then, some dominant ideology or cause which sustained these Australian soldiers when fighting against the Japanese? Few war novels and stories of the time seem to express extreme patriotism or beliefs which would justify their war with the Japanese. In many stories the Australian soldiers often declare they fight not because it is what they wanted but because there was no alternative. Oscar White, a Sydney department store clerk who found he had become a young soldier in the jungle of New Guinea, joined the army not from patriotism, but because it was what everybody else did. Eventually, he starts to feel 'cheated' for what he has to go through (Hungerford 1971:30).

The issue of race, which had been problematic since Australia became conscious of Japan, was surely one of the motivations to fight, both official and private. However, although each individual in the novel may have had some degree of bias against the Japanese, this is not presented as a strong motivational force for any of the characters in most of the novels and stories of the time. Racial hatred on the battlefield is not revealed to be strong enough to sustain the daily fight. Rather the Australian soldier became 'not a human being who pursued other human beings, but a creature with the means to murder who pitted his cunning and endurance against a similarly equipped creature' (Lambert 1954:173).

Faith in one's capability, in religion, or in mateship, is described as the motivating force for Australian soldiers to remain on the battlefield. For Australians it was more often than not because of simple faith, rather than ideology, politics, diplomacy or economic necessity that the soldiers needed to endure. Ron Fisher, a young Bren gunner, describes faith as 'a shield that a man built around himself' and it 'lay in those parts of life which experience had proved reliable in time of need' (Forrest 1985:141). For Kevin Manetta, son of humble Sicilian parents from Redfern, faith in God is what keeps him going (Hungerford 1971:27) while for Howard and his mate Wallace, who had 'nerves of steel' and believes in the power of arms, there is a love of the Bren gun and because of that a dedication to killing (Hungerford 1971:35:43:178). For Farr, a veteran back in the New Guinea jungle, it is humanity that he thinks he is able to believe in. For others of a simpler kind it is 'their instinctive courage and goodness, their inarticulate beliefs' (Lambert 1954:174). So when this faith is shaken and replaced by despair or 'hopeless nihilism' it can be fatal. Kevin Manetta, although he has his faith in Christianity, is 'overcome, almost terrified, by the futility, the no-meaning of what they were doing' (Hungerford cited in Gerster 1992:142). Krauth also points out that 'self-respect', which was the most-assaulted human trait in war time, especially in the private war in the confinement of 'jungle cocoons', was the key for regeneration of each soldier (Krauth 1983:18).

The Australians were also fighting against the Japanese in order to defeat Japan's imperialism and expansive militarism. As Farr, the protagonist in *The Veterans*, states, 'the knowledge that [they] were fighting in a just cause, that fascism must not come to their homeland, must triumph nowhere', was their armour which kept them going (Lambert 1954:119). However, at the same time as an integral part of British Empire they were also involved in Western imperialism and militarism themselves.

In *The Long Pursuit*, the only female fugitive Elizabeth Blinker—daughter of a rich Dutch plantation owner—who once believed in 'their Divine right to rule', realises how much the Sumatrans actually hated them. Kamar, an English-speaking Javanese who served as the fugitives' guide, lets the Europeans know from time to time what it has really been like for the natives in the past 300 years of English or Dutch colonisation, every time adding his favourite phrase, 'No offence, Sir'. Kamar, who later turns out to be the leader of the local Communist group, tries to sell the Europeans to the Japanese, believing in the uncertain promise of Japanese co-operation in freeing their country from Western imperialism, and is stabbed by Maynard. According to Cleary, for some of the Australians this was a war in which they first looked at imperialism in practice from both sides and that for the people who had long been victimised, history was 'just the propaganda of the victors' (1955:238).

In Eric Lambert's *The Dark Backward* (1958), which expresses the author's denial of imperialism and his espousal of socialism, Anthony Harding realises that although he is fighting against the Japanese with the Malayan communist guerilla force, once the Japanese are out of the picture he will be on the side of another form of imperialism—from the Western side which threatens the Malay people's liberation. His Chinese comrade and lover Liu-Sun refuses to go to Australia with him because of Australians' perceived difference in ideology and race. As Caesar (1988:149) points out, Australian nationalism at this time was 'not in opposition to British imperialism but rather contributed to, and is contained by, that imperialism'.

In some novels the Japanese are described in a similar state: they were not fighting for their faith in Imperial Japan, but for their own survival. Their acts and attitudes are bound by the set of Japanese military codes, 'Senjinkun', advocated by Hideki Tojo, then Army General. It was the overall control of the codes of the Japanese that was driving them, rather than their own faith in them. While Ron Fisher fights against the Japanese 'for the most elemental reason of all, to stay alive', he realises that 'the enemy were no longer fighting for the Emperor but fighting because they were driven there by their officers' (Forrest 1985edn:156:165). Young private Turner in Bartlett's *Island Victory* calls out for his mother when he bails out from his plane, just as the pilots of the 'kamikaze' squad, in their high teens and early twenties, called out for their mothers when they made their suicidal dash at the enemy, instead of the laudably believed phrase: 'Banzai—Long live, the Emperor!' (Bartlett 1955a:104).

Degenerating war for both parties

War offers an extraordinary condition for fiction writers. Those who were in it for a long period are described as living only for the 'here and now'. The Australian soldiers in *The Ridge and the River* who are 'from all over Australia, from all walks of life' after living so long together and sharing their fate in such a long battle in the New Guinea jungle, become 'stateless, belonging only to the war, to their unit, and to one another' (Hungerford 1971:198). This ambiguous 'mateship' accompanying their hatred and anger toward the enemy kept them going; and the enemy here does not necessarily mean only the Japanese, but also the jungle, the officers of higher ranks, and the whole course of things that brought them there. One of the Australian platoons spent their Christmas Day shooting a company of starving Japanese who had come to a taro plantation in search of food thus marking the day as 'a festival of carnage and filth'. This everyday atrocity produced 'men forever changed' (Lambert 1953:154) in the same way as was private Tamura who turned to cannibalism in *Fires on the Plain*.

For the Australian characters in these war novels, war turns out to be never glorious, unlike the implication of the Anzac legend. As Tully, an older platoon member and a good husband and father back in Australia, confesses, 'none wished this war' and they did not deserve it. After so many losses, he believes they should never let it happen again (Lambert 1953:158–159). The Japanese and the jungle have given soldiers a common expression: 'a look of exhausted resignation' after a long battle in New Guinea rain forests, and '[t]hey had lost their enthusiasm for the war and would fight now only for their own survival. Ideals and causes, patriotism and anti-fascism were buried somewhere in the black slime of the past three weeks' (Cleary 1955:232). An old lady predicts to Farr when he is being sent to New Guinea for another three years of combat: 'this war will make people come to their senses; they will know it'll have to be the last war…' (Lambert 1954:21). An ex-university lecturer of English and now senior flight lieutenant Philip Masters cynically concludes that 'it was [an] American war in the end' (Bartlett 1955:84), and that he and other Australians fighting on the Kamiri island are only co-operating for General Douglas MacArthur to gain another stepping stone on his road to Tokyo (Bartlett 1955:1).

The long battle and isolation in the jungle deeply affected the Japanese, too. On the run in the jungle, Private Tamura in Ooka's *Fires on the Plain* (1967) falls into a most devastating condition. In the style of diaries written in a mental home for the purpose of treatment after the war, Tamura looks back and sees how isolation, strangeness and hunger in the jungle can drive one into an abnormal state of mind. On Leyte Island in the Philippines in 1944 when the American landings and their all-out attacks started, the Japanese troops begin to scatter and run away to a port which was believed to be the last resort for them. Tamura, who is suffering from tuberculosis, is refused admission to the hospital where (like everywhere on the island) food is a major preoccupation and food rations are the ticket to anything. He is also rejected by his own squad, threatened by his leader and told to put his 'hand grenade to good use and make an end to it all' (Ooka 1967:4).

Tamura, who does not have 'the slightest will either to fight or to kill' (Ooka 1967:19) since he landed on the island, is different from most other soldiers, and he is vaguely aware of the approach of his death as the solution. He wanders through the hills, shoots a native woman and robs her of salt, and starts to wander again. However when the salt, his life-savior, is all consumed and starvation reaches such a height, Tamura starts to feel like eating anything, even the flesh of the dead. He tries to eat the flesh, but somebody, either the dead Filipino woman or something more divine, seems to be watching and disturbing him, preventing him from eating another human being. This represents the last thin line between Tamura's humanity and non-humanity in the jungle, whether or not to eat human flesh, even when hallucinations invite him and the dying body itself gives permission to be eaten (Ooka 1967:186). In many Australian war novels and stories we find this problem of each soldier's consciousness and conscience, although it is often to a lesser degree. Harsh weather, physical and mental fatigue and torment, a strange and alien background, all rip off a man's surface and reveal a very basic side of himself.

At the critical moment of dying, Tamura is offered a piece of dried meat by a fellow soldier, and eats it as if it was monkey's flesh. That is the moment, the ultimate transgression, when he has changed. He asks God to destroy his former self. War offers such a hard opportunity to giving testimony of one's humanity, not only for the Australians but also for the Japanese. In the asylum after the war, Tamura thinks that the gentlemen who oversee wars 'will not understand until they have gone through experiences like those [he] had in the Philippine mountains'. And that it is only then that their eyes will be opened (Ooka 1967:232).

Enemy Japanese as human beings

TAG Hungerford is one Australian author who, by presenting the Japanese in a devastating condition, emphasises their more human side rather than offering a flat and hostile description of them as the enemy. As Cowan points out, Hungerford shows the enemy both as a fellow human being, caught in the same circumstances, and also as a mere cypher to be destroyed in his stories. He brings a new notion of the enemy into his story which leads to 'an admission that in some things there is no difference between sides, nations, individuals'. By doing so he proves that 'there may be no real winners to this kind of conflict' (Cowan in Hungerford 1989:8). His short stories 'Letter' and 'The Last Entry in Red' are different from other writers' in that they are written from the enemy's perspective.

One of the stories, 'The Letter', which was first published in *The Bulletin* in 1949, compares two equivalent soldiers, Australian and Japanese. Mort, from Western Australia, is now assigned to duty in New Guinea and continues writing to his wife from the station there, but has no chance to send the letters. The Australians ambush a Japanese unit and Mort clubs a Japanese soldier to death.

In the Japanese soldier's pocket Mort finds a roll of oiled silk which contains a piece of paper. It is sent to the intelligence section for translation. It turns out to be not a secret military document, but a letter written by the dead Japanese soldier to his wife more than a year earlier, asking exactly the same things as Mort: '*How's the kids, how's the weather, how's the crops?*' In the futility of war, every time one kills, one is killing his counterpart. As Johnston points out, Australians were to see the evidence of the humane side when they examined the corpses of their enemy (Johnston 2004:133).

Hungerford's other story, 'Last Entry in Red', which was first published in *The Bulletin* in 1950, is about the discovery of a war diary written by a Japanese lieutenant called Ayashi. When an Australian division takes over from the Americans and lands on Bougainville Island, the Japanese troops divided into small units are all scattered. The Australians destroy these units one by one through an operation called 'dawn attack.' Ayashi's diary is obtained after one such operation and is translated. It turns out to be 'a tale of cunning and desperation, hunger and homesickness' (Hungerford 1950:81). In his diary Ayashi always dreams of home and 'bowls of white rice, heaped, steaming' (Hungerford 1950:81). Because of such starvation, ugly behaviour erupts among fellow soldiers. Food, which consists of only small pieces of dried fish, lead to fights and even murders, just as in Ooka's *Fires on the Plain*. 'Men had coveted it, schemed for it, cheated and lied and murdered to get it, and had lost it' (Hungerford 1950:88). Ayashi's diary ends with the 'last entry,' 'which was written in red...but not in ink; which had no words, but was most easily translated of all...'(Hungerford 1950:81). Starvation, as in *Fires on the Plain* and as we will again see in the next chapter on POW narratives, could defeat any sense of comradeship and create a most aggressive character in human beings.

'Song of War', a prelude to *End of a Hate* by Russell Braddon, is also written from the enemy's perspective.[34] It describes a Japanese second-class private called Yamamoto, an ignorant peasant-born young man whose hands are made for hoes and ploughs rather than for weapons. He is despised by his higher ranks, platoon members, and even POWs for his clumsiness and stupidity. Eventually by his own mistake, Yamamoto invites a British platoon to attack them. A soldier, Anderson, is to take out Yamamoto on sentry-duty; however, when he is about to kill this ignorant soldier, and sees his 'strong, good natured face' and hears him singing—although the words were incomprehensible—the tune of 'Auld Lang Syne', he becomes awe-stricken. Yamamoto's 'utter defencelessness, unsuspecting contentedness and the plaintive melancholy of the song all combined to fill Anderson with fearful revulsion for what he had to do', and he stabs the Japanese, crying. In his dying moments, Yamamoto understands Anderson's tears, the 'savage sadness' on his face, for he knows that Anderson, as a soldier, has to kill 'a man who sings', not one who is fighting. Soon after that event Anderson is also killed, and their momentary mutual understanding is nullified as their corpses lie side-by-side in the jungle.

For both Australians and the Japanese, jungle warfare demanded such immense sacrifice. On the battleground, however, they were equal in that they were the enemy of each other and they were both the victims of jungle, the combat, the rank and standing of the military, and the war itself. They were of different races, of different historical, cultural, and social backgrounds, and of different ideologies, but they were alike in many ways. This was perhaps the first time that the ordinary Japanese were treated as major subjects and described together with Australians in the form of fiction. Out of that situation of equivalence, similar points of view and, furthermore, a balanced way of looking at the enemy eventually produced different options for describing the Japanese who had now emerged distinctly for the first time in Australian narratives. The actual crisis of war against the Japanese had thus provided Australian writing with an opportunity to reflect on racial issues, national and international policies and ideologies, on themselves and on the 'Other'. This came about because they were fighting on the same battlefield as equals. As Cox and other invasion novel writers had predicted, when the Japanese became conquerors of the Australians for a time during the course of war, we were to see very different writing about the Japanese by Australian prisoner-of-war writers.

chapter four

Prisoner-of-war narratives in the 1940s and the 1950s

It has been pointed out by Dower and others that the Second World War was a 'racial war' in which various kinds of racial misunderstandings, discrimination, hatred and unfairness were revealed, not only in the relationships between enemies in the war theatre but also within one's own territories. Some Allied nations blamed Germany's doctrine of 'Aryan supremacy' over Jews, Romany and other minorities, but at the same time contradicted their own position by not allowing citizenship to the natives or non-Caucasians in their own countries. Japan's outward propaganda was to free white-dominated colonies in Asia under the scheme of the 'Greater Asia Co-Prosperity Sphere', fuelling what Dower calls 'Asian racial dreams and Western racial fears' (Dower 1986:6). However, it was a hollow gesture that ended in the attempt to impose another form of imperial dominance over the already suffering Southeast Asian nations.

In the Pacific War, Japan was 'challenging the entire mystique of white supremacism' (Dower 1986:6), and its extreme case was realised in the relationship between white prisoners of war and their Japanese captors. As we have seen in previous chapters, race issues raised fear and hatred in the Australians against the Japanese. However as soldiers on battlefields, they were equals. Once the Australians surrendered and were captured by the Japanese, they were relegated to a lower status by another race, which until this point had never happened in Australian white history and had only been imagined in the scare novels of the 'yellow peril' invasion genre. Australian prisoner-of-war experiences at the hands of the Japanese thus formed a very different kind of writing to earlier narratives, not only because of the frightening facts of wartime atrocities in the prison camps, but also because they recorded the overthrow of supposed white supremacy.

Australian prisoner-of-war memoirs written about the Pacific War present a unique category, both in Australian writing and in war narratives. This category provides the first experience-based accounts of white Australians in degraded circumstances under Japan, the old enemy in their imagination from the 19th century. It also gives a very different image of the brave and strong Australian soldiers represented by many writers and journalists. The fact that they were dominated by a race that they considered to be 'inferior', and placed into such a humiliating position in alien lands and cultures provided Australians with a totally different viewpoint not only of their enemy but also of themselves.

Prisoner-of-war experiences had such a strong impact on those who went through them that memoirs were written from soon after the end of the war in 1945 to well into the 1990s. The reasons for recording these experiences were many: some hoped not to forget but to remember what had happened, some wished to record history and let others at home and in coming generations know what had happened, while still others wrote as a form of therapy. However, most publications did not occur immediately after the prisoners' release, with ex-prisoners being aware of 'the gap between their own memories and popular knowledge' (Nelson 1985:5–6). It took some time for the ex-prisoners to face what really happened and to try and understand it. Only after a considerable time lapse were they able to tell their stories. But with the passing of time, popular mythology sometimes replaced direct memory.

A few writers, however, chose to tell their stories straightaway. While spending his years as a POW in the labour camps of the Thai-Burma Railway, Rohan Rivett was urged by other fellow prisoners to record all—'Everybody's counting on you to tell our story'—which led to the publication of his book a year after his release (Rivett 1946:204). Some memoirs, which were published soon after the war, still carry the excitement of the aftermath of such extreme events as war and captivity. Examples include Walter Summons' *Twice Their Prisoner* (1946), in which he states in his introduction that his story is a warning of how close the Japanese were to invading Australia and what 'terrible nature of life' they could expect under the Japanese, (Summons 1946:16) as well as Brigadier Blackburn's comment in the foreword of the same book, that '[every prisoner's sacrifice] contributed in no small measure to the fact that Australia was saved from invasion' (Summons 1946:13).

In this chapter, memoirs written and published in the 1940s and 1950s, which seem to present more spontaneous and fresh accounts of prisoner-of-war experiences than those in later decades, will be examined to see how the relationships between Australians and the Japanese under such unusual and extreme circumstances are portrayed.

Australian prisoners under the Japanese

Unlike fictitious war literature, prisoner-of-war memoirs are meant to be 'true' stories. In their acknowledgements or forewords, the authors declare that what they describe is 'fact' and 'truth'. Russell Braddon's first of his sequential memoirs, *The Naked Island* (1952), is said by the author to give 'the naked truth' from a 'private soldier's angle'. For Rohan Rivett, his 'inside story of the Japanese Prison Camp' is 'a personal record', 'not merely one man's book' but the result of his fellow prisoners' collaborative assistance. Betty Jeffrey's *White Coolies* (1954) is 'the story' of Australian Army nursing sisters taken prisoner by the Japanese and is based on excerpts from her diary hidden in her pillow in the POW camps. Roy Whitecross asserts that in his memoirs, 'the personal story of an Australian prisoner of the Jap', 'every word of [the] story is the truth', and 'the incidents are real'. These authors all suggest that the aim of writing their POW memoirs is to disclose as vividly as possible their extraordinary experiences under Japanese captivity.

Of course there is not only one type of POW memoir that could be called '*the* POW life and experiences'. There were differences among the camps, and the prisoners' well-being or 'mal-being' depended greatly on the Japanese camp leaders and guards. For example, Roy Whitecross (1951:10) calls Changi 'a haven of rest' compared with other prison camps. The difference in rank between officers and soldiers made a crucial difference as well, as a British memoirist John Coast admits.[35] As a Lieutenant Officer, Summons acknowledges that there was some 'luxury' enjoyed by himself during the captivity, including owning a car at the very beginning of his captivity in Sumatra and relatively light duties inflicted on him later (Summons 1946:73–74). Thus, as McQueen (1991:332) points out, 'the differential treatment [by the Japanese] according to rank shows that there was more than one value system at work in determining Japanese behaviour'. In addition, the physical and mental condition of each prisoner as well as his position among his own men determined how he survived POW life (which also applied to female captives as seen in Betty Jeffrey's memoir). All the authors wrote about what they underwent and how they suffered during their POW experiences with the Japanese. Consciously or subconsciously, they selected what to write and perhaps what not to write.

To explore what these Australians wrote about their Japanese captors is to see how they first wished to express their feelings about their enemy-master. Almost all the memoirs are written in the first person, thus putting the author in a more responsible position than in third-person narratives. Often these memoirs are based on the facts and impressions they had recorded in their diaries or memos. At the time of publication, there may have been some self-censorship and editing, especially about themselves, for 'unmediated reporting' is achieved more in fiction than in non-fiction in many cases (Malcolm 1999:viii). However, there seems to be little censorship in writing about the enemy-captor. The authors seem to express their 'true' and unabashed impression of the Japanese. They were also able to write about how human beings, enemies and allies alike, became dehumanised in the extraordinary circumstance of war, a situation which, unless experienced first-hand is beyond the wildest imagination of many writers. The eagerness of POW memoirists to let readers know what they went through seems to be apparent from the efforts authors made with their books—most of the POW memoirs provide maps which show the courses of their progress or retreat and the positions of POW camps, figures and tables as well as glossaries of Japanese and other local languages. All this lends an air of authenticity to the accounts that follow.

One of the strong appeals to readers of the prisoner-of-war memoirs seems to be the authors' initial astonishment at being taken prisoner and enslaved by the Japanese. This is often expressed in the titles of their books. Betty Jeffrey's 'White *Coolies*' or Roy Whitecross's '*Slaves* of the Son of Heaven', Kent Hughes's '*Slaves* of the Samurai' (1946) all sum up their sense of humiliation. The prevailing Australian image of the Japanese as the enemy had presented them as something less than human beings—childish, monkey-like and primitive. Collective madness was often suggested in the propaganda against the Japanese before and during the Pacific War (Dower 1986). In this degraded situation, where the 'sub-human' enemy became their slave master, a reversal of perceived 'normal' racial relationships is exacerbated. Pearl Buck warned that the Pacific War would be 'the racial war…the bitterest and longest of human wars…between the East and the West' (Dower 1986:210–211). It is in this context that the Australian prisoners-of-war first looked at and recorded the Japanese at close range, with much humiliation and dismay. Summons, who was taken prisoner twice—first by the Vichy French army and then by the Japanese army—clearly distinguishes between the two. The first captivity, because it was an indirect and reluctant one by the French, who were acting for the Germans, was not so hard as there was enough food and the climate was mild. In such circumstances, there seems to be some room for compassion toward the enemy. After Summons's release, however, the second captivity is described in a very different way. The shock he experienced on first seeing his new captors is very strongly described:

> [their Japanese captors were] unshaven, untidy, small, ugly, repulsive to [his] eyes…these were the troops who had forced the Dutch and [the Australians] into surrender…in the press as magnificent soldiers, and here [the Australians] were subdued by these Asiatics who had faces like backward troglodytes (Summons 1946:64).

Summons further laments that Australian prisoners were forced into a degraded and uncivilised condition by the Japanese, saying that [they] were living 'in exactly the same way as the natives, under the same conditions, with the same primitive arrangements' (Summons 1946:87).

Some characteristics of Australian prisoner-of-war writings on the Japanese

From 1942 to 1945, over 22,000 Australians became prisoners-of-war of the Japanese in Southeast Asia, the Pacific islands and New Guinea and about one-third of them did not survive captivity. Such figures themselves reveal the tremendous hardship of POW life, which included tropical diseases, malnutrition, slave labour, torture and also the depression of being 'prisoners of indeterminate sentence' (Nelson 1985:23). Above all, Australian prisoners-of-war, like other European prisoners, were put into the Japanese system without any means of resistance. Without any preparation, they had to adapt themselves to Japanese military ways. Through this, they had very different experiences resulting from the East–West dichotomy, which no Australian could probably have learnt in any other way. Roy Whitecross started his book *Slaves of the Son of Heaven* (1951) by writing: '[the Japanese] cannot be judged or examined by Western standards as their mentality and their ideology is utterly different...Behaviour that is normal to them is, by Western standards, unspeakably cruel and ruthless' (Whitecross 1951:155). This introduction shows how unprepared Australians were in their appraisal of their enemy.

To become prisoners-of-war under the Japanese brought some changes to Australian notions about the East, the relationship of East and West and the simple dichotomy of the Orient and the Occident. There were many Japanese army customs that were incomprehensible to Australians and they had to accept 'cultural compromise'. The Japanese custom of bowing is one subject that often appears in POW memoirs. The need to bow to the Japanese was not easily accepted by many Australians and they were often physically punished for neglecting this 'ritual'. Bowing to one another is one of the first social behaviours among equals that Japanese people learn in childhood and it does not necessarily imply obedience or flattery. But to bow, especially to the Japanese, was felt to be an undignified act for many Australians. Eventually, some Australians realised that if they bowed, the Japanese would bow back and that this salutation was 'just their way of life' (Nelson 1985:19).

'Tenko' (sometimes misspelled as 'tanko') or rollcall, was another Japanese formality that annoyed Australians. It occurs not only in the army but everywhere in Japan. However, the repetitive effort of checking the number of hundreds and thousands of prisoners and soldiers, who all had to stand to attention, was something beyond comprehension for many Australians. Betty Jeffrey (1954:50) called it 'one infuriating habit our masters have' and Graeme McCabe (1946:74) thought it 'maniac', fuelling the negative feeling against the Japanese.

While standing against the Japanese, Australians often found themselves in solidarity with other Asians. When being stricken by hunger and thirst on the roads or railways in Singapore, Malaya, Thailand, Burma or the Dutch West Indies, they appreciated kindness shown by the local natives. Despite the threat from the Japanese, these natives acted like their own 'flesh and blood' (Whitecross 1951:6). Graeme McCabe's escape from the Japanese for two months along the Malay coast described in *Pacific Sunset* (1946), would not have been possible without the help of the local Chinese. Japan was clearly conscious of the European bias against Asians, as is shown in Karenko Camp Commandant Captain Imamura's speech noted in Kent Hughes's *Slaves of the Samurai* (1946:xvii). Captain Imamura said that 'the Americans and the British [were] not allowed to have the haughty attitude over the peoples of Asia or to look down on them, which [had] been their common sense for a long time'. However, prisoners-of-war witnessed that once the Japanese became 'the powerful', it was the same old story and other Asians once again became the 'powerless', despite being included in Japan's scheme of the 'Greater Asia Co-Prosperity'. When Kent Hughes was sent with other officers to Formosa (Taiwan), he saw in the eyes of the Taiwanese 'no sign of hate nor hostility [against Australians], but the incurious, disinterested, mute, immobile piercing stare of Orientals' (Hughes 1946:121–122). During that period Taiwan was also 'conquered', with the Taiwanese being captives in their own country. Rivett wrote that despite

> 'fine words about the 'co-prosperity sphere' and the brotherhood of all Asiatics, the Japanese Army had no hope of inducing this feeling in the occupied areas ....You cannot preach love to a people when you constantly assert your dominance with ostentatious arrogance backed by ruthless brutality' (Rivett 1946:132).

Thus the Japanese were specifically described as an oppressor-figure with a strong sense of imperialism.

When Australians learnt to look at Japan as imperialists from the same point of view as other local Asians, some began to realise that they had already colluded in Western imperialism and colonialism themselves, willingly or not. When some prisoners-of-war escaped the Japanese camps, some became part of the guerilla force of the British, French and Dutch colonies where they suffered a worse survival rate than in POW camps (Nelson 1985:137). This became the subject of such war novels as Eric Lambert's *The Dark Backward* (1958), as seen in the previous chapter. Among the prisoners-of-war were some who sympathised with the colonised against the coloniser. After being in close contact with the Indonesians, some prisoners were said to have become 'increasingly reconciled with [the Indonesians'] aims as they realised the issue was that it was not race that was important but the colonial mentality, and they had to be free of it' (Nelson 1985:201). These Australians were caught in a dilemma when the war was over and the old imperialists came back, as seen in *Dark Backward* in Chapter Three. Due to their sympathies with plans for rebellion or revolution by the local guerilias, some were under 'some sort of house arrest' until they were flown back to Australia (Nelson 1985:202). On the other hand, prisoners like Betty Jeffrey who had had enough of the local natives would rather not see the fall of the old imperialism. When they heard that 'the Japs [were] going to get [them] all out of Sumatra and give the country its independence', they would hate to see 'this rich country run by the types [they had] seen loose in it' (Jeffrey 1954:175).

In almost all memoirs, Australian prisoners saw Japanese soldiers' arrogance and oppression over Korean and Taiwanese guards and soldiers, who in turn took it out on the prisoners in still harsher ways. It was important for these Koreans and Taiwanese to show that they were at least superior to the prisoners and that they were actually working diligently for the Imperial Army. This racial hierarchy is evident as well in Cowra prisoner-of-war memoirs, as discussed in Chapter Five. The arrogance and cruelty of the Japanese are often described without questioning. More critically, McQueen warns against a continuing tendency in Australian writings to sweepingly attribute such damning characteristics to the 'supposedly inherited national character' and suggests that efforts to seek and examine the causes should be made (McQueen 1991).

Attitudes toward prisoners

Clashes between Australian prisoners and the Japanese during captivity were severe, both physically and mentally. One memoirist, Graeme McCabe, includes extracts from the Geneva Convention at the end of his book, *Slaves of the Son of Heaven,* in protest against Japanese atrocities towards its prisoners. The Geneva Convention of 1929 was signed, but not ratified by Japan, although Japan notified that it would apply the Convention in February 1942 (Japan had ratified the Hague Convention of 1907). However, as is often pointed out, *Senjinkun* or Japan's Military Code, issued by Hideki Tojo, the then Commander-General, meant much more than the Geneva Convention for ordinary Japanese military men (examples can be found in Gerster 1987:229). For Australian soldiers, once they had surrendered and were taken prisoner, it was their right to be treated as human beings (although there may be some submerged complex feelings of shame or guilt for not living up to the ANZAC legend they were following). However for the Japanese, the Code states as an unconditional command, 'one should rather prepare to die, not to disgrace oneself alive when captured by the enemy...' It was shameful for the Japanese to be prisoners-of-war, while for Australians, it was not considered as such. When Russell Braddon fell into enemy hands in Malaya, he recorded in *The Naked Island* that they were treated by the Japanese in such cruel ways that it seemed the Japanese had never heard of the Hague Convention's protocols concerning the treatment of prisoners-of-war (Braddon 1952:88). He later realised that they were not 'official prisoners-of-war but only slave labour to be used' (1952:103) and that 'warlike Nippon did not greatly admire men who surrendered' (1952:110). For the Japanese, at least ostensibly, it was more sublime to die 'like the cherry blossoms fell' as the then popular military song put it. The other alternative was to resort to being a suicide kamikaze bomber pilot, which meant a total and manly self-sacrifice. As a consequence of these cultural differences, the Japanese expressed their most severe attitudes toward the 'living' prisoners. Braddon writes in his memoirs that 'as the coffin of the dead Australian went, the Jap guard at the main gate stood up off his chair, saluted and bowed... "[i]t was the only time those little apes cared a hoot for us", muttered Hugh' (1952:127). Betty Jeffrey also notes that the Japanese guards paid respect to the military funeral. When Australian nurses, all in uniform, conducted the military funeral for a sister nurse, the Japanese guards also 'stood to attention and removed their caps as [the coffin] went past their quarters, a thing they had never done before' (Jeffrey 1954:150). Prisoners were respected only when dead, which was coded in Japanese military ways. This behaviour would again be noted by the Australians in the Cowra uprising.

Japan's neglect of the Geneva Convention led to the notorious use of prisoners as slave labour in all camps, especially in the construction of the Burma–Thai railway. Although Japan was allowed to make prisoners work on condition that a certain amount of wage was paid to them, and that the work did not have any direct connection with the operations of the war, prisoners still worked for their enemy's benefit. The way the Japanese used the prisoners as well as the locals was described in every POW memoir as something atrocious and incomprehensible, as though it was hell on earth. The captives were forced to work with much violence and little care for medication and food. This maltreatment coupled with the harsh natural circumstances, eventually lead many of them to die. The treatment of prisoners by the Japanese was a bit like that of the pawns in *shyogi*, Japanese chess. Although it originated from the Indian board game over two thousand years ago with the same origins as Western chess, Japanese chess has one particular difference: one can use one's enemy's pieces as one's own once they are captured. It was already a military custom in the Age of Provincial Wars in Japan in the 16th century that when warriors surrendered, they were put by their enemy in the frontline to fight against their own side (Sakaiya 2000:38–39). Prisoners were not exactly used as combatants, however, as the stories of the

Australian prisoners of the Japanese show; rather they were treated as pawns and used at the will of their captors.

Another major cause of conflict between the prisoners and the Japanese concerning the Hague/Geneva Convention often described in the memoirs was the 'non-escape contracts' requested by the Japanese to be signed by all the prisoners in each camp. It was forbidden for prisoners to attempt escape and if they did so, the contract stated the consequence: they would be shot when recaptured. The Allied prisoners, including the Australians, were against such a pledge at first, saying it was against the Geneva Convention and that they had been instructed, as per their duty, to try to escape when captured (Tanaka 1996:18–19). McCabe, in his *Pacific Sunset* (1946:62–63), wondered if the Japanese order would be 'in direct contravention of British military law, for the first duty of a war prisoner [was] to escape if possible'. Kent Hughes, in his *Slaves of the Samurai*, lamented in his verse memoirs that it was a 'misunderstanding of each nation's code/ [which] increased the burden of the prisoner's load' and regretted the signing of the contract which involved the death penalty for escapees (1946:126).

Prisoners-of-war experienced the Japanese military system on a day-to-day basis and saw its position within Japanese society. The Emperor was the head of the nation and power was concentrated only at the very top level of the government or military offices. Graeme McCabe observed, when transported to Japan, that the Army was paramount in society and that the Imperial edicts were more like 'rescripts' than 'commands', stronger than anything (1946:77–80). In a camp in Taiwan, Kent Hughes, along with other prisoners, was told by the commander-colonel that they should learn *Bushido* or the Code of the Samurai and they should appreciate the Emperor's grace in sparing their lives, a pronouncement that to the prisoners seemed hypocritical and meant nothing (1946:184). The Japanese kept telling the prisoners about Japan's determination to let the war last 'at least a hundred years or so'—a Japanese war-slogan of those days, which showed their unquestioning belief in Japan's military power (Hughes 1946:183).

The tendency of the Japanese to save face and to give priority to superficial principles had already been observed by Japanese prisoners-of-war before Ruth Benedict published *The Chrysanthemum and the Sword* in 1946, a book which enabled the Allied world to learn of the Japanese mentality and their way of life. Rhetorical speech and the hypocritical actions of the Japanese army are often targeted by the prisoners in their memoirs. McCabe notes one such speech delivered by the camp-commander when they arrived at Kobe Camp in Japan. In it the prisoners were told that they should have been put to death as war criminals who 'butchered good Japanese soldiers', however, 'by the divine goodness of Imperial Hirohito they had been spared'. So the prisoners were ordered to 'work hard and diligently as they were housed, fed, and clothed by the Imperial Japanese Army' (McCabe 1946:75). Rivett felt disgusted hearing such speeches delivered in Batavia or Thailand by Japanese commanders. In one speech prisoners were told that their lives were generously preserved by the Japanese Military at a time when material goods were short and hence the captives should show their gratitude by labouring for the construction of the railway, which was of 'the great interest to the world' (Rivett 1946:123). In another speech prisoners were reminded that the commander regretted not finding 'seriousness' in them because of their lack of conviction and eagerness for work. The commander maintained it came from the fact that, unlike the Japanese, they did not have such firm beliefs as 'Health follows will' and 'Cease only when the enemy is completely annihilated' (Rivett 1946:124).

Being captives, the strongest feeling the prisoners held against their Japanese captors was hatred. Braddon notes that to see 'the young prisoner-soldiers suddenly become old men, shrunken and desperate' because of constantly insufficient food and various diseases, caused the captives to be 'filled with...a hatred for the enemy that nothing can remove' (Braddon 1952:109). According to Whitecross, 'the only things [those brutal guards] were skilled in were torturing [the prisoners] and teaching [them] to hate' (1951:92). He thought he could happily kill them and it would be 'an exquisite joy in seeing them die'. However in the end, he 'had learned to hate with such a hatred' that there could be 'no fitting punishment for the acts that had bred this hatred' (1951:241). McQueen, in commenting on Braddon's *The Naked Island* as being closer to 'a fictionalised account than an eyewitness testament', suggests that Braddon, with his own racial prejudice and his 'ironic, entertaining and self-deprecatory manner,' made the book successful as a popular quasi-fiction rather than as a reflective analysis. McQueen cites Braddon's speech delivered in 1958, in which he said 'This was an age of hatreds: and I was in there hating with the worst of them' (McQueen 1991:296–303). The popularity of *The Naked Island* (it sold more than a million copies from 1952 to 1974) may then be the result of the author's exaggerated style and his attitudes toward the Japanese, which suited contemporary readerships. Summons also refers to his hatred, saying that the hope to return home was the prisoners' incentive to live on and make 'them despise the Japanese for their barbarisms' (Summons 1946:96). Such comments, in memoirs written and published soon after the war, offer a more honest and spontaneous appraisal than later, more analytical works.

Closer observation of the 'Other'

In the earlier invasion novels, the Japanese, the authors' imaginary foe, are hated or feared not as individuals but 'en masse'. In war novels and stories, the distance between Australians and Japanese becomes closer and the enemy is presented through clearer images, although the encounter is often brief and momentary. In prisoner-of-war stories, prisoners are almost forced to have a close look at the Japanese, who are now described individually. Rivett once thought that 'the average Anglo-Saxon or European was inclined to regard the Japanese as something in the nature of a joke' and materials concerning Japan were treated superficially or propagandistically. Now he realised it caused misunderstanding of the country's true nature (Rivett 1946:119–120). When Whitecross (1951:6) first saw the Japanese soldiers in Singapore, he thought that they were 'small, dark, not yellow but dark brown...their uniforms were nondescript and ill-fitting...some of the Privates had patched knees to their breeches...[they looked] insignificant but they had beaten us...' The first impression of the Japanese as dull-looking, small soldiers was to change quickly as they started to behave as slave masters. Summons describes the Japanese as a whole, deciding that 'every Japanese hates to lose "face"', 'their whole nature is a mixture of complexes and superstitions' and their 'appearance is revolting to [the Western] eye' (Summons 1946:142–143). Summons also concludes, (although he admits that the prisoners 'had dealings only with the army class') that the '"nature of the brute" is very similar throughout the nation' (1946:140).

Many Japanese soldiers and guards (or sometimes their Taiwanese and Korean equivalents) are called by nicknames in prisoner-of-war memoirs: 'Charlie Chaplin', 'Ah Fat', 'Almond Eye' and 'Prune Face' was for their physical characteristics. For their harshness towards the captives, they were also called 'The Snake', 'Bully' or 'Dillinger'—after John Dillinger (1902–34) a criminal who was said to be Public Enemy No 1 in Chicago. Although the diaries and memos were hidden from the Japanese in the camps, it was safer to use nicknames in case they were discovered. Moreover, some prisoners declared that they did not care for Japanese names. Using nicknames or code-like names also gave the captives pleasure as well as a sense of solidarity with fellow prisoners. It was a small form of rebellion against their captors, and brought amusement to their monotonous camp life.

The prisoners sometimes even managed to laugh at the antics of their captors. Rivett records an episode of a Japanese guard who was trying to shoot an animal just outside its cage to provide meat for the next meal. He was only about three yards from the beast. However, the more the guard tried to shoot, the more he missed, while the prisoners looked on laughing. The guard, highly infuriated, finally brought the animal down at the fourth or fifth shot and happily 'waddles' off. Observing the whole comical scene, Rivett records that he 'felt, not for the first time, that it is almost impossible to hate anything which is alternately ludicrous and pathetic' (Rivett 1946:207).

On the other hand, personal names also appear in some memoirs and these lend an air of realism to the stories. Those Japanese mentioned by their real names are of various ranks. Kanemoto, a first-class Private and guard in one of the railway camps in Thailand, is described as one of the typically cruel guards found in any camp in Braddon's *The Naked Island*. He is a short, stocky and unpleasant man, who calls repeatedly 'Speedo! Speedo!' (ie 'Speed! Hurry up!'). The author and his fellow prisoners would often have clashes with Kanemoto and were frequently belted and bashed (1952:185–187). Terai, a Japanese interpreter, was a professor of English in a Japanese University during peacetime and is thus pro-British. He also holds anti-war feelings and is rather sympathetic to the prisoners, so he becomes distressed when he sees them punished over trivial matters. Terai keeps visiting Braddon to inform him of his mates' whereabouts or to ask for Braddon's opinion on a play he wrote. Without the language barrier, they could have become closer, particularly as they have the same liking for literature; however, Braddon finds Terai strange and hard to understand. Although a pacifist, Terai is deeply involved in Japan's war (as he sees it) as his confession of belief in the slogan 'the war will last one hundred years' indicates. When the war ends with Japan's surrender, Braddon hears that Terai has committed suicide by 'hara-kiri' (1952:165–260). Contradictory attitudes evident in such 'middlemen' as Terai are often observed in other memoirs and stories. Such characters seem to be torn between the publicly reinforced dichotomy of East and West and are unable to bridge the gap. The only solution for them is to destroy themselves.[36] Such varieties in Japanese characters provide the memoirs with the multi-dimensions that help provide a realistic picture of prisoners' lives.

In a Burma camp, Rivett and his fellow prisoners are for a while under 'the reign of terror' of Lieutenant Naito, who also appears in many other memoirs including that by Summons. Naito has a double personality that's affected by alcohol and thus provides 'an interesting study in the more educated type of Japanese'. When Naito is sober he is 'an extremely efficient officer' and more reasonable for prisoners to deal with than most Japanese. Once he is under the influence of drink, Naito transforms into a tyrant. His behaviour becomes worse after Mussolini's overthrow and Italy's surrender is reported. Colonel Black, POW camp commander, never knows which of the 'two' Naitos he is to meet for his daily report, 'Jekyll the Sober' or 'Hyde the Drunk'. Even the nerves of the Japanese guards are 'worn as thin as those of any prisoner' when his 'drinking bout' lasts for several weeks. They are not willing to assist Naito in his drunken murder of prisoners. When Naito is forced out of the camp into the hospital, the Japanese guards hold parties to celebrate the end of the 'terror', in which they all get drunk (Rivett 1946:216–221).

During the war, German atrocities were often described as 'Nazi' crimes by Allied critics rather than 'behaviour rooted in culture or personality structure'. But in the Asian war theatre, 'enemy brutality was almost always presented as being simply 'Japanese' (Dower 1986:34,78). Because of the racial difference of the Japanese and ignorance of Japan by the West, the Japanese were more hated than any other race and conventionally treated as 'a group' by the Allied countries. Prisoners-of-war at least knew there were different grades of 'bad' among the Japanese based on their own experiences, despite some sweeping observations and comments made from time to time.

Environment of prisoners—food, language and religion

Along with such diseases as beri-beri, dysentery, tropical ulcers, malaria and pellagra, extremely hard labour and everyday atrocities committed by the captors, scarcity of food and subsequent malnutrition were some of the main reasons captives lost their lives. Indeed, in the memoirs of prisoners-of-war, hardly a chapter goes by without the mention of hunger and food. Food became the main interest of prisoners and it dominated their lives. Hunger was the 'test of character' which 'only captives can with truth concur' when sharing food becomes such a sublime act (Hughes 1946:142). Whitecross realises that Australian prisoners knew what real hunger was like when captured; what they previously thought to be hunger was 'just a healthy appetite' (Whitecross 1951:7).

Then came rice, perceived as a most unwelcome type of food. What was the soul food for one race group became the embodiment of hate for the other group. For many Japanese soldiers from poverty-stricken towns and rural villages, the only merit or reason for being in the military was to be able to eat rice. For many Australian prisoners, rice meant porridge with sugar or a dessert like pudding or custard. Now they had to sit down to a meal of rice, 'but a plain, badly boiled rice' all through their captivity (Whitecross 1951:8). Rice became the symbol of the East, Japan and the captors, whereas 'bread' became the symbol of the West, Christianity, relief and home. The change from a European diet to an all rice fare caused much sickness in the camps; when prisoners '[were] suffering from mental worry and maladjustment, [a rice diet speeded] up physical debility and general bad health' (McCabe 1946:60). So awful was the 'rice monotony' that the prisoners longed to find anything that could break it, perhaps a pinch of salt or stinking sun-dried prawns, which were used as a paste (Hughes 1946:75).

One day in a Burmese camp, Whitecross and his fellow prisoners received bread and this 'staggering event swept through camp and brought everyone to the Quartermaster's Hut'. It was only half of a small bun, weighing about three ounces that was distributed to each prisoner; however, the bun gave such pleasure and even hope in their dark life as prisoners-of-war (Whitecross 1951:34). When Kent Hughes and his fellow men are transferred to and arrive in Taiwan (Formosa), to their surprise bread is issued to every man and to them it tastes better than anything. The author realises that 'The simple things of life and simple fare / Are far more precious than the rich and rare' (Hughes 1946:122). In the freezing camp of Liaoyuanchow, Manchuria, when captives viewed the months to come and their hearts sank, they were 'greatly cheered / When two large rolls of bread appeared...They soon forgot the raw black biting cold outside, / As soon as breakfast was supplied' (Hughes 1946:241–242).

When food became more and more scarce and their rations were reduced, 'Shadow Meals', or discussions of food, 'became again a vice; / And everyone talked food' till their brains became replete (as opposed to their stomachs) (Hughes 1946:276). Male captives as well as female prisoners, such as Betty Jeffrey and her fellow nurses, exchanged recipes and talked about their mothers' cooking constantly. Rice represented the alien culture and diet but also captured life and the relationship of captors to the prisoners. It was all the more hated because they had to take it for their own survival.

The Japanese language was one of the most difficult and perplexing aspects of prison camp life under Japan's military system. Some prisoners-of-war were given easy counting and reading exercises but most were confronted with the reality that not understanding the language could be fatal. However, prisoners did not show much enthusiasm in acquiring the master's language. Summons records that the Japanese were 'very disappointed at the lack of interest displayed in the Japanese language by the prisoners'. It was necessary for the prisoners to understand what the Japanese were requiring from them at work and Summons laments that 'many misunderstandings developed' generated by the lack of verbal communication (Summons 1946:82, 93). Rivett notes in his memoirs the 'incessant barrage of shouting and screaming' incomprehensible Japanese uttered by guards and engineers while working on the railway construction (Rivett 1946:154). 'The shattering shrieks with which the guards at the guard-house on the road saluted the passing of an officer's car' are worse than any 'screaming of the gibbons' or 'the howling of the pariah dogs' in the jungle around their camp (1946:159). Prisoners hated the language and speech sounds of Japanese but they had to try and understand it for their own survival. In Kent Hughes's memoirs, Captain Imamura's speech delivered at Karenko Camp on 11 August 1942, declared that 'the language spoken daily to [prisoners-of-war] is the

Nippon language...[They] must, therefore, make diligent effort to understand Nipponese for [their] daily use' (Hughes 1946:xvii). Orders shouted in Japanese, such as *Kiwotsuke* (Attention), *Yasmae* (At ease), *Kashira Migi* (Eyes right), *Naore* (As you were) resounded in the camp and made all the prisoners tense. As 'one veteran solder said, "Shellfire in Flanders was much less nervous strain"' (Rivett 1946:104). In most of the memoirs, once they acquired enough vocabulary for survival, few prisoners seem to have made serious efforts to learn the language of their captor. Still the impact of the alien orders remained strong and many memoirists have recorded Japanese words and phrases in Roman letters as they heard them.[37]

Because of this difference in language, the strangeness and inscrutability of the Japanese are emphasised: incomprehensible language combined with other differences such as religion or lifestyle are targeted as the causes of their savagery and barbarous behaviour as well as their inhumane attitudes towards the prisoners-of-war. As such, any Japanese who were Christian soldiers or English-speaking were generally described in more favourable terms as they were at least a little closer to the prisoners' own cultural background. Among the very few Japanese characters depicted favourably in Summons's *Twice Their Prisoner* is 'Hank-the-Yank', an interpreter who had been educated in America (1946:149). However, as we have seen in the case of Terai the interpreter in *The Naked Island* or Lieutenant Takanaka, the commander of Kobe camp in *Pacific Sunset*, there are other cases. Takanaka insists that he is a Christian, but Graeme McCabe (1946:83) and his fellow prisoners find 'Jap Army Christians [are] worse than Shintoists' with such hideous examples as Takanaka, who, because of his lack of sympathy with the prisoners, will 'go and live with Satan' at the end of the war.

Australian interpreters, then, bore a very important role between the prisoners and the Japanese. Many of them were Commissioned Officers who had to deal with the Japanese every day. When these interpreters/mediators became aware of the enemy's figures of speech and physical gestures (sometimes prisoners could be bashed simply because they stared into the eyes of the Japanese, without realising that it was seen as an impolite gesture), they served as a good 'buffer' and their requests were sometimes met by the Japanese. When they failed to interpret, they themselves were at risk of being victimised by both sides. One such example was Erik, an interpreter for the Allied captives on the railway construction site in *Kura!* by Cornel Lumiere (1966), which is discussed in Chapter Seven.

The prisoners-of-war discovered the importance of a common language when dealing with the locals as well. When trying to escape on a boat along the Sumatra coast, Rivett (1946:57–58) and his mates are cordially cared for by Chinese locals because one of them speaks fluent Chinese. Similar occasions with Malays and Indonesians reinforce the importance of prisoners' knowing and talking in other languages/cultures. The glossaries of Japanese or other local words attached to the memoirs seem to point to the importance of languages in their POW life. According to Braddon (1961:29), the 'lingua franca' in the camp in Singapore was 'a mixture of Japanese, Malay and English and both the prisoners and the guards used it for their own ends. Prisoners even started to understand the rhetorical use of words by the Japanese. When Japanese guards said *Ashita* (tomorrow) following a prisoner's request, it was often meant to express the 'near future', but eventually 'never' came to be its true meaning. *Ashita* thus became a negative response rather than positive.[38] In Japanese society, a direct decline of a request is regarded as impolite. But prisoners, without knowledge of the Japanese language-context, have to read beneath the surface of words.

Life with the 'Other'

There were many differences between Australian prisoners-of-war and the Japanese soldiers. Some behaviours, even minor, revealed marked differences and allowed the prisoners to see how ideas could have different meanings in different cultures. One example refers to the prisoners' singing. Besides camp concerts held on special occasions, there were many sing-songs in everyday life. For the Japanese, this was incomprehensible. Whitecross finds that the prisoners' behaviour confounded the Japanese soldiers on the Burma–Thailand railway construction:

> after working all day and on through the hours of darkness...[they] raise their voices in song as they splashed, slipped and staggered along the waterlogged road...the guards shrugged their shoulders, pointed to [the prisoners] with one hand and made circular motions round their heads with the other' (a gesture for 'you must be crazy') (Whitecross 1951:104–105) .

Betty Jeffrey and her fellow nurses surprised the Japanese guards with their eagerness to practise 'voice orchestra'—the guards wondered 'why [they] could sing while [their] people are being killed' (Jeffrey 1954:100). What may seem improper and inappropriate to one group, such as singing in serious circumstances, can raise morale for another group. Such discoveries of cross-cultural differences offer both parties new notions about each other.

As is constantly suggested in the prisoners' memoirs, the authors presume there is an immense gap between other people and themselves. The bond between the prisoners became very strong after having supported and sustained each other during such times when they could not be sure of their survival. They were mates who shared the hardest days. Even after their release, they tended to support each other mentally, socially and often financially (Nelson 1985). Many of the memoirs were dedicated to their fellow prisoners who shared the same experiences. There were more dedications to those who died while in captivity than to those who waited for them back home or to those who came to liberate them at the end of the war. Many times in the memoirs it was recorded that the mateship among Australians helped their survival: dividing whatever food could be obtained, attending the sick, helping others with work loads, protecting others from harassment by the Japanese, or simply being there to provide support. Their mateship often includes other American, British or Dutch prisoners as well, but their 'Australian-ness' is often emphasised within their own rank. According to Braddon, their prisoner-of-war life was 'devoid of friction' and there were no cases of murder, and few of theft or suicide, which he concludes was the result of 'the Anglo-Saxon's ability to live together' (Braddon 1952:143). It was a close kept 'good society', which they had built for themselves 'out of a chaos of disease and starvation and degradation and brutality' (Braddon 1958:47–48). It was a 'family' for Betty Jeffrey and her fellow nurses. While they traded with and worked for other Dutch, British, and German prisoners for money, in many cases they did things voluntarily for their Australian 'family' members (Braddon 1958:47–48).

There are not many recorded instances that tarnished the sacredness of the 'mateship' concept in prisoner-of-war memoirs. However, despite Braddon's comment in the previous paragraph, he had to admit that there were some who occasionally cheated or stole from their own mates during captivity and these are sometimes described in the memoirs. Even after his release, one prisoner stole sets of bed sheets in the hotel that accommodated them in Singapore. Another who was angry with a friend who had refused to help over obtaining drinking water while in captivity, sent an invoice to him for a glass of water long after their release, back in Sydney (Braddon 1961:218). Unpleasant memories and episodes seem to be regulated by the authors' self-censorship to maintain the consistency and simple structure of East versus West, captor versus captive, or wrongdoer versus victim dichotomy, as often seen in some post-colonial literature of accusation. As the memoirs discussed here were written and published soon after the end of the war, certain kinds of censorship introduced by the author, the publisher and readership might have been practised.

Often described in the Australian prisoners' memoirs was the need for tolerance towards people from other countries. They made contacts with men of other nationalities and shared hardships with them against the common enemy. As Rivett says, 'many men, particularly those who had never left Australia before the war, acquired a new outlook on many things as a result of conversations with men from other lands with vastly different backgrounds, interests and points of view' (1946:291). Many memoirs show that some prisoners-of-war learnt tolerance. While suffering extreme starvation, Whitecross agreed to allow some Dutch prisoners to eat dogs and a fellow prisoner called Maurice suggested the best way was to accept 'any ways' and not just *the* way' (1951:155–156).

In terms of sexuality, few memoirists recorded explicit observations or experiences in their writings, except for some excitement caused from glimpses of half-naked local women and so on. Summons concludes that if a man's interests are concentrated on the three essentials: life itself, food and women, 'for a prisoner the first two were the only ones that counted' (Summons 1946:153). When his observation extends to the Japanese, he is surprised at their peculiar morals. In Java, for example, he was informed that 'there were practically no cases of rape at the time of the capture of the island'. At the same time, there was a fair proportion of venereal disease among the Japanese soldiers and they had 'comfort girls' with them wherever they went' (Summons 1946:148–149). He also decides that homosexuality is 'rife' among the Japanese, but refrains from talking about the prisoners themselves (1946:149). This may be where self-censorship was applied, although the enemy's sexual tendencies were freely speculated on.

Humour also played a crucial role in the recorded life of prisoners-of-war. In almost all the memoirs, humour is revered as crucial for survival. It was also used to make a clear distinction between the prisoners and the Japanese, the latter whom are regularly described as being 'humour-less', as is seen in the case of 'sing-songs' discussed in the earlier part of this chapter. Whitecross confirms that 'the Australians never lost their native sense of humour…[and] often it was coupled with ingenuity' (1951:28). Kent Hughes notes that 'A sense of humour is a saving grace, / When famished minds give temper pride of place' (1946:143). Australian prisoners' mischievousness and tendencies to look at their captors from an ironic, humorous point of view are often observed in the memoirs. Betty Jeffrey (1954:110–111) notes that there is always something to laugh at in their camp: once it is 'Ah Fat' the guard, who is bathing in a tub of water 'far too small for himself, having a nice warm bath in the sunshine', not suspecting that he is being peeped at. He is a miserable sort, who is always confiding to the prisoners of his wish to go home to his family and trying to gain their sympathy. The way Kent Hughes looks at a Japanese officer in charge, who tries 'to enforce / The order by a crude display of force', is to compare him to the haughty queen of Lewis Carroll's *Alice in Wonderland*, who strides 'in a raging storm / Of temper, and contemptuously would say: / 'Off with his head! Off with his head! Away!' (1946:126). The Australians maintained their sense of humour, calling their camps and cells nicknames like 'Shangri-la' or using funny mottos; it was to reflect an eagerness and hope for survival. Their humour could become ironic or cynical, as Kent Hughes's tone did during successive transportations to different camps (1946:xvi). When prisoners lose their sense of humour, it often leads to the loss of will to endure captivity, sometimes even leading the captives to drop out of the race for survival. Humour is their defence against despair. As Jones and Andrews point out, 'individuals manipulated by circumstances, or a destiny they are unable to control, wryly resign themselves to their own powerlessness' (Jones & Andrews 1988:60). Thus humour seen in POW writings is 'an acknowledgement of the status quo' for themselves in their captivity by the 'Other' (Jones & Andrews 1988:74).

Betty Jeffrey's prisoner-of-war accounts from a female point of view give us a different perspective on the relationships between the Australian prisoners and the Japanese. Out of 65 Australian Army Nurses who escaped the fall of Singapore in February 1942 on the ship Vyner Brooke, 32 survived the aerial bombing by the Japanese and the sinking of the boat between Sumatra and Banka Island. They were subsequently not involved in the Radji beach massacre. Betty Jeffrey was one of the survivors.

Being female captives, their power-relationship with the Japanese often had sexual overtones. They faced harassment and had to scheme about averting potential Japanese sexual demands. When these nurses were asked to 'entertain' officers, they all showed up in front of them in dirty, dishevelled outfits and hair, presenting a 'most unattractive sight' in order to dispirit the enemy. The 'mental strain' they suffered during this event was 'worse than being bombed and shipwrecked' (Jeffrey 1954:30–33). Army nurse camps also interned civilians and natives and there were 'girlfriends' of the Japanese among them. To choose to be a girlfriend was one way to survive camp life. Without the protection of the powerful, their 'inmate-ship' or 'family' became an important factor for their survival.

The nurses observed funny sides of the enemy as well, as mentioned earlier. When the allied bombing over Borneo intensified and became frequent in the later years of captivity, Captain Siki, the Japanese camp commander, said that when the bombs come, they will look after the nurses and take them into the rubber plantation for safety. The captain also mentioned he will die with them in the rubber plantation, to which the nurses all 'cheered'—a reaction the Japanese did not expect when talking about the dignified topic of dying—and he becomes 'nonplussed' (Jeffrey 1954:103–104). When some of the nurses are accused by a guard, 'the Snake', for no particular reason, he severely punishes them, then afterwards brings them some soap and Chinese biscuits either as compensation or as a reward, an action which puzzles the punished (Jeffrey 1954:111–112).

The various observations and experiences of the Japanese as captors given by Jeffrey's female captives offer a more ambiguous perspective than those of male captives.

Prisoner-of-war memoirs provided eye-witness accounts that surpassed anything that those back in Australia could ever imagined. Although the Australian prisoners did not think they fully understood the Japanese as captors, there were moments in their POW experiences when they recognised new aspects of the Japanese, which had not appeared in Australian writing before. It would be easy for the Japanese to be categorised as the powerful captor-master with an incompatible racial and cultural background. However, those described in POW memoirs are seen as more than the stereotypical barbaric enemy as depicted in invasion novels, for now they had names (even if only nicknames) and faces. When a Japanese military band visits the camp where Betty Jeffrey and her fellow nurse-prisoners are interned, they are at first determined not to listen. However, as the music goes on, they begin to realise that these men are not militaristic at all but just a group of 'people' with a love for music who happen to be Japanese (1954:105). Whitecross is surprised to observe that something unexpected can be taboo to the Japanese. When Japanese guards pester prisoners to sell their possessions, they state that these are gifts from their wives. With that magic phrase they become untouchable and the Japanese withdraw (1951:59). When Japanese soldiers entered military service, they were officially supposed to give their life away for their country. So when they left their family, keepsakes or farewell gifts were often exchanged and such mementoes became more sacred than anything else, as they represented the family for many Japanese soldiers. Australian prisoners-of-war may have been the first Australians to know of such customs.

As McCabe observes, some prisoners-of-war witnessed war-time Japan and saw the domination of the Japanese military in society. War changed people and gave extraordinary power to many military men who did not know how to use it. McCabe (1946:101–103) concludes that upon seeing Hiroshima's disaster after the atomic bombing, the 'heathen' Japanese realised that they were misled by the Emperor and his system and that was the result. As mentioned in Chapter Three, Dower says the Japanese and Japanese military are often described as an inseparable unit unlike the Germans and the Nazis, and thus 'the malice' was thought of as a feature of the whole society (Dower 1993:43). However, Australian prisoners-of-war recorded in their memoirs not only the Japanese military as a whole but also individual soldiers. Kent Hughes reminds us that 'Australians with the West pre-occupied, / Like football barrackers, have been one-eyed', a dangerous state to be because it can breed 'smug isolationists'. Even when he is a POW of Japan (or perhaps because he is one), he hopes that

Australia, being situated 'in the Orient', will become aware that the 'white man's burden is to learn to know/ These Eastern people', an idea that was very different from that of Kipling (1946:19–20). After seeing the worst of Japan and the Japanese, there also came the possibility of looking at something as not simply 'bad' or 'incomprehensible'. The authors' perception of themselves as victims, with their own ideology and prejudices, may mean that prisoners-of-war memoirs lack a certain objectivity. However, they are not carefully calculated or designed as literature to appeal to general readers, and in that sense, they may provide more realistic observations of Japanese as the 'Other'. McQueen, in criticising Rivett's memoir, raises a question as to why the author, with his journalistic background, failed to give an explanation for why the Japanese race are seen as base, degenerate and atrocious in his work (1991:307). As McQueen again points out, it may be necessary for the ex-prisoner-memoirists to have some time for detachment in order to come to objective analysts. His example includes Braddon's next title after *The Naked Island*, *End of a Hate*, which seems to have achieved some freedom from the 'hatred' that permeated the former memoir (1991:299). Citing 'Weary' Dunlop's phrase, McQueen concludes that the prisoner-of-war question has to be discussed more freely, so that Australians may escape being 'prisoners of propaganda' (1991:321).

Prisoner-of-war narratives offer further direct representations of the Japanese following the war literature discussed in the previous chapter. During the war years there were some Japanese, although few and limited, who became prisoners-of-war of the Australians and were confined in Australia. These Japanese prisoners provided the Australians with the opportunity of direct contact and gave non-combatants a chance to observe the 'Other'. After the end of the war, Australians, also went to the territory of the 'Other', in the Occupation Forces, this time as captors themselves. The writings that emerged from these experiences will be discussed in the next chapter.

chapter five

Narratives of the Cowra Breakout and the Occupation Force experiences

Compared with previous images, memoirs written about Australian experiences as prisoners-of-war of the Japanese present very different perspectives on the Japanese. The Japanese, who were usually described only 'en masse' in the imaginary invasion novels, start to have names, faces, and characters when they become the actual enemy of Australians. In Australian POW memoirs, a wide range of Japanese characters are afforded with more individual descriptions rather than the simple stereotypes of atrocious and incomprehensible captors. Captivity for Australians, (and the British, Dutch and Americans), by the Japanese was a unique event, not only in Australian history but in the whole Western experience. This 'reversal' of roles led to distinctive modes of representing the 'Other' in Australian narratives.

In Australia there were a few Japanese held in captivity as prisoners-of-war during the Second World War, though they were very small in number compared to the Australians in the Asia–Pacific area. It was a new experience for Australians to hold Japanese captives; that is, to face the Japanese as their enemy not on the battlefield but in their own territory where their power-relationship was quite clear. During the captivity of the Japanese by the Australians, the profound cultural and mental differences between them became evident, with the ultimate expression of this difference being marked by the mass breakout in Cowra in 1944. There were also civilian Japanese interned in Australia during the Pacific War and about 4,300 people kept in captivity, from both Australia and nearby areas. They were divided into three camps. Research has been done on these internees, a major example is Yuriko Nagata's *Unwanted Aliens: Japanese Internment in Australia* (1996). Nagata attributes these civilian internees' acceptance of their camp life to the fact that 70% of them were from nearby areas and thus did not have negative feelings against Australia and that their living conditions were in fact better in the camps than in their normal lives (1996:152–153).

When the Pacific War was over, this power-relationship appeared again in another form when Australians became part of the Occupation Force in Japan and played the role of the conqueror, with the Japanese being the conquered. These postwar experiences of Australians as the 'master' in the enemy's territory gave yet another dimension to the relationship with the Japanese and led to new (and often unique) descriptions of the Japanese, in both fiction and non-fictional stories.

In this chapter, experiences generated from the cross-cultural relationships between the Australians and the Japanese as they have been described in fiction and non-fictional works will be examined. They differ according to the year and circumstances of each publication, reflecting the respective contemporary situation of both countries.

Cowra narratives

A particular incident that took place at the Prisoner-of-War Camp in Cowra has been regarded by many Australians as the embodiment of the differences in ideas and behaviour between Australians and the Japanese. The Japanese mass-breakout from the camp, however, was not fully understood for over twenty years. It was not until the 1960s and 1970s, when journalist-authors like Hugh Clarke and Harry Gordon started to research the 'Cowra' incident that the story could be reconstructed and made fully public. They examined the government archives, bringing to light official documents, records and materials,.

On the Japanese side, prisoners who had survived the breakout and eventually returned to Japan when the war was over kept silent. It was only in the 1970s that some of these ex-prisoners started to tell their stories and the Japanese version of the event slowly became known. Publications include Teruhiko Asada's *The Night of A Thousand Suicides* (1970), which was translated into English from his original Japanese version published in 1967. In Japan, to reveal oneself as an ex-prisoner of war was still considered to be a great shame, a humiliation which might affect one's family even many years after the war. Some ex-prisoners even refused to admit having been in Cowra, which hampered the whole process of unearthing the facts. Nevertheless, interviews and memoirs were eventually collected, which, combined with information and evidence collected by the Australian side, led to further publications about the event in the 1980s.

The Japanese breakout from the Cowra prisoner-of-war camp occurred in the early morning of 5 August 1944, almost a year before the war ended. This camp, known as Number 12 Prisoner of War Group, was established 3 kilometres northeast of the township of Cowra, 318 kilometres west of Sydney, in New South Wales in 1941. The camp was then guarded by the 22nd Australian Garrison

Battalion. It consisted of four 17-acre compounds, identified from A to D, each catering for a thousand prisoners. In addition, there was an army compound outside. Compounds A and C housed the Italian inmates. Compound B housed the Japanese inmates, while Compound D housed Japanese officers, Formosans (Taiwanese) and Koreans. The number of prisoners in Compound B exceeded 1,000 in 1944. For security reasons, it was decided Non-Commissioned Officers were to be separated from Other Ranks in Compound B, the latter to be sent to another POW camp in Hay. The Japanese camp leaders were notified of this decision beforehand on the morning of 4 August. These leaders held a secret meeting to discuss the possible separation and eventually with all the inmates of the compound involved, they voted to rouse themselves to action—with a breakout. It was a swift decision, although there had long been rumours of such an event among both Australians and the Japanese.

At 1.50 am the following morning, with the signal of the bugle, over 900 prisoners attacked the barbed wire fences in three places around the compound, with makeshift weapons such as table knives, bats and clubs in hand. The huts were set on fire, while the invalids and some others remained inside and committed suicide. Most of the escapees used baseball gloves, blankets and toilet paper to get over the triple barbed wire fences; however, many were just blocked and subsequently shot. Over 300 prisoners actually managed to escape. Among those 25 died, mostly by taking their own lives. The rest were recaptured, both by the AMF and civilians and brought back to the camp. The total death toll of the prisoners in the breakout was 231, while 108 were wounded.[39] There were four Australian victims—three were killed during the riot and one during the search for the escapees.

Dead men rising

Censorship of the media at the time and the subsequent classification of the whole affair as 'confidential' by the authorities, meant that very few contemporary Australian authors wrote about the event.[40] Kenneth 'Seaforth' Mackenzie was one of the few authors who did, using the event as the setting of a novel and describing it from the point of view of one of the witnesses. The first impression one receives from his novel *Dead Men Rising* (1951) is the author's 'indifference'—to Australian–Japanese relationships and to the cross-cultural experiences between both groups. As has been pointed out by others,[41] Mackenzie's main interest was not in Japanese psychology, or in the 'extraordinary situation' in which the prisoners found themselves, but rather in the protagonist's love story and of the relationships formed while enduring the boredom of garrison life and military bureaucracy. It was only later that non-fiction writers such as Harry Gordon or Hugh Clarke posed the first simple question: 'why did the Japanese do it?' The prisoners were well fed, clothed and sheltered—their fish was imported from New Zealand and their copper pots were replaced by iron ones in order to cook rice better. They were given a certain degree of freedom, even allowed to grow their own vegetables and play baseball or sumo wrestling. Despite these concessions, the Japanese prisoners were desperate enough to revolt. In his novel, Mackenzie does not try to pursue the reasons why and through one of his characters—a Russian–Chinese interpreter named Orloff, simply ascribes it to the unbearable shame felt at being captives.

The title, *Dead Men Rising*, referring to the prisoners, is taken from an epigraph quoted by Mackenzie from Michael Paul's *The Anatomy of Failure*, which refers to prisoners who escaped, but were eventually captured and killed. Mackenzie's story seems to be chiefly about the garrison life itself in Cowra, (which is called Shotley in the story) rather than the Japanese breakout and its consequences. In the author's note written in 1949, Mackenzie emphasises two things: the first is that the 'garrison men were human, intelligent, and on occasion brave'. The second was that the 'greatest POW mass-escape in Christian history occurred in Australia in the first week of August 1944, almost a year to the day before the final defeat of the Japanese Army in the Pacific'. For the author, the main role of the 'great breakout' seems to be to provide a climax in which the protagonist John Sargent becomes embroiled and killed.

Besides the love story, garrison life appears to be the author's second main theme. It is often described with harshness and in candid, colloquial language. The camp troop is a patchwork of 'ragtag and bobtail recruits from city and country', of 'aging solders, B2 men—younger fellows in spectacles or half-crippled, and permanently grumbling veterans of an earlier world war' (1951:18). There is a prevailing friction among the ranks as well as within groups in the camp. Self-interested officers and inquisitive sergeants make the daily work difficult for their subordinates. There are many cases of absence from the camp without official leave, including that of the protagonist. Rumours about officers' mistresses in nearby towns are whispered and one of the sergeants is believed to have gone out to see his at the Army's expense. As Carr-Gregg points out, their garrison life 'lacked not only the excitement generated by active combat duty but also the spirit of comradeship which tends to develop among soldiers who share danger and hardship,' an ethos close to the legendary 'mateship' (Carr-Gregg 1978:60). On the battlefield, the existence of the enemy helps to heighten morale and confirms comradeship. However in the POW camp, the subjugated Japanese become only a burden and a nuisance and do not arouse any feelings of solidarity. As Jones (1969:9) points out, the existence of the Japanese means the intrusion 'of aliens upon the protagonist's life', as in other

Mackenzie novels. Clarke also mentions the garrison men's own deficiencies, their 'unfitness' for active service and 'the secret contempt of civilians and scorn of younger combatant troops in training' in Cowra 'because of the nature of garrison men's duties' (Clarke 1994:33). Australian soldiers in Cowra were also 'prisoners in a dull, mechanical round of garrison duty' (Mackenzie 1951:33). Mackenzie's protagonist sees that there is 'no liberty...on either side of that barbed wire' (1951:36). A negative mindset on the Australian side is revealed, including an ignorance and lack of preparation by those in authority for the eventual Japanese breakout.

In his author's note, Mackenzie asserts that this is a work of fiction and 'not one character can in any way be taken to represent the likeness of any living man or woman'. However, he had written to George Ferguson, publishing director of Angus and Robertson, 'that all the characters in the novel were "real people"' (Carr-Gregg 1978:56). Besides the military secrecy over the breakout itself, this might be one of the reasons why the book was not immediately published in Australia. While Mackenzie had won a fellowship from the Board of the Australian Commonwealth Literary Fund to complete this book in 1949, it was not published in Australia until 1969, although it was published both in the United Kingdom and in the United States in 1951. This English/American version was not circulated in Australia (Gerster 1992:226).

Mackenzie himself was one of the guards in the Italian compound in 1944 and he provides some observations and personal stories of Italian prisoners. He does not fully describe the Japanese prisoners, nor speculate why they were driven to their action. For Mackenzie, the Japanese prisoners were little more than aliens and the protagonist's interest in them remains the same from their arrival to the end of the story: '[they were] squat, ape-like and apparently sub-normal men... Technically dead to their families and their war office, the yellow-brown soldiers, ugly to Western eyes and grotesque in their burgundy uniforms crowded their quarter-share of the huge camp...' (Mackenzie 1951:21).

The protagonist, John Sargent, working as a corporal clerk whose job is to type official documents, shows very little interest in the prisoners throughout the story. One of the very few occasions when Sargent gives his impression of the Japanese prisoners is when he sees them doing Swedish drills. He compares them to mass 'automatons', exactly the same word used later in Hal Porter's short story called '*Irasshaimashi*', which was written about the postwar Japanese. As Jones points out, the Japanese prisoners, 'throughout the novel still remain an almost totally unindividuated mass of small, similar and incomprehensible figures off-stage' (Jones 1969:11).

The Japanese may be 'incidental to the main business'[42] and not the main purpose of Mackenzie's novel; however, there are details which only witnesses could reveal, making this novel unique. In Mackenzie's novel one character who shows an interest in the concerns of Japanese prisoners and talks on behalf of the Japanese is sergeant-interpreter Orloff, who is probably based on a real figure, a Japanese–Russian interpreter called Negerevich (Gordon 1978:85–86). Orloff, a Chinese–Russian interpreter who studied in Tokyo before the war, carries out the role of the middle-man between the Australians and the Japanese. He speaks several languages, knows something about both Eastern and Western cultures and can conveniently explain the Japanese mentality and social background. Orloff's position makes him appear to betray the Japanese prisoners; he feels frustrated because he is the only one who can read these seemingly tame and quiet prisoners' insulting gestures or scornful remarks. Orloff scorns both the Japanese and the Australians—the former for their contempt for the generosity and patience shown by their captors and the latter for the ignorance and carelessness shown by their captives.

In the novel, Orloff's listener and friend, Sergeant Major Poole represents ordinary Australians as a whole. Poole is continually surprised by Orloff's comments about the Japanese, especially their 'codes' of fighting and dying. He is the son of a grazier in his civilian life and 'more inclined to listen to nature's course of change rather than to hear about the incomprehensible heathen mentality' (Mackenzie 1951:61). These Japanese soldiers, were 'technically dead to their families and their War Office' because of their Military Code *Senjinkun*—which forbade the status of 'prisoner-hood' (Mackenzie 1951:ch4). They were a source of puzzlement and mystery to Poole. Yet Poole becomes one of the few Australians who begins to take Orloff's warning about a crisis seriously and 'by his make-up and honest simplicity of mind' prepares himself for what might happen.

In the novel there is an episode where a Japanese lieutenant slaps a mean Australian Major across the face and then demands he execute himself. Orloff explains to Poole that this is derived from their 'code' of behaviour and that from the Japanese point of view it is the best way to die (Mackenzie 1951:148). Poole, from his Western viewpoint, thinks that logically the Japanese lieutenant should be happy being spared, but he is corrected by Orloff, who explains that the young and vain Japanese lieutenant seeks 'dying in action' as a way of avoiding a dishonourable and miserable life of captivity. With Orloff's ambiguous use of the word 'ingenuity', Poole gets the idea that the Japanese may be both 'ingenious' and 'ingenuous'. Thus, through the ambiguities of language, Poole starts to see the necessity of recognising Eastern logic and not to try and interpret things through Western eyes, even if he finds it difficult to accept such a difference.

This episode concerning the Japanese lieutenant reaches a climax in the court hearing when the Australians, except for Orloff, are astounded to realise that the silent lieutenant in fact understands English perfectly, this showing his contempt for and rejection of his captors (Mackenzie 1951:192).

With his own 'simple knowledge and code of living', Poole is unable to wholly believe in what Orloff says or to take action in response to his warnings of a crisis (Mackenzie 1951:152). He eventually dismisses the urgency of Orloff's warning as being too pessimistic. Major Shawe of the Japanese compound, who holds an anti-White-Australia policy opinion and maintains 'fair' attitudes towards the Japanese prisoners, finds Orloff too defensive and 'getting on his nerves'. Orloff's repeated phrase, 'wait and see', does not meet with a positive reaction and the prisoners' outbreak is not prevented. Australians' ignorance, indifference and negligence with respect to the Japanese are thus emphasised.

Some of the characteristics described in *Dead Men Rising* convey the atmosphere of the camp at the time of the outbreak. In Mackenzie's novel, the tranquillity and superficial peacefulness of the camp, as well as the surroundings, are emphasised throughout the story. Under the blue sky, with abundant sunshine, or under the cool moonlight, the camp is presented in a pastoral context, without any violent or terrifying images of the war and its combatants. However, it is partly because of this quiet and calm that both sides, captors and captives, become nullified and like the 'dead'. Australian soldiers are tired of the Army life, which lacks any 'passion of action and movement, no swaggering thrills from foreign lands and foreign girls under other skies' (Mackenzie 1951:36). When finally the mass escape happens, it creates much excitement for Australian soldiers, who are finally able to 'shoot into mortal flesh', even causing random shots to ricochet into their own troops. One Japanese writer even blames the environment for the breakout, saying that 'the tranquillity of the place made the suicidal breakout possible' (Nagase 1990:180). The outside tranquillity is believed to have been a tremendous burden to the Japanese prisoners, who were ashamed of themselves for not fighting against the enemy in the harsh atmosphere of the jungle.[13] Instead, they were protected and fed in the enemy's land, which in turn drove them to their desperate act.

The moon in *Dead Men Rising* is also described as symbolic of the night of the breakout. In reality, the breakout was carried out under a bright moon, which, as later writers often point out, shows the Japanese's aim was not a successful escape but rather a suicidal act in order to achieve an honourable death. They had no intention of hiding or escaping. In *Dead Men Rising*, Orloff warns that the Japanese breakout is close at hand because the moon will be full, and they were taking baths all day. For Australians, only lunatics would carry out an escape at night under the full moon. However, according to Orloff, Japanese *are* lunatics and they are cleansing themselves before the final act. Later writers of non-fiction like Clarke and Gordon and Japanese memoirists almost always mention this brightness of the moon.

The literary weakness of *Dead Men Rising* seems to lie in the fact that the author's two main themes—the love affair of the protagonist and the garrison life of the Australians in Cowra—are too separate from the extraordinary situation in which the Australians and Japanese find themselves and the eventual breakout. Jones believes that the love story '...has no potentially significant relation to [the event] and [Mackenzie's novel] fails to be a tense fictional account of the break-out' (Jones 1969:11). Nevertheless, this is one of very few 'authentic' stories by an Australian author who witnessed and experienced the breakout. The story also coincidentally shows how surprised and unprepared contemporary Australians were, with little knowledge about the Japanese of the time.

Cowra reconstructed in non-fiction

Mackenzie's novel can be regarded as a fairly immediate contemporary response to the Japanese breakout in novelistic form. When the official records were finally made available after 20 years, later non-fiction writers using these records took a very different approach in reconstructing the events. In the 1960s and 1970s, when Japan had recovered from the immediate aftermath of the war, the relationship between Australia and Japan once again changed dramatically—this time their political and economic ties became closer. The ideas and images of the Japanese held by Australians changed too. Australian society had become more ethnically diverse and from 1972 a policy of multiculturalism was formally adopted. There was no longer the 'implied' power-relationship of the Australian occupation force as the conqueror or the Japanese as a conquered people.

When official documents became available, Hugh V Clarke and Harry Gordon were among the first writers to try and reconstruct the outbreak. Clarke himself had been a prisoner of the Japanese in Malaya, Thailand and Japan.[44] Gordon was a newspaperman whose senior colleague was unable to write about the breakout because of censorship enforced by the government. This was at a time when 'censorship of war information was being tightened in Australia for political rather than security reasons' (Gordon 1994:228). Both writers used official documents and conducted interviews with ex-prisoners in Cowra, and reconstructed the event from both Japanese and Australian perspectives for their first books. Both then revised their books in 1994, commemorating 50 years since the breakout. Clarke's first book, *Break-Out*, was the 'first full inside story' of the event when it was published in 1965; it was later revised and published in

1994 as *Escape to Death: The Japanese Break-Out at Cowra, 1944*. Gordon's *Die Like the Carp!* was first published in 1978. He conducted many interviews and correspondence, both in Australia and Japan and tried not only to elaborate on the facts he discovered but also to uncover new and previously unpublished information. The discovery of the court-hearing transcripts of the first ringleader, Sergeant Major Kanazawa and exclusive interviews with him became central to *Die Like the Carp!,* Gordon's first book. In his next book, *Voyage from Shame*, he observes some changes in Kanazawa's state of mind as time passed—from shame to regained pride. Gordon also reveals that one of the ringleaders who blew the bugle and signalled the breakout had assumed a false name as had many other prisoners. He is still buried in Cowra's Japanese cemetery under that name. Some of the facts Clarke and Gordon disclose in their books were taboo for Japanese memoirists and writers in Japan. Even in the 1980s and 1990s, the remaining ex-prisoners often wished to withhold their names.[45]

As the titles of their books show, one of the major aims and attempts of both Gordon and Clarke was to reveal the nature of the uprising and the reason why the Japanese prisoners chose this suicidal act. The title of Gordon's first book, *Die Like the Carp!*, is a phrase actually uttered by one of the hut-leaders to his members at the outbreak. The carp, traditionally the Japanese symbol of bravery, has excellent health with the strength to swim up waterfalls. It 'knows how to die—it doesn't flinch when the time comes to plunge the knife into it' (Gordon 1978:16). Thus one of the leaders called Ogi, a storyteller in the story reconstructed by Gordon, tells his men to show dignity in their death. Clarke's contradictory title, *Escape to Death*, also reveals the nature of the act. It was to gain 'life-in-death' for the Japanese prisoners because to go on living with dishonour and shame meant 'death-in-life' to them. The later version of Gordon's book, *Voyage from Shame*, traces the mental change of the prisoners over the fifty years and as mentioned earlier, he records the process whereby they recover their self-pride. Examples include the Masaru Morimoto episode in which Morimoto, one of the survivors of the breakout, regained his courage to revisit Cowra 50 years later.

The first aim of these Australian writers, or their strongest motive, is to reveal *why* the event happened. It was much easier for Australians to see it as a Japanese attempt for a successful escape and their eventual unification with the Japanese Army advancing southward (Clarke 1994:81). But Clarke and Gordon did not try to solve the puzzle with 'Western logic'; rather, they chose to listen to Japanese voices and let them tell their stories as a means of reconstructing the whole event. While Mackenzie had not been able to do this because of his limited opportunity to communicate with the Japanese, as well as his own narrow viewpoint, later writers and novelists were able to take this approach through research and interviews.[46] Gordon and Clarke both start their books with the experiences of Japanese soldiers from the war in New Guinea, how they fought and were captured and how they became prisoners and were sent to Cowra. The authors attempt to research the Japanese mentality, to understand it, and to let it come through in their stories; to reveal something of the cultural and psychological characteristics of the Japanese mind, which until this point had not been a focus of attention in Australian writing. This was also the time when such journalist-authors as Christopher Koch, Blanche d'Alpuget, Robert Drewe and other writers started to write about Asia, constructing their novels through their own experiences and cautiously employing indigenous characters.

Through Gordon's and Clarke's observations, the attempt to retell the whole affair from both sides is made, especially with Gordon's numerous and often painstaking interviews with both the Japanese and Australians involved. Important points in the psychology of the Japanese prisoners are revealed, some of which had been previously incomprehensible to most Australians. One such paradoxical revelation is the fact that the Japanese prisoners were driven to act under pressure of being treated 'humanely'. As Gordon observes, the difference between the Allied POWs and the Japanese lies in their ignorance of how to behave as prisoners. Because of their 'code', there was ostensibly no state of 'prisonerhood' for the Japanese, thus no room for them to claim their right of survival. They even felt contempt for their captors for their kindness, regarding it as a major sign of weakness (Gordon 1978:42). Prisoners of war should expect nothing from their captors, as has been revealed in the memoirs of POWs of both sides. The incident of the young lieutenant who slapped an Australian officer in the face in Mackenzie's novel suggests that some Japanese wanted an easier and quicker solution to their dilemma, using the enemy as a tool to achieve that end.

The Australian official records stress that the treatment of Japanese prisoners of war had been:

> humane and generous [and that] the conditions at the camp prior to the mutiny were exemplary and fully in accordance with the provisions of the International Convention Relative to the Treatment of Prisoners of War (Geneva 1929)...No complaints concerning their treatment had been made by or on behalf of the prisoners of war in Camp B to the Camp Commandant immediately prior to the mutiny' (Clarke 1994:104).

Almost all the Japanese ex-prisoners from Cowra admit that they were lucky in terms of their treatment.

The direct trigger for the breakout is thoroughly discussed in the works of Clarke and Gordon. The prisoners' frustration and despair was generated from the sense of shame and hopelessness at being abandoned by their homeland and the fear of ostracism for their families at home in case their captivity became known. But still there were no elaborate plans to escape from the camp. Rather the idea developed as a spontaneous, if conditioned, response to the decision by the Australian authorities that Non Commissioned Officers and Other Ranks were to be separated. This swift and sudden action bore a resemblance to the Featherston mutiny by Japanese prisoners in New Zealand the year before. Mateship was an important means for survival for the Australian prisoners during their captivity. For the Japanese captives, sharing their 'massive, collective sense of shame' was just as important, as shown in *Die Like the Carp!* (1978:29. Gordon cites the Russian interpreter's words that describe the relationship among the Japanese prisoners as 'brotherly like the Mafia'. He also borrows a Japanese ex-prisoner's words: with 'a greater degree of frankness by the camp authorities (and) a better knowledge of the Japanese mentality' the revolt need never have occurred (1978:87). Clarke calls it, in *Escape to Death*, a 'dreadful bond' that tied the Japanese prisoners together. They 'all shared the same cheerless conviction...They could not go back to Japan and sooner or later, all must die in this foreign country' (1994:49).

However, Clarke also challenges the notion of a perfect collectivity of the prisoners. He emphasises that among the thousand and more Japanese from B Compound, 138 prisoners did not leave the camp nor take their own lives there (1994:71). These men, although they shared the same fear and despair, were unable to simply obey the majority who carried out their mass suicide. In both Gordon's and Clarke's stories, these recalcitrant Japanese prisoners (and in some cases the Korean prisoners) show their unwillingness to support the plan by secretly informing their captors about the possibility of a breakout. One even presented himself to the Australian authorities as a 'troublemaker' so he would be kept in the cell and thereby avoid participating in the breakout. With such episodes collected from both the Australian and the Japanese sides, Clarke and Gordon were able to reconstruct the event with a fuller and more accurate picture, with different perceptions and understandings based on different cultural interpretations about what was going on at that time.

The Cowra breakout has also been used to describe Japanese idiosyncrasies by later novelists such as Roger Pulvers, who used the event as the background to his novel, *The Death of Urashima Taro* (1981), set in the 1980s. This will be further discussed in Chapter Eight. Based on both fictional and non-fictional literary works and records, Pulvers uses the Cowra event to explore in greater depth what the war meant to the Japanese and Australians. He also tries to come to grips with the problem of the Emperor's responsibility for the war, a topic that is generally avoided in Japan.

Writings on the experiences of the occupation forces

Soon after the Soviet Union declared war on Japan and the two fatal atomic bombs were dropped on Hiroshima and Nagasaki early in August 1945, Japan announced its surrender on 15 August and the Pacific War was over. Japan was then placed under Allied occupation. Contingents from the Australian Imperial Force became part of the British Commonwealth Occupation Force (BCOF) and were garrisoned in the mid-southern part of Chugoku-region in Japan, which included Kure and Hiroshima as major cities. The experiences of such postings provided some Australian writers who were members of the Army of Occupation with a unique opportunity to live in Japan and have direct contact with its people and culture.

After so many atrocities committed during the war, with race hatred a very strong motive on both sides, one might have expected a cruel and violent occupation in Japan, with the Western conquerors' vengeance being wreaked over the conquered. Macmahon Ball, the representative of the British Commonwealth in the Allied Council for Japan, points out that Australian policy toward Japan in the period of early occupation was shaped by 'the emotional aftermath of the war years, by fear and bitterness' (Ball 1969:107). He explains the attitudes of the Australians in his writings in 1948 as follows:

> To Australia, where we escaped invasion and occupation in 1942, whose soldiers went through long years of fighting or captivity in the Pacific, the first interest in Japan is undoubtedly a negative one: to assure by every possible means that she shall not regain the power to become an aggressor in the foreseeable future. This is not revenge, not even retribution. It is an unavoidable impulse of self-preservation. I was often told in Tokyo, not only by Japanese, but by Americans and others, that Australians seemed more bitter and revengeful towards the Japanese people than any other of the Allied peoples. I once had the disagreeable distinction of being described in part of the United States press as the 'leader of the revenge school' in Japan (Ball 1948:11–12).

While early occupation novels reflect this 'negative interest', Dower points out that the actual 'peaceful nature of the Allied occupation of Japan' and the goodwill that developed between the occupants and the occupied were evident, and that racial hatred dissipated relatively quickly. He explains this by saying 'the simplest of [answers is] that the dominant wartime stereotypes on both sides were wrong' (Dower 1986:301). Both sides were tired of war. The Allies discovered that 'the Japanese people—unlike their militarist leaders—welcomed peace' (Dower 1986:301). Despite slogans such as 'Kichiku-Bei Ei' (Beast–Barbarian Americans and British) propagated during the war, the Japanese found that the Westerners were not as the propagandists had portrayed. While racial discrimination and hatred did not vanish, each side discovered that the other was human too, and so started to communicate as human beings. From this time a new kind of story started to emerge, generated by the occupation experience and subsequent encounters between Australia and Japan.

The power relationship was still clearly that of the conqueror and the conquered. Australian writing generated from the experiences of the occupation reflects this relationship first and foremost. The servicemen of the Occupation Forces were fresh from the war and were affected by its aftermath, both mentally and physically. Most authors of occupation novels were among these servicemen, including such writers as TAG Hungerford, Stephen Kelen and Leonard H Evers. Hal Porter was an exception, being a teacher in a school attached to the Occupation Forces.

If the Australia–Japan relationship in the Cowra narratives was masculine and inter-group focused, stories written from the Occupation experiences are dominantly male–female and personal. As the title of Evers' novel indicates, the 'pattern of conquest' was clear. In this West–East, Australian–Japanese relationship, the West was an empowered group of people. The first actions of these people were those of the 'conqueror.' Pop, a serviceman, describes the nature of their existence in Kure:

> ...a conquered city was always burned, looted, and its women ravished...that was the pattern in ancient times...I don't mean we soldiers bust into houses, tear jewels off lovely throats, then toss the women on to the nearest bed—but the effect's the same (Evers 1954:28–29).

Pop suggests to the protagonist Mark Foster that they are inevitably drawn into this pattern.

Before the subordinate Japanese, the Australians are often portrayed by Australian authors as being like lords and masters, despite their usual role in Australian society. They take whatever opportunities are available—status, honour, money, women. Even though they often use vulgar language and lack education and status in their own society, they are honoured and privileged in their occupied land. George Smith in Kelen's novel *Goshu* (1965) says that he 'had to travel half-way round [the world] to find a bloke who reckons he ain't good enough to sit next to [him]' when a Japanese man, with customary politeness, says he is unworthy of sitting with Smith at a dinner table (1965:57–58).

The black market is described as a very common and necessary means for allied soldiers to obtain funds to behave like masters. It is also one of the main ways in which servicemen are able to have direct contact with the Japanese, even if it is characterised by the tricks and tactics of both parties. Mark Foster, the protagonist of *Pattern of Conquest* (Evers 1954), unexpectedly murders a Japanese black-marketeer in order to obtain 'funds' to keep a Japanese woman. Ron Prothero in TAG Hungerford's novel, *Sowers of the Wind* (1954), engages in secret trades by manipulating the Japanese. When troubles occur, Prothero retaliates by bashing the Japanese men and raping their wives. By doing so, he believes he is taking revenge for his brothers who were killed in Changi.

Japanese wartime atrocities against Australian soldiers during the Pacific War become a major reason for Australians abusing the Japanese during the Occupation. Captain Dugald in Porter's novel *A Handful of Pennies* (1958) treats his Japanese subordinates badly, saying he had seen plenty of atrocities by the Japanese during the war. He also mocks those who show tolerance to the Japanese, accusing them of sentimentalism, weakness and sloppiness. He hits an aged gardener and fractures his jaw for failing to build a kennel for his cocker spaniel (Porter 1958:30). The gardener then conspires with a house-girl and kills the dog in revenge.

According to Porter in the introductory chapter to *A Handful of Pennies*, the occupation is a game in which 'neither Conqueror nor Conquered had experience'. Eventually both sides become 'disconcerted, fascinated, and disappointed with each other' (Porter 1958:3). In such a game, people like Andy Waller in Hungerford's novel, *Sowers of the Wind,* who regard themselves as 'on holiday' and take as their motto 'easy come, easy go' are the most comfortable of all. He has never considered that he is 'in effect an ambassador' for his country; nor has he 'the foggiest notion of what the Force was doing, or of what it [hopes to] accomplish' (Porter 1958:165). Besides his mission to remove the hidden ammunition from Kira-jima (island), Bob Twindle in *Goshu* tries to gain as much as possible through black-marketeering, saying that he:

> didn't come here to save the Nips from themselves...[he] just came here to see how they live, have a bit of fun, adventure, and when [he] discovered there's a bit of good honest trading around the place...that made [him] sign up for a second term (Porter 1958:35).

For such people as Waller and Twindle, 'women' are the most tangible trophies of the occupation. As the 'pattern of conquest' goes, so the women in an occupied land are conquered. 'Cho-Cho-San'-like stories repeat themselves. Soldiers with money and goods, with saviour-like generosity, come and obtain temporary comfort. Then, when they have to return home, they are gone forever, leaving their wailing 'Japanese wives' at the harbour—a scene exactly the same as that described by authors such as Carlton Dawe some 60 years before. In *Sowers of the Wind* (Hungerford 1954), most of the characters (including the protagonist Rod McNaughton, who is more compassionate towards the Japanese than his fellow compatriots and had determined not to have any children with his girlfriend Fumie) eventually leave their pregnant Japanese wives and their 'half-caste bastards', thus 'sowing the wind and reaping the whirlwind', in other words, 'sowing a wind of hatred for the future' (Wilde, Hooton & Andrews 1994:389).

McNaughton, who 'saves' Fumie from a Japanese cabaret bar and takes her under his protection, treats her humanely. Fumie becomes his 'funny, dear, loyal companion', almost 'home' to him. With her in his life the faces he had known in his memory back home fade (Hungerford 1954:238). A more experienced friend of McNaughton's, Norm Craigie, sees the whole thing as 'loneliness and hunger masquerading as love' which only takes place in this extraordinary circumstance of war (Hungerford 1954:199). In Hal Porter's *A Handful of Pennies*, young Captain Truscott, takes dancer Imiko from a cabaret while on leave. His experience is 'a symbol between youth and manhood, West and East, loneliness and fulfilment' (Porter 1958:60). She relieves his 'homesickness of the spirit' (1958:83) and becomes very much attached to him. But Truscott does not see the difference between 'lust and tenderness, need and thievery' (Porter 1958:89). When he receives a telegram informing him of his promotion and urging his quick return to Australia, he does not hesitate to leave Imiko. Imiko's words: 'Come back the day before yesterday!' ('never come again', a kind of a parting shot) and 'Can't be helped!' while shrugging her shoulders in a gesture of unhappiness, was the 'cry of the East,' and the cry of the abandoned women who have resigned themselves to their fate with full knowledge. Unlike Americans, the BCOF did not allow interracial marriage, which is described as follows in *Pattern of Conquest*;: 'love 'm and leave 'm' was their policy, thus leaving many 'madam butterflies' (Evers 1954:81).[47]

The policy of non-fraternisation enforced by the BCOF has been condemned as impractical by many critics today. Examples include Wood (1998:93), who believes that they should have introduced a practical and flexible attitude. Wood attributes this policy (the non-fraternisation policy was first introduced in 1946 and then reaffirmed in 1949) to the Australian government's deliberate intention to keep the war wounds open (Wood 1998:95). Davies also believes that the policy should have been abandoned 'once it became obvious that both [Japanese] repatriated servicemen and the population generally were cooperative and submissive [to the Force]' (Davies 2001:314). In reality, however, this non-fraternisation policy failed on 'thousands of young soldiers, who, overcome by the boredom and loneliness of the conqueror, turned hungrily and furtively to the inevitable distractions of oriental life' (Evers 1954:cover blurb).

Complications of legitimacy or illegitimacy aside, the men from the Occupation Forces who devoted themselves to sexual encounters are often depicted as straightforward, crude and coarse. Andy Waller, 'on a good holiday' in *Sowers of the Wind*, practises what he had fantasised during the voyage to

Japan and contracts a venereal disease in the process, but it does not worry him: 'Penicillin and the Army would take care of that' (1954:164). In Kure, the town where the Occupation Forces are stationed, 'another night of civilised looting and raping [begins], woe to the conquered' (Evers 1954:62). The Occupation Forces, alarmed at the soaring venereal disease rate, started to plan licensed brothels, but that was stopped when a female journalist from Australia threatened to report this 'back home' (Evers 1954:81).

Other members of the Forces deplored this situation. Johnny in *Goshu* warns his fellows, saying that '…All over Kure…Australians [are] looking for females. And the Japanese threw their poor, infected, degraded women at us, and we fell into those dirty, stinking pits of disease just as they wanted us to do', but he is just ignored as being 'a bloody hypocrite' (Kelen 1965:138)

The conquest is described through various episodes in a variety of literary texts. In Porter's *A Handful of Pennies*, Padre Hamilton seduces a Japanese bar boy, a 'naval officer's son, a student of engineering, nineteen-years-old, heterosexual…and anxious to do the right thing' (Porter 1958:35). This boy wishes to learn everything about the West and the Padre's seduction is part of his lesson. In the same novel, an Australian teacher called Paula Groot picks up a university student called Kazuo, her house-girl's brother. She takes the lead in the relationship with Kazuo, convincing herself that 'since thousands of men played the double-backed game with Oriental women, she was justified in exchanging flesh with an Oriental man' (Porter 1958:171). But her 'East–West double standard' fails, for the innocent-looking Kazuo is actually a frequent brothel visitor and Paula Groot ends up contracting syphilis. Both the teacher and Padre are deported back to Australia and are thus punished for their deeds. In this process, Porter shows the naivety of his Australian characters' presumption in these cross-cultural, sexual encounters.

In the occupation novels, Japanese women are often depicted as commodities and as an inferior group of people. However, their characters are more distinct than those in the stories half a century earlier, and despite their 'Cho-Cho-San'-like fate, they are given more human qualities. While Meriko in *Pattern of Conquest* (Evers 1954) who has to sell herself to save the family from hunger, is still typical of the sacrificial female figure of the East, there are other stronger, postwar 'new women'. Imiko in *A Handful of Pennies* is dropped by Truscott because of his promotion and at one point she decides to return to her hometown, where she plans to settle down as a farmer's wife. City life and memories of her times with Truscott have made Imiko a totally different person, thus giving her a chance, helped by money from Truscott, and motivation to become independent from the Japanese traditional framework. As Clancy describes her story, it is a 'tragedy' in which Imiko has to 'return to the city knowing what her fate will be' (Clancy 1992:186). However, unlike her predecessors, Imiko has the 'choice', at least. Tohana, a Canadian-born Japanese woman in *Pattern of Conquest*, who speaks fluent English and knows the Western advantages for women, tries to use Mark Foster as her means to get out of Japan and live in the West. When it turns out to be difficult because of the 'non-fraternisation policy', she ditches him for another Australian who appears better able to fulfil her desire. This eventually leads Foster to murder the man. Mama Watanabe in Kelen's novel *Goshu*, the wife of the head of Kira-jima, as a result of the critical situation arising from the presence of the Goshu-jin (Australians), gains courage to speak out in public without her husband's permission, an action, to that point, considered impolite and against tradition (Kelen 1965:184).

In most of the Australian male-authored novels about the occupation of Japan, Australian women do not have impressive or influential characters. They are silent and unseen, their names are sometimes omitted, and they are portrayed neither as their soldiers' saviours nor as deterrents to amorous adventures in Japan. Rod McNaughton, in *Sowers of the Wind* (Hungerford 1954), is dropped by his girl friend Merle while he is away fighting in the jungle, and thus seeks comfort and companionship from Fumie. Mark Flannery, Merle's brother, cannot escape from his alcoholism and infatuation for women. He loses his fiancée back home when somebody informs her of his dissolute state, and eventually through desperation he commits suicide.

Australian women who belong to the Occupation Forces in Japan are no more kindly portrayed than those back home. Gloria Linden, a mistress to a married officer called Mercier in *Sowers of the Wind* (Hungerford 1954), follows the military from Europe to Japan, and when the 'dependents scheme' for families is enforced and Mercier's family goes to Japan, she is dumped without hesitation (Hungerford 1954:ch 13). As has been mentioned, Paula Groot in *Handful of Pennies* (Porter 1958) tries to take the same opportunities as the men from the forces do, but ends up like many of them, with venereal disease. Thus women of both sides somehow become victims of the circumstances in which they find themselves.

Although Japanese female characters still dominate, Japanese civilian men also start to appear in more distinct roles in the occupation novels, something new in Australian writing on the Japanese. Many are black-marketeers who have more opportunities for direct contact with the Occupation Forces. People like Andy Waller worry about their lack of Japanese language ability and learn words 'necessary to love-making or the operation of his black-market interest', and so through their broken Japanese are able to communicate with the Japanese (Hungerford 1954:165).

These black-marketeers are described in similar terms in most of the stories. They are greedy and tricky, trying to manipulate both their own people and the Occupation Forces, exploiting whomever they can. For example, Osada, an immensely fat owner of a brewery in *Sowers of the Wind*, sells his beer to the forces and earns enough to build a lavishly ornate house on the hill, abusing his subordinates along the way (Hungerford 1954). Nomura buys girls from poor families to work at the dance-hall where McNaughton discovers Fumie. When, like Fumie, girls are bought out by their Australian boyfriends, Nomura waits for the girls to be dumped, then gets them working for him again. Such exploitative fathers as Meriko's urge their daughters to go and sell themselves (Evers 1954). Nijori owns a boat and does black-marketeering with his uncle, uncle's wife and his cousin, thus showing some Australian soldier-business partners how a 'Japanese family business' is run (Hungerford 1954). Akiyama Yashira's episode from *Pattern of Conquest* shows that both the Japanese and Australians try to trick and outwit each other in business. Akiyama tries to use counterfeit money to buy 'cigaretto' from an Occupation Forces soldier only to find the cartons he buys are packed with rolled paper. Thus in this black-marketing business the two sides become matched opponents.

Among the Japanese characters in the occupation novels are some bellicose nationalists left over from the war. In *Goshu*, a Japanese ex-corporal called Yonemitsu and his mentor priest Harunobu are frustrated by the fact that the Australians are required to remove explosives from their island. They urge the villagers to keep the buried bombs as a sacred token from the Emperor by trying to build a shrine on the ammunition dump. Yonemitsu, who was once admired as a hero-soldier by the villagers and swore never to surrender, is desperate not to suffer the 'barbarians' on their island, and tries every means to resist the Australians' attempts.

Osada, the rich brewer in *Sowers of the Wind*, maintains patience and silence when accompanying the 'barbarians', but believes that 'Tenno Heiko[sic], the Son of Heaven, had asked his people to endure the presence of the invader, and endure they would....When [the occupation] was finished...[they would] begin once more to build Nippon to greatness' (Hungerford 1954:137). They regard the occupation as a 'defilement', an extreme form of shame and dishonour as was seen among the Japanese prisoners in Cowra, and they believe that it will not last forever. Among the postwar Japanese notions observed by these writers, (particularly by Hal Porter on his second visit to Japan in the late 1960s), was the Japanese eagerness for rehabilitation, reconstruction, recovery and eventual prosperity, so strong it was akin to a form of revenge.

Like Orloff, the interpreter in *Dead Men Rising*, those who are placed in-between West and East during the occupation are often depicted as lone figures. They do not belong to either side. Trying to please both sides, they suffer a 'middleman's burden'; they fail to please anyone. Sato, a *nisei* (second-generation) interpreter from the United States, is a tragicomic character in *Goshu*. He has decided to be the 'twain', to build the 'bridge of understanding between East and West' (Kelen 1965:155). But he is American-born, and the language and manners of Australian soldiers perplex him. With his Asian appearance and Western education and knowledge, he wants to help his ancestor's land rise from the ruins. He tries to 'balance his fate between East and West', only to find he belongs to neither side. His interpretation of information from both sides is sometimes circuitous, free-ranging and altered in order to make the messages acceptable to both sides. Sato's tragicomic efforts to please both Australians and Japanese tear him apart, revealing the immensity of the gap and the tenuousness of any bridge.

'Jimmu' Murimoto, a peace-time architect and now storeman to Rod McNaughton in *Sowers of the Wind*, is another tragic figure. Having lost his four sons as well as his career, fortune and health in the war, Murimoto invites McNaughton, who is about the same age as his sons, to his house. He and his wife show McNaughton how ordinary Japanese live, think and survive in the aftermath of the war. McNaughton exacted racial hatred on a man named Weisman, calling him 'wogs...bloody foreigners', so Weisman takes his revenge by pursuing Murimoto (Hungerford 1954:235). Xenophobic attitudes hamper the process of reconciliation not only between the conquerors and the conquered, but between the conquerors as well, among whom there are also considerable differences of national background, manners, attitudes and values.

Among the conquerors there are some, though small in number, who are portrayed as the 'bridge-to-be', and Major Everard-Hopkins in Porter's *A Handful of Pennies* is one of them. He 'admire[s]...and love[s] Orientals' (1958:19) and is intensely interested in observing the results of East–West encounters, dichotomies and their effects. He is disappointed by his first view of the East, just as the author himself was, having been filled with Orientalist illusions through childhood stories.[48] However, Porter's alter-ego, Everard-Hopkins, gradually finds that those who are conquered are not merely subordinate, and that the conquerors are themselves being conquered through the Japanese people's abundant energy for life and eagerness to recover from the war (Porter 1958:46–47). Everard-Hopkins tries to understand the 'Other' through observation, tries to reason and to look inside the Japanese. He observes that 'Orientals [are] poverty's most delightful offspring...they live on "taboo and ritual"' (Porter 1958:17) and realises that 'Democracy is a Western foible whose ideas of freedom, politics, religion are not based on [as] firm sand as [the] Oriental'. The latter is based 'on a philosophy or a harmony of subordination, on those unwritten codes so much more logical than ethics typewritten in triplicate' (Porter 1958:18). Everard-Hopkins, however, before reaching 'inward', trying to be part of the whole, is 'flicked' out. When he is lost in the enchanted circle of *Bon-Odori*, a dance to welcome the soul of the deceased with 'repetitions, reappearances and layers of sounds', he suddenly realises that 'these barbarians are differently stronger' (Porter 1958:167–170). Unable to regain strength in his already weakened body, he dies in despair and loneliness.

Everard-Hopkins's efforts to comprehend Japan were unsuccessful, suggesting a difficulty in the mutual understanding between East and West perceived by Porter. However, witnessing Japanese in their cultural context and having direct contact with local people did result in a gradual gaining of knowledge that is in turn reflected in the writings from the period. In *Goshu*, the importance for men, either of lower or higher class, not to lose 'mentsu'—face— is comically exaggerated, revealing the male-centred, public-oriented aspect of Japanese society. The toughness and resolve of the Japanese to survive the aftermath of the war is observed, not only in the wily black-marketeers but also through the life of ordinary people—workers for the Occupation Forces, who appear submissive but subversively take what they can get from their masters. These include people like Imiko or Kazuo in *A Handful of Pennies*, who not only are used by the conquerors but also use them as stepping stones for their own purposes. Japanese customs like *Bon-odori* are mentioned in various works such as in *A Handful of Pennies* and *Goshu*. The importance of these customs is that, despite minor errors in Japanese given and family names, or in Japanese words transcribed in Roman letters, the authors have attempted to bring the atmosphere of the country to their readers.

Most of the authors from the Occupation Forces witnessed the ruins of Hiroshima and put some aspect of this experience in their stories. In *Sowers of the Wind* an American tells the Australians how it was like 'hell' just after the atomic bomb exploded above them. In the same novel, a Japanese translator, Akiru Tesuo, also tells the Australians about his experiences. In *Patterns of Conquest*, in the totally shattered remains of the city, even the most flippant soldier of the group becomes silent and thoughtful (Evers 1954:182). In *Goshu*, Johnny talks about his experiences in Hiroshima with his company, about how much the bomb afflicted the ordinary citizens with 'their festering wounds that will never heal' (Kelen 1965:139). But despite this, Johnny believes that dropping the bomb was necessary to stop the war and save millions of lives on both sides (Kelen 1965:140). Later, when villagers of Kira-jima want to celebrate the removal of ammunition with a fireworks display, Johnny is killed in a fire on the boat full of ammunition, ignited by a special firework ironically called the 'Atom'. Justification or condemnation over the inevitability of the bomb aside, these authors were among the first witnesses of conquered Japan, and thus were able to inform their readers of one aspect of the war not widely talked about in public, either in Australia or Japan.

As Porter puts it in *A Handful of Pennies*, the 'Mess' of the Occupation Forces is a place, which, 'like oldmen's home or prison, is a unique zone having a climate of its own,' and the people there are a unique group of soldiers, many of whom are 'self-exiled, escaped from a Western *milieu* that knew their meagre shameful failings' (Porter 1958:27). They have a special atmosphere and status, thus not representing the 'West' as a whole. Under such extraordinary circumstances, to be conquerors does not necessarily mean to be victorious or heroic. Despite the fact that Hungerford's novel *Sowers of the Wind* won a prize in the *Sydney Morning Herald* Literary Competition in 1949, it was not published until five years later because of the publisher's concerns: 'Australian exploitations of the conquered Japanese, economically and sexually, reveal such a distasteful side to the character of the young Australian troops that…Angus and Robertson kept it back until 1954' (Wilde, Hooton & Andrews 1994:389). As a 'realist', Hungerford was not interested in depicting his Australians as heroic conquerors, but the Australian reading public were perhaps not yet ready for this approach.

Australians are often portrayed as victims themselves. On their arrival in Japan, Australian garrison men are disappointed to see that 'it [is] just like home, just like Fremantle' (Hungerford 1985). Like Mark Foster, they are inevitably drawn into the 'pattern of conquest'. Some characters like Charlie Rogers (*Pattern of Conquest*) or Johnny (*Goshu*) have strong wills, often supported by Christian religious beliefs, know the signs of danger and vice well and have enough moral strength not to fall into the traps. Some, like Pop or Honest John in *Pattern of Conquest* take it as an opportunity. Naïve characters like Mark Foster, who do not know the pattern, fall into the trap, becoming tragic figures. It is much easier for people like Captain Truscott (*A Handful of Pennies*), who 'touch' the pattern and then move on. The morale and the sense of morality of the garrison men cannot be raised when they do not understand the importance of their contact with the 'other', and eventually 'novelty' turns to 'ennui' (Evers 1954:80). 'Beer and Women' become the only two subjects of their conversation (Hungerford 1954:173), and their famous 'mateship' that sustained them in the hardship of war dissolves in peacetime.

However, it also seems true in the occupation writings that through the boredom of garrison life and the petty missions of everyday life, and through the black-marketeering and penicillin-treatment for STDs, they establish some cross-cultural relationships. However partial and imperfect, they are able to gain impressions of Japan and the Japanese, as well as give their Japanese counterparts impressions of Australia and Australians. What the Australian occupation servicemen actually did in Japan may have been quite different from what was originally expected. In the 'Objects and Role of the BCOF', it was stated that one of the objects is 'to maintain and enhance British Commonwealth prestige in the eyes of the Japanese and of [their] allies' (Wood 1998:93). Through their direct contact and interaction with the 'Other', Australian soldiers perhaps presented different images to what had been intended. It may be, as one of the characters in *Sowers of the Wind* says, that when the occupation is over,

> the politicians and the blasted priests will make their tours of Japan and assure the press that everything's hunkey-dorey, no black market, no VD (venereal disease), no nothing. And if anyone says anything different, he'll be howled down for besmirching the glorious name of our fighting forces (Hungerford 1954:142).

But the first-hand stories narrated by those who experienced the postwar occupation of Japan give a real account of what went on, and a good description of the 'Other'. Even the ultimate 'sacrifices' as with the deaths of Major Sholto Everard-Hopkins or Captain MM Wilkinson in *A Handful of Pennies,* who return home in china jars, provide a silent account of the continuing impact of the 'Other.'

Part Three

Post-Second World War to the 1990s

chapter six

New writing on Japan from the 1950s to the 1970s

Although it was on the winners' side at the end of the Second World War, Australia was preoccupied with its recovery due to losses in its work force and delay in national development during the war. Like many other war-exhausted countries, Australia's postwar rehabilitation was the country's main priority, which eventually led to changes in thinking and behaviour. Australia also faced the need to reshape its national orientation in accordance with the major structural changes that were taking place in world politics, diplomacy and economics.

With the conclusion of the ANZUS Treaty in 1951, Australia entered into a new phase of diplomacy, which involved a closer relationship with the United States. It had already dispatched troops to Korea in the previous year to join the United States-led United Nations forces. The lesson learned from the Pacific War was that an imaginary invasion from the North could become a reality. Together with the newly perceived threat from communist Asia, Australia was increasingly influenced by American rather than British thinking on world affairs. The eventual decision by the United Kingdom to enter the European community in 1973 further distanced the once close relationship between the two nations. In fact, as Blainey wrote in *The Tyranny of Distance*, Australia probably started its transition 'from its traditional role as echo and image of Britain and an outpost of Europe' right from the start of the Pacific War (Blainey 1983:326).

However, Australia's relationship with its mentor, the United States, was rather ambivalent. Australian participation in the Vietnam War from 1965 generated some antipathy towards the United States among those who interpreted the United States' action as a display of imperialistic power politics in the region. The evolution of a youthful counter-culture in the late 1960s and 1970s provided a strong outlet for the expression of these sentiments. Anti-authoritarian and anti-American feelings were expressed in a variety of forms, especially through demonstrations, although by doing so Australia 'paradoxically found itself imitating American modes of expression' (Bennett 1998:240). The rejection of the Vietnam War meant 'a blanket rejection of almost everything associated with the world of their parents', thus resulting in changes of previously held values and ideas (Bennett cited in Gerster & Bassett 1991:241). According to Hughes, because of the Vietnam War, people started to perceive Asia as not the 'Far East' but rather as the 'Near North'. As such, there was a shift in focus from the 'old world' of Europe to Australia's near neighbours in Asia and the Pacific (in Gerster 1995:294).

Together with such social re-orientation, the change in the Migration Act, which abolished the dictation tests in European languages in 1959, was the first step towards Australia officially becoming a multicultural nation. As shown in Chapter Five, Japanese war brides, who were first allowed into Australia in 1952, signalled a breakthrough towards the abolition of the strict immigration policy. The increase in Australia's population, 10 million at that time, would later include more and more people from Asia along with non-English speaking Europeans and other ethnic groups. Before the 1960s, for many Australians, Asia was a stepping stone or port of call, a necessary step on the way 'Home' to the old world of Britain and Europe (Gerster 1995:293). Now Asia started to become the main focus for young travellers, with their main interest being Asian food, culture and adventure, all available at relatively cheap prices.

Donald Horne, who removed the slogan 'Australia for the White Man' from *The Bulletin* when he became the editor in 1960, suggested in *The Lucky Country* that Asia lost its meaning as being the 'opposite' to Europe. There was no longer the concept of 'Pan-Asianism' that had been seen as a threat to Australia after the Second World War. People started to see that there were 'divisions between the nations of Asia and…there are immense feelings of difference between races' (Horne 1998:110). As Horne notes in the fifth edition of *The Lucky Country* (in 1998), the first edition of the book published in 1964 did not mention 'multiculturalism', nor had the word 'ethnic' become part of everyday Australian vocabulary (Horne 1998:xii). However, by the late 1950s and 1960s such notions had probably started to emerge within Australian society. As Gerster puts it, Horne's famous declaration, 'We're all Asians now', might have sounded a little too daring in 1964 (Horne 1998:121; Gerster 1995:295) and yet the apparent changes from the pre-war and immediate postwar atmosphere within Australian society were becoming apparent and so was the new emergent relationship between Australia and Asia.

One of the earliest turning points in Australia's growing interest in Asia was the inauguration of the Colombo Plan. In 1950, at the meeting of British Commonwealth foreign ministers in Colombo, Sir Percy Spender, then Minister for External Affairs in the Menzies government, initiated a project which aimed to further the economic development of Southeast Asia. Soon after he was appointed as Minister, Spender had indicated that his 'intention was to examine and strengthen Australia's relationship with her neighbours in Southeast Asia' and that 'Australia...should make her primary foreign relations effort in Asia and the Pacific', even though he himself thought it was 'quite a new concept in Australian foreign policy' at the time (Spender 1969:195). The primary goal of the plan was to encourage stability in both the economies and politics of Southeast Asia by developing human resources and providing financial aid, which in turn was based on the political intention to ensure Australian security by stabilising an unstable Asia. Positive reciprocal interchange was not on the initial agenda. With other non-Commonwealth countries such as Nepal, Thailand and Indonesia included as recipients of this aid, and with the United States and later Japan joining as providers, the project provided a strong symbol of the positive interrelationships between countries in the region, with Australia at its centre.

After the Treaty of Peace between the Allied Powers and Japan was signed in San Francisco and since the Australian occupation force in Japan ceased its operations in 1951, Australia and Japan started to form a new relationship, which was mainly economic and political in nature. With the significant efforts made by the Japanese for postwar rehabilitation (described by Hal Porter in his essays and fiction), Australia established a cooperative relationship with Japan by supplying the materials needed for postwar recovery. In 1957 both countries signed a trade agreement on most-favoured-nation terms and nine years later, Japan replaced Britain as Australia's largest customer.

With the memories of the atrocities committed during the war concealed beneath the surface, a more practical relationship in terms of trade and business developed more smoothly and quickly than human and social relationships. As mentioned earlier, it was not until 1952 that Japanese war brides of Australian servicemen were allowed into Australia and it was not until 1957 that they were allowed to become Australian citizens. However, the arrival of these brides may be regarded as 'a chip, albeit a tiny one, in the White Australia Policy' (Easton 1995:14) and the war brides became the first Asian women to enter Australia on a permanent basis in the 20th century.

With such changes starting to happen both inside and outside Australia, a new form of writing about Japan began to emerge during this postwar period. As an introduction, this chapter starts with a brief examination of short stories and novels other than war literature before, during and just after the Second World War. Such stories, written by authors like Xavier Herbert, Katharine Susannah Prichard and later writers such as Tom Ronan, are few in number. Nonetheless they are remarkable for employing Japanese characters in their plots, not as enemies but as ordinary community members, albeit within special locations such as Darwin and Broome. This is followed by a discussion of novels written in the 1950s and 1960s by such authors as Nevil Shute, Thomas Keneally and Randolph Stow, whose stories reflect ordinary people's lives in Australian society during the war years and explore how Japan was seen as the enemy.

This chapter then focuses on those authors who spent some time in Japan through the war to the occupation period and who expressed their views in fiction. Elizabeth Kata is one of these writers who, as the Australian-born wife of a Japanese man, had the unique experience of being detained in Japan during the war. Hal Porter, as was discussed in the previous chapter, spent a year in Japan during the occupation period and revisited Japan in the 1960s, writing about his experiences in a series of essays and short stories. Later in the 1970s, there emerged Australians who had direct contact with Japan and the Japanese. The observations of diplomats and journalists, such as Alison Broinowski and Morris West, presented a new set of images of Japan in postwar Australian literature.

Pre-war and immediate postwar novels and short stories

As we have seen in previous chapters, most stories written by Australian authors from the beginning of the 20th century to the end of the Second World War, which included Japan as a theme, were war-oriented. Either imaginary or real, the Japanese were almost always 'the enemy'. An exception to this genre is evident in the writings of Xavier Herbert in the 1930s, Katharine Susannah Prichard in the 1940s and Tom Ronan in the 1950s, who all wrote short stories and novels about the pearling industry in northern Australia. Like Ion Idriess and Henrietta Drake-Brockman discussed in Chapter Two, these authors incorporated the Japanese, not as outsiders but rather as insiders, although they were still not fully regarded as Australian citizens. While their stories do not cover the whole spectrum of Australian society nor represent the ideas and images of the Japanese held by the majority of Australians at the time, (which ranged from enemy to courtesan), they may be regarded as the forerunners of more recent 'multicultural' writing. In particular, they give different perspectives of the Japanese against the stereotypes usually found in the war literature genre of that period.

Xavier Herbert is perhaps better known for his writings about Aborigines in such novels as *Capricornia* and *Poor Fellow My Country* than for his writings about the Japanese. Yet he had a continuing interest in Japan and the Japanese people. Early in his literary life, Herbert wrote several short stories, sometimes under pseudonyms, on the adventurous life of pearling masters, divers and shell-openers in the north of Australia. Such stories include 'Living Dangerously', 'Sounding Brass', 'Sailor Bring Joy' and 'Miss Tanaka'.[49] According to de Groen, most Australians in the 1920s and 1930s were condescending towards the Japanese and distrustful of their motives. Herbert remained fascinated by Japanese men, establishing friendships in the Japanese community in Darwin during the late 1920s and 1930s, writing sympathetically about Japanese pearlers and naval officers and planning a novel about the Japanese community in Darwin. In the 1940s his enthusiasm for Japan would bring him to the attention of Australian Naval Intelligence (de Groen 1998:47–48).

Except for 'Miss Tanaka', in Herbert's stories, the protagonist is typically either a young energetic Australian or British man seeking adventure and romance with a young woman. With various ethnic groups (including the Japanese), pearling in the northern tropical seas of Australia provided an exotic atmosphere and background for romantic adventures, which evolved from the earlier short stories of the late 19th century. However, Herbert's stories are unique in that the Japanese characters are variously good and bad, young and old, men and women. They have their own names, faces and voices and they are probably based on the author's own experiences.

'Living Dangerously' was published as 'a true story' in *Wide World* under the pseudonym 'E Norden'. Herbert even attached a hoax-photo to help support its authenticity, for the magazine only published true stories with photos to verify them (McDougall 1980:336). The storyteller, a leading seaman on a naval Cruiser becomes bored with the monotony of life on the boat and deserts while it is sailing in the Arafura Sea. The course of events rather typically leads to the punishment of a bad Japanese. The protagonist outwits the Japanese baddie and retrieves a most precious pearl, thus helping the deceived owner of the shell boat and his daughter-heroine. The heroine is half-Australian and half-Japanese and this racial mix makes it easier for Australian readers 'to feel more familiar with' her, as observed in the short stories of the 19th century discussed in Chapter One. However, unlike the earlier stories discussed in that chapter, the author's observations of the Japanese are not limited to generalisations and his descriptions of Japanese characters are as people with individual characteristics, rather than stereotypes or impersonal symbols that were often the case when Japanese were described in pre-war narratives.

In remote pearling towns in the 1920s and 1930s, there was often a hierarchy of people, determined by ethnicity or by law. Pearling masters had to be Australians by law, shell-openers white men only, while good Japanese divers were financially better-off than Japanese workers such as tenders (who help the divers by holding their lifelines) and other ethnic groups. In discussing the peculiarity of Broome as a pearling town, Cowan cites JM Harcourt and his novel *The Pearlers* (1933) to illustrate the power-relationship between the Japanese and others. The Japanese divers, admitted to the country under licence but prohibited by law from operating boats, manipulate the dummy boats—'[the] yellow man was master, and in a thousand sly ways he kept the white man conscious of it' (Harcourt in Cowan 1983:89–90).

Moreover, within that social structure and given the peculiar background of the pearling industry in Herbert's stories, people at sea, regardless of whether they are Australian, Japanese, or any other racial group, have to be strong, proficient in reading the waves, winds and mastering boats and have a confidence-inspiring personality. They sometimes include women, as seen in 'Sounding Brass'.

'Miss Tanaka' has significance in two ways. First, it is perhaps one of the very few Australian stories that deals exclusively with the Japanese. Second, it is comical. Words such as 'humour' and 'comedy' are seldom applied to Japanese characters in Australian literature. The Japanese are always seen as serious, polite, quiet, sullen, incomprehensible, mysterious or fierce, but not very funny, witty, merry or humorous. In Herbert's story Miss Kitso Tanaka, the niece of a storekeeper in Port Darwin, is the only young 'pure-blooded' Japanese female in the community. Two deadly rivals, scrambling to win her favour, follow her uncle's instructions in order to be her future husband. The willowy girl with downcast eyes, presumably because of her natural shyness, turns out to be Tanaka's young son in disguise. He successfully cons the suitors into parting with all their money. The characters' dialogues in their pidgin English and the description of Japanese lifestyle, from wooing a bride to wearing traditional garments—a mixture of the author's own observation and creation—present a different scenario from conventional short stories of the time.

About a decade later, Katharine Susannah Prichard used Japanese characters in her novel, *Moon of Desire*, again set in a pearling town. Prichard's *Moon of Desire* was published in 1941, the very year the Pacific War started. However, her story does not reflect any war-influenced sentiment. As the author herself admits, the book was 'rotten', for it was 'written in hopes of a money-making film' (Broinowski 1992:38). Unlike Prichard's other more politically and socially conscious novels, the plot of *Moon of Desire* is very melodramatic; the story improbable.

The novel is set in Broome in the 1930s, with a young couple, Ann and Alec, as the central figures. In the course of events they become estranged, attributable to Ann's malicious husband, and then reunited through various misadventures concerning a priceless pearl called 'Moon of Desire'. The villain of the story, who once caused the separation of the couple because of his greed for the pearl, decides to reunite the couple by retrieving the lost pearl, out of regret and self-pride. Through all kinds of adventures, deals and tricks, both in Australia and in Singapore, the villain finally gets hold of the treasure, reveals the truth and saves Ann from her husband, which enables her to return to Alec.

In this melodramatic plot, there are few Japanese characters who play important roles except the pearl diver called Matsumoto. He is the first smuggler of the 'Moon of Desire', only to lose it and drown in the first quarter of the book. There are however, other Japanese characters who are not depicted as villains. Although it seems like another formula novel set in an exotic pearling town with many ethnic groups, and then later in Asia, where anything can happen away from 'home', *Moon of Desire* does present ordinary Japanese people (mainly men) living in Australia in the pre-Second World War period, a depiction that is very scarce in literary works of the time. Broome itself was a 'half-colonial, half-oriental township' (Prichard 1941:35) and very different from the rest of Australia. The author also notes in the novel the ways and customs of the Japanese inhabitants in Broome, such as *Obon*, when souls of the dead are supposed to visit the world of the living. It describes how the Japanese brothels once did a roaring trade when pearling ports used to flourish, how Japanese shell polishers worked silently in the quiet corner of the township, how white men acted as dummy-owners of ships for the Japanese who were not authorised to own their own pearling boats and how a Japanese mother-in-law bullies the newly-wed wife of an interracial marriage because she does not conform to the Japanese traditional ideas of daughter-in-law. Such episodes in the story lend an air of exoticism to the township of Broome but also reveal that the Japanese had their own everyday life there as community members. This in turn, actually shows that there existed Australian authors and readers who had the desire and the opportunity to obtain access to this sort of information about the 'Other'.

Tom Ronan's novel *The Pearling Master* (1958) is a 'descendant' of Herbert and Prichard's stories and it was one of the first books written after the war that dealt with Japanese people as other than 'the war enemy'. Ronan was a writer who used life in the bush at the beginning of the 19th century to the 1950s as topics for his novels as well as his experiences working on pearling boats based in Broome.

The Pearling Master is set in a town called Flotsam in the early 20th century, when there is only one motorcar in the whole town. The central figures are Maud, ex-companion to the Doctor's wife, and Alfred, whom she decides to marry to secure her future. Although a little too gentlemanly in the rough and tough society of Flotsam, Alfred eventually advances and prospers to become the mayor of the town, with Maud the driving force behind him. The story traces their rise and fall, the accompanying decline of the pearling industry and their son Oliver's downfall.

This novel is a short chronicle of two generations of a family as well as the history of a pearling town in northern Australia, where the Japanese are again described not as aliens but as community members. The time is set before and during the First World War. When Maud arrives in Flotsam from England, it is a polyglot community and its inhabitants' only common trait is their desire for the profit brought by pearls. The streets are full of strikingly different people. '[S]turdy, short-legged little brown Japanese men...all with a vaguely simian manner of movement'; coastal Malays, 'chocolate coloured, handsome, walking with almost feminine grace...sarong-wearers and knife-users'; 'the Ambon men...even shorter and almost as sturdy as the Japs'; 'a few Filipinos...in whose features there was still a trace of the Spanish strain' and West Indian mulattos. For the Bishop who observes this busy street, each can be 'a potential enemy of the soil on which he trod and of the flag across the road' (Ronan 1958:10–11).

Despite the Bishop's anxiety and his prejudice against the Japanese, they, as well as other non-white groups, have their roles in society. There is a Japanese professional photographer who takes pictures of Maud and Alfred's wedding. Their new Japanese cook-houseboy, Moto, takes pride in his racial heritage and national dignity. He used to work for a Colonel and was knocked down by the employer when he hoisted 'the Rising Sun' higher than the Australian flag on some special Japanese holiday. At the time Maud gives birth, Alec, who cares for the good opinions of the Japanese, recommends that she consult a Japanese doctor who has 'a mouthful of gold teeth and an American degree'. However, Maud declines and chooses an ex-Indian Army medical officer instead. When at Alfred's pearling company a white supercargo man is appointed to replace an old Japanese one, the Japanese commits suicide. The Japanese characters are not major ones, but they are not incidental and they have particular roles in the plot. They are not always portrayed as favourable neighbours. For example, Maud shows her disgust at Alec's amicable attitude toward the Japanese, concluding that it may derive from the common characteristic that both possess; a complete lack of gratitude. Nevertheless the portrayal of the Japanese seems to be relatively open and fair when the book's publication date is considered. The Japanese are depicted as part of everyday life in a pearling town, but the novel also provides Australian readers with the suggestion that the Japanese are more worthwhile than previously thought, as seen in the comment made by Alfred:

> The whole future of pearling rests on the Japanese divers and crews. The day is past when they can be trampled down as the other coloured races are. We must handle them with diplomacy. It will pay us to forget these silly tales of white supremacy (Ronan 1958:139–140).

This admission was rare at such a time in Australian society and as we have seen in Chapter Two, Idriess had already made a similar comment in his *Forty Fathoms Deep* published just before the outbreak of the Second World War. Broome became 'an integral part of the Australian legend' for its uniqueness (Drake-Brockman cited in Cowan 1983:76) in offering Australian writers an opportunity to express a more intimate view of the 'Other'.

However, because such an experience was not usual in Australia, these novels set in or about the pearling ports of northern Australia remained a minor part of Australian narratives. Such works by Herbert, Prichard and Ronan are not at this point considered to be central to Australian culture. The Pacific War had such an impact on Australians, that hardly any literary works dealing with Japan were subsequently free from that impact. Both in direct and indirect ways, Japan and the Japanese were represented in a war-related way in postwar Australian literature in the 1950s and 1960s, together with a set of new images observed in new settings, which will be discussed in the following part of this chapter.

New writings in the 1950s and 1960s

The 1950s and 1960s were, according to Donald Horne, still a time when Australian society had 'certainties', for it had 'an imposed outward conformity'. As Horne puts it, these 'certainties' or 'conformity' may have been based on the remains of the White Australia policy and many have arisen from an 'ignorance' of how and what things can be changed in the course of time (Horne 1998:xvi). However, as mentioned at the beginning of this chapter, it was also a time when significant social changes were taking place. It was a time when mass immigration from non-English-speaking and then non-white groups had started and this 'conformity' was no longer as solid or fixed as it had been before and during the war. This change can also be seen in the novels and through the descriptions of the Japanese in these novels at the time.

Nevil Shute's *A Town Like Alice* (1956) may be considered as somewhere in between war memoirs and postwar novels, where the plots are influenced by the war and its aftermath. The author himself was from Britain and had lived permanently in Australia since 1950 when the book was published. The book is about a young Australian woman who leads a party of women prisoners seized by the Japanese in Malaya. It is based on the true story of the march of a party of Dutch women prisoners in Sumatra, Indonesia.[50]

In the first part of the novel the suffering and struggle of the women as prisoners of the Japanese Army and the atrocities committed upon them by the Japanese are emphasised. The Australian sergeant Joe Harman, is tortured and sentenced to be crucified by a cruel Japanese captain for having stolen his chicken to feed the women. This Captain Sugamo is depicted as an 'incomprehensible mixture of sadistic barbarism and reverence' (Gerster 1992:229). Although he had given the death sentence to Harman, Sugamo lets him live when Harman's dying wish—a pint of beer—cannot be fulfilled. Death is a 'ritual' for him and whether his captive is dead or alive does not really matter if the formality is incomplete. This behaviour provides another example of Japanese 'incomprehensibility' (Shute 1956:129–130).

Instances of Japanese atrocities notwithstanding, there seems to be a certain balance in the way this author tells the story in *A Town Like Alice*. These victims in Malaya, as Broinowski points out, 'do not hate the Japanese, observing human strength and weakness among friends and enemies alike' (1992:64). This may be because the author himself did not experience such barbarities, or perhaps because such 'enmity could be dissipated by time' (Broinowski 1992:64). Although the atrocious behaviour of Captain Sugamo is described, some goodness and humanity in the behaviour of other Japanese are also portrayed. For example, another Japanese captain was a 'good thing'; he always gets up and bows when the women approach (Shute 1956:46). On their journey on foot in the jungle of Malaya, they found 'the Japanese guards to be humane and reasonable' (Shute 1956:70). One of the Japanese guards weeps bitterly when they have to bury a captive's child who dies of a tropical disease (Shute 1956:102). There is 'a queer companionship' between the women and the guards under the same circumstances, and to the captives the Japanese soldiers are mostly humane and helpful, although within certain limits (Shute 1956:50)

In the latter half of the novel, Jean's ambition to set up a shoe-making factory and transform a dull outback town into a lively one like Alice Springs seems to be a symbolic gesture at the time when Australia was trying to recover and develop in the aftermath of the war. Leaving the Old Country to try her luck with her wartime hero who had returned to Australia as a stockman, Jean embodies Australia's idealistic future. The climax comes when the couple conquer the adversities of nature and succeed in saving an injured man left alone in the bush. As a popular novel, which was both filmed and serialised for television, *A Town Like Alice* gives hope, suggesting both the rebirth of Australia and its future prosperity, while the description of the nightmare of war and the cruel and inhumane Japanese behaviour fade in significance.

In the 1960s, Thomas Keneally and Randolph Stow wrote 'mainstream' novels on Australian society and its people and in them the authors show how Japan as the enemy affected people's everyday lives. Keneally's second novel *The Fear* (1965) is set during the time of the Pacific War. The main plot is about the narrator, a boy just before puberty and his relationships with his friends and two brothers in a suburb of Sydney. These brothers are sons of 'the Comrade', a communist, and as the title shows, it is the fear of unknown communism and the way the family reflects that fear that cast a dark shadow over the boy in the first half of the book.

The boy, Daniel Jordan, is surrounded by other fears, too. 'The Comrade' himself is a strong menacing figure with an alcohol problem and a reputation for domestic violence. The children's everyday life is filled with fear—an accidentally found hand-grenade, a death scare over the disabled brother, the sisters' stories about the uncertainties of the world at his Catholic school, and the Comrade's rage towards Daniel when he discovers that Daniel has 'baptised' the ill boy so that the dying boy can go to heaven. Daniel is left with the unsolvable uncertainty of why death is defined by dogma, politics and ideology and how the adults seem to become obsessed by them.

During all these events, the fear of Japan is always present. The story starts in 1942, the year when Singapore falls to the Japanese army and Australians become frightened because they are 'naked before invasion'. There are rumours that the Japanese might bomb Sydney. Daniel's aunt hesitates to take a job in Queensland, for she is afraid that 'the little yellow beasts will get there'. The ultimate fear of the Japanese is the main topic of the latter half of the novel, when Daniel's family move to the mother's parental home on the coast, while his father, a civilian militiaman, is called up for duty. As Pierce has observed, *The Fear* drew on Keneally's memories of Sydney during the Second World War, 'of trains passing the back of his Homebush house carrying troops, or sometimes POWs' (Pierce 1995:8).

In one part of that coastal area the Army decides to establish a Japanese Prisoner-of-War camp, which horrifies the locals and puts them in a flurry. Keneally uses the actual event of the Cowra breakout as the basis for this camp and adds episodes employing different types of Japanese. However, the real Japanese are not depicted as fearful figures; on the contrary, the Australian side are made to realise that they are nothing to be afraid of. One of the guards called Hogan is shocked to see that 'the race beyond the wire was human'. This forces Hogan to 'mistrust the War Cabinet, the films and the newspapers, who, in the interests of total war, had convinced him of the sub-humanity of Japs'. His reaction highlights the prejudice generated among Australians like Daniel's aunt who harbours racist views without having seen any Japanese (Keneally 1965:183–184).

There are dramas within the breakout. A Private called Aggai Haduchi, becomes isolated because he cannot convince other inmates that there is no hope of the Japanese Army's invading the Australian continent. He is murdered with other dissidents. The Liaison Officer betrays the other escapees and tells them to go north, so that he with his chosen officers can go south by boat unnoticed.

One of the officers, Captain Saito, is a 'neo-samurai' and with his subordinates takes hostages including Daniel and the Comrade. The boy is now experiencing the ultimate fear that Australians all harboured through the war years and yet, at that moment his 'proximate emotion [is] a humanist interest in the men facing [them]—the peasants and fishermen and business men of Japan' (Keneally 1965:204). The children escape at the climax of the second half of the novel when the Comrade is killed by the Japanese and eventually the Japanese are killed or recaptured.

The revised edition of this novel, entitled *By the Line*, was published in 1989. In this version the first half of *The Fear* remains intact but all the episodes about the Japanese Prisoner-of-War camp and the captivity of Australians by the Japanese are omitted. The focus of the former novel, *The Fear*, may be a little diffuse and the compactness of the revised novel which concentrates on the life of the boy living in the suburb 'by the line' of trains may have a stronger impact on readers. However, as we have seen, there were not many novels that included Japanese in their storyline and described them as individuals as Keneally's *The Fear*. From this perspective, it seems a pity that the latter half of the novel was deleted. The editing may indicate that by the 1980s the memories of the war had become distant and were starting to be forgotten.

Randolph Stow's novel *The Merry-Go-Round in the Sea* was published in 1965, in the same year as *The Fear*. It is also a 'nostalgic re-creation of an Australian childhood' (Wilde, Hooton & Andrews 1994:531), of a boy called Rob Coram, set in Geraldton, Western Australia, during and after the Pacific War. The growth of Rob and the war experiences of Rick Maplestead, his adored cousin, form the central themes of the novel.

For the boy, Rick is a role-model hero. However, when Rick returns after the war as an ex-prisoner-of-war of the Japanese in Malaya, Rob finds he has changed and no one except his old 'inmates' can understand him. Rick's 'humiliation' and 'shame' embarrass not only himself but also his mates, fellow ex-prisoners and family members. The boy starts to hate it when Rick has nightmares and becomes resentful and restless. This kind of shellshock phenomenon among the returned prisoners and their families has, as we have seen in POW memoirs in Chapter Four, recurred in both fiction and non-fiction, and reflect a shared experience among ex-POWs in the postwar years. After being tortured and seeing others die one after another in the construction of the Burma-Thai Railway, Rick cannot put himself at ease nor find a solution to his despair, unlike his mate who gets married, settles down and finds stability. In *The Merry-Go-Round in the Sea* the emphasis is not put on the cause—the brutal cruelty of the enemy—but rather on the effect. Neither university education, nor sweetheart, or even family support can resolve or reduce Rick's frustration and instability. Rick could not find the 'firmness' of the mirage-like merry-go-round, which makes 'his circle just, and makes him end, where he begun' (Stow 1965:220). Rick regards Australia as an 'Anglo-Celtic vacuum in the South Seas' and decides to leave.

For the younger Rob, fear of Japan is more remote and faceless, something that only indirectly affects his circle of life. The war is 'a curse, a mystery, an enchantment', when 'people don't have maids or there would never be paper flowers again from Japan'. 'The people in Japan [are] suddenly wicked, far wickeder than the Germans, though once they [had] only been funny, like Chinamen' (Stow 1965:4) Because of the war against Japan, the boy cannot reach the barge, which is broken and sunk in the sea and looks like a merry-go-round. Soon this faceless enemy starts to intrude closer to his own territory with the aerial bombardment of Broome, an event that has more direct and immediate implications to the Japanese southward movements than those overseas as in Batavia or Surabaya. The fear of the Japanese invasion becomes a reality when the tennis courts are turned into air-raid trenches and the boy's family evacuates to a relative's station. Here the description of the Japanese by the author is fair, for the Japanese are not depicted with groundlessly biased comment but from the child's point of view.

'His world [has] changed' and the eternal circle of childhood innocence is not possible anymore when the war ends. Rob's life moves into the era of postwar revival and prosperity in the suburbs of Geraldton. Through his experiences in seeing Aboriginal hand-prints at the 'Hand Cave' and of having an Aboriginal boy in his class, he further realises that 'his world [is] not one world'. It seems that a resistance has started against the notion of 'conformity' or 'certainty' as Horne suggests (1998:xvi), which on the surface, seemed to have existed during the 1950s and 1960s.

Japan is portrayed principally as a 'fear' in Australian society during and after the Pacific War in both Keneally's and Stow's novels; however it is not depicted as the direct or only cause of people's anxiety or the target of special hatred. Rather, it serves as the trigger for people to reflect a bit more during the turbulence of war and its aftermath. When authors who spent their childhood during the Pacific War write about it, they seem to be affected less directly than their seniors and hence are more capable of offering a more detached and balanced view of the enemy Japanese. Another author of an autobiographical memoir is Gavin Souter, who wrote about his own childhood in *The Idle Hill of Summer: An Australian Childhood 1939–1945* (1972). For the boy protagonist, the author in his childhood, Germany has meaning only in his stamp collection while Japan is the object of ridicule, with such phrases as 'made in Japan' being used in negative ways. Although there is a direct fear of being bombed by the Japanese after the bombing of Broome and Sydney, with the boy's family digging trenches and practising blackouts at night, to the boy, the war is a 'friendly silhouette in the sky...some fabulous beast like the centaur or Pegasus' (Souter 1972:85). To him it's 'a spectacle rather than an ordeal' (Souter 1972:115). When these authors start to write about their experience of 'unseen' Japan and the Japanese in later decades, bitterness, fear and antipathy against the enemy has thus become attenuated.

There were some writers who published their direct experiences of Japan and the Japanese people in the 1960s, and among them are Elizabeth Kata and Hal Porter. Kata was a civilian in Japan, while Porter was with the Occupation Force as a schoolteacher. They were not journalists or diplomats, although Porter had a brief career as a journalist in Australia in his early days. Porter had already published *A Handful of Pennies*, a novel about his experiences during the occupation, which was discussed in the previous chapter. After his return to Japan in 1967 he wrote critically and satirically about the changes he perceived, the new Japan in the postwar recovery period and its people in *The Actors: An Image of the New Japan* (1968) and later in several short stories in the 1960s and 1970s, including the collection *Mr Butterfry [sic] and Other Tales of New Japan* (1970). Kata, on the other hand, lived in Japan during the war as the Australian wife of a Japanese husband, a social circumstance that gave her a very different set of opportunities to observe and write about the Japanese.

Elizabeth Kata, originally from Neutral Bay, NSW, went to Japan to be married to a Japanese pianist Shinshiro Katayama in 1937, just before the Second World War broke out. During the Pacific War she spent some difficult years in Karuizawa in the Japanese Alps under the close and suspicious eyes of the authorities. After the war she returned to Australia and wrote her most popular novel *Be Ready with Bells and Drums* (1961, later entitled *A Patch of Blue*), and then a year later *Someone Will Conquer Them*, using her experiences as a non-Japanese person in Japan during and after the war.

The story of *Someone Will Conquer Them* is of Mary, the young American wife of a Japanese scientist. She becomes an embarrassment to her husband, Goro Ogata, who comes from a traditional Japanese family. When the Pacific War begins, she is sent to a village among the mountains especially set aside for aliens in Japan. The central plot is about Mary's adventures, including her murder of a police captain and the discovery of true love with another man, Ludi Hoffer, a German-Polish black-marketeer. The first part of the novel is set during the war and the second part during the occupation. In the first half of the novel, Mary and Ludi Hoffer save and hide an American airman from a crashed B29 fighter. She thinks she is in love with the airman but finally realises that her true love lies not in the hero-American but in Hoffer,, who has always stood by her, despite his negative words and behaviour.

There are a number of Japanese sub-characters surrounding the main ones, some of them probably based on the author's own observations and experience. Mary's husband Goro Ogata is an obscure figure who does not provide much basis for understanding the problems of a cross-cultural, inter-racial marriage of this time. The somewhat comical Japanese servant who attends Mary is an old, lively and determined woman called Suzuki, who bears the same name as the maid of 'Cho-Cho-San' in *Madame Butterfly*. Captain Tanaka from the local police force casts a vigilant eye on the heroine, mainly because of his infatuation with her. There's a lady doctor, Kimura, a fervent feminist who secretly amputates the American airman's arm in rebellion against the male-chauvinistic authorities and who also used to conduct illegal abortions for helpless women. Yuriko, a Japanese detective's daughter, eventually falls in love with the airman and decides to marry him despite her father's objection. She is killed in a car accident when she steps into the street 'as if she were a butterfly fluttering, in her gay kimono'. All these characters retain typical elements of the 'East' presented by the 'West', and yet provide many voices, both male and female, young and old, which are new in Australian narratives.

Some interesting observations and descriptions of the Japanese are also presented in the novel. Ludi, living among the Japanese and having little sense of belonging, is amazed at why they could be so ignorantly patriotic and nationalistic (Kata 1962:17). He also wonders why 'so many Japanese people take refusal of their offer as a personal insult' (Kata 1962:104). When the occupation starts, it was a 'bewildering time for both conquerors and conquered', for the Americans 'had fought long and bloody battles against these [Japanese] people, had entered Japan with hearts stalwart, and ready for anything', only to find 'the shabby, down-trodden, depressed Japanese'. On the other hand, the Japanese civilians 'had been fed a propaganda of lies and truth, exaggerations and underestimations', and 'instead of the bullying iron heel of the conqueror they had awaited, it was bewildering to find that this was not so' (Kata 1962:161-162). Interestingly, Kata does not mention the Australian Forces in her novel. It may be because the protagonist is American, or the occupation force she encounters is from Tokyo, while the Commonwealth Occupation Force was based in Kure and Hiroshima.[51] The latter part of the novel presents a less poignant though more detailed description of the occupation than that given in Hal Porter's novel, partly because Kata was a captive herself among the Japanese. Unlike Porter, who always remains on the side of the empowered master, Kata experienced both sides, thus enabling her to provide a description of what it was like to be both a captor and a captive of the Japanese. Kata's novel, like Rosa Praed's *Madame Izàn* discussed in Chapter One, has significance also as one of very few works by a female author in what has traditionally been a world depicted chiefly by men. Though not explicitly, Kata also offers insights in her novel about the problem of sexual relations between female self and the male 'Other'.

Hal Porter describes 'the gulf between Occidental and Oriental culture' during the occupation in *A Handful of Pennies* as we have seen in the previous chapter. On his second visit to Japan, the gulf seems to have widened and the Japanese have become more incomprehensible as the whole nation dashes for economic prosperity. Besides essays on Japan, Porter wrote short stories from this visit in 1967, which reveal a deep chasm between West and East, or more specifically, Australia and Japan.

The characters in almost every story of Porter's, both Australians and Japanese, are more or less victims of this chasm, caused by the rapid changes of the postwar society. In 'Irasshaimashi' from *Mr Butterfry and Other Tales of New Japan* is a young Japanese girl called Fumiko. As an attendant in the elevator of a department store in a big city in Japan, she keeps greeting the customers every day, saying 'Irasshaimashi'—welcome. She becomes like an 'automaton' and falls into a 'state of vacuum' until she is stabbed by a passer-by, and given an 'exemption' from monotony. She is among those who have fled their hometowns that are full of 'fish guts and animism' in order to be invisible in the obscurity of the metropolis, but now find they no longer belong to either. This was the time when the population of Japan passed 100 million and its GNP became the second highest in the world. In the author's eyes, Japan's almost self-destructive Westernisation and frantic devotion to economic development results in the 'death' of each individual. Japanese 'en masse', once described as the massive invading force in Australian invasion novels, is now described as a different type of 'mass', which is reoriented in a materialistic and physical direction.

Australians can also be the victims of Japan's desire for prosperity. 'Mr Butterfry', from the story of the same name, is one of them. In this story it is not a helpless lady of the East, but a Western male, who is used and cast aside. This Australian ex-corporal from the occupation force has become rich from black market profits and yet is totally 'conquered' and exploited by his wife, an ex-housegirl, who is devoted to promoting their daughters as fashion models. His intention to exploit his opportunity as a conqueror turns out to have the opposite effect. This once 'oh-so-sweet-and-cute-housegirl' is one of many Japanese whom Porter describes as being deprived of 'their powers of discernment, discrimination and control...incapable of interpreting the times, the results of actions and themselves' (Porter 1968:55). She is described as a formerly conquered but now empowered woman who is able to turn the tables on a gullible Australian who was once the conqueror. Porter's fiction contains many such reversals.

Other examples of Western victims of Eastern guile in Porter's short fiction include two artists—Simon Hart-Browne, in 'My Pal Rembrandt' and Perrot in 'The House on the Hill' from *Mr Butterfry and Other Tales of New Japan*. Hart-Browne, both in Hong Kong and Tokyo, uses Asian friends, lovers and acquaintances to hold exhibitions and sell his paintings. While he thinks he is doing well, he eventually finds himself caught in a 'Yakuza' (Japanese mafia) net and is killed. Perrot, who revisits Japan on his sketch tours 20 years after the 'après-guerre ruin', is braced for its transformation. He finds that Japan's 'mock-humility' after the war has become 'near arrogance', as the author himself expresses it in *The Actors*. He is falsely accused of sexual harassment by a Japanese college student. Unable to prove his innocence, he is banished.

As Lord points out, Porter on his second visit to Japan seems to have decided to 'savagely denounce' the country and its people and accuse the new Japan of being different from the old Japan in *The Actors* (Lord 1993:225). According to the author himself, Porter's admiration for Japan, started at the age of five with a 'paper-flower floating' in the water, like Rob in *The Merry-Go-Round in the Sea*, who is fascinated with the china tea set and a kimono clad lady with a parasol. Later, when Porter finally reached Japan for the first time he became 'addicted' to Hearn, Loti, *The Mikado*, *Madame Butterfly*, *haiku*, Hokusai, etc—all the typical Western images of old Japan (Porter 1968:7–8). A traditionalist, Porter was bitterly disappointed with modern, rehabilitating Japan. His short stories and essays seem to show the author's stance as a 'Westerner looking at the East'.

Porter's view is revealed in his treatment of a number of master-pupil relationships between Australians and the Japanese throughout his work. In *A Handful of Pennies*, the female teacher, Paula Groot, seduces a young Japanese college student and is infected with syphilis and expelled from the school. It shows how the master-Australia, though being the empowered nation at this time, becomes victim to the subordinate Japan. In his play *The Professor*, which was originally called *Toda-San*,[52] a university student called Toda worships his master, Professor Medlin, to the extent of letting his Japanese girlfriend sell her body in order to make money to get a gift for the professor. To Medlin's horror, Toda cuts off his own tongue to punish himself for telling lies to his adored professor. Both masters are unexpectedly betrayed by their outwardly quiet and tamed pupils. Lord summarises: 'On closer inspection, Porter finds postwar Japan and the Japanese not "quaint and exotic" as he had first thought, but "cruelly sadistic or downright perverse or wantonly childish"'.[53] Porter's works, unlike those of other Australian authors, present a series of versatile and idiosyncratic perceptions of Japan. However, like other authors they also reflect his paternalistic Western attitudes.

In the 1970s, a small number of professional people who worked in Japan started to use the country as the setting and source of characters for their fiction. One such person is Alison Broinowski, who stayed in Japan for three years as a diplomat. Her first novel, *Take One Ambassador* (1973), is a mixture of adventure and suspense based around the kidnapping of an Australian ambassador. The main character is a journalist called Andy Xenos from the *Daily Mirror*, who is dispatched to investigate and report on the case. The main plot involves his encounter with Japan and his discovery of Asia, much in the same way as Koch, Drewe, and D'Alpuget did in the 1970s.

This theme of 'discovery' and disillusionment recur throughout Broinowski's story. Andy Xenos, a Greek-Australian from Bondi Beach, remains ambivalent not only about Japan but about Australia and is unable to decide what his country really means to him. The Australian ambassador, who is kidnapped in the story (he was the kidnappers' second choice after the American ambassador), finds out during his captivity that he does not know anything about the country in which he resides and so wishes for a safe return so he can start again. Through the busy, social life of the embassy, his wife re-discovers things about herself while on her own. Another journalist from the *Herald* confesses that although he enjoys the opportunity, he regards Japan as a 'hot-pot', as a strange place—'the longer I'm here, the less I understand it', for this is a country full of contradictions (Broinowski 1970:56). Japan thus offers the chance for Australians away from home to rediscover (or reveal the true nature of) their notions of self and nation.

The Japanese portrayed in Broinowski's story represent various characters and types ranging from university students involved in leftist political activities to right-wing, old-style Japanese nationalists who organise the kidnapping. In the end, it turns out that both parties share the same ground in rejecting the growing American influence, which Porter and others satirised. They both believed in the need to regain a new, truer Japan. Australia, on the other hand, is regarded in Japan as being a 'part' of America. This novel was published a year after Okinawa was returned to Japan after more than 20 years of occupation by the United States and when there was a significant movement against the United States. At the end of the novel, the head of the society who organised the kidnapping commits *harakiri* (ritual suicide) to demonstrate the importance of his ideology. It is the same act committed for the same reasons by Yukio Mishima, a right-wing author, at one of the offices of the Self-Defence Force in Tokyo in 1970. Broinowski's novel thus reflects the social atmosphere of Japan and its people in the 1970s, not only through the eyes of an outsider but also partly through those of an insider who sees patterns of recurrence across apparent political difference.

Prior to Broinowski's novel, Australian novelist Morris West also portrayed a diplomatic figure in *The Ambassador* (1965). Although West's main character is an American ambassador who is posted to Tokyo before being transferred to Saigon at the beginning of the conflict between North and South Vietnam, the author's focus is on the anguish of the diplomat caught between the West and the East. The protagonist, Maxwell Amberley, falls into this dilemma when he is ordered to support the assassination plot of the President of South Vietnam by collaborating under cover with the military attempting a coup. West shows that America and other Western nations, including Australia, have their own political agendas when co-operating with or manipulating the churches, sects, military and the government of South Vietnam. However, Amberley's sympathy goes to the President of South Vietnam. As the First Secretary of the Australian Embassy puts it, he has doubts about 'Western logic over Asian ambition'. While posted to Japan, Amberley becomes a disciple of Zen and actively practises it. As a diplomat, he has 'a flair for language, a taste for exotic custom, an ear for the minor key' (West 1965:11). With his devotion to the teachings of his Zen master and capacity to understand Asian religion and culture, he bears a 'middleman's burden' and the decisions he makes for the United States become the hardest of all, almost unbearable. After the coup is over and the President is killed, Amberley returns to his master in Kyoto, where he realises the gulf between the different sides—West and East—is immense and, as his Zen master puts it, they must not accept the difference too readily nor reject it too quickly (1965:240). Based on his understanding of the historical events of the military coup in South Vietnam, West presented in his novel the harsh reality of the irreconcilability of cultures, ideas and power-relationships between West and East. Amberley's experiences gained in Japan provide a bridge for the middleman who tries to reconcile the policies and practices of opposed ideologies and nations.

As seen in this chapter, despite the fact that war memories were still alive and real, there were some authors who used modernising, postwar Japan and the Japanese as a focus for their novels and stories. It was a time when political, diplomatic and economic changes came first, followed slowly by cultural exchanges from professional writers, journalists and teachers. Examples include the poet, Harold Stewart, who moved to Japan in 1966 to live there permanently. Stewart had had an interest in the Orient since his childhood and by the early 1940s he believed that 'the East afforded a new realm awaiting conquest by an English-language poet' (Ackland 2000:149–151). The Ern Malley hoax (in which Stewart and James McAuley made up a non-existing poet and fabricated his poetry in 1944) had 'more corrosive and long-term effects on Stewart' and his accomplice McAuley than the actually deceived Max Harris (Mead 1995:85). Stewart seems to have sought 'sanctuary' in Japan where he was able to escape from what he felt was social and literary ostracism in Australia. Stewart claims he chose to live in Japan because of his spiritual quest, in which he attempted to 'shed his modern Western limitations and prejudices' (Stewart 1981:xvi). Japan may have provided Stewart with a place to escape from what he wanted to leave behind—including his notion of being a 'sexual outcast in violently homophobic Australia' especially in the 1930s–40s (Ackland 2000:151). Yet he was able to serve as an introducer of Japanese culture and literature to the West. With his three volumes of collected haiku translated into English, as well as his own collection of poems with prose commentaries on Kyoto, he served for more than 20 years as 'Australia's unofficial, unappointed and unpaid cultural attaché in Kyoto'.[54]

Although the first and direct motives for expatriation to Japan may be complex, as Tipping points out, literary figures such as Stewart may be an important 'touchstone' of the distances between Australia and the Japanese, when the future for Australia in Asia and the Pacific will be decided 'by the extent to which [Australians] understand and address fundamental differences in cultural value systems and social structure' among different cultures.[55] This kind of exchange would eventually contribute to a more versatile literary interest and enhance Australia's multicultural writing in the 1980s and 1990s. Before examining such writings, we will look at recent novels and memoirs of the Pacific War in the next chapter to see whether these writings differed from earlier war literature written immediately after the war and if so, how.

chapter seven

Reflections on the Pacific War since the 1960s

Novels, short stories and memoirs about the Second World War continued to be written by Australian authors well after the war was over. Non-Australian writers also wrote about their experiences during the war with Japan—examples other than Norman Mailer mentioned in Chapter Three include Laurence Jan Van Der Post (*Venture to the Interior*, 1952, *The Seed and the Sower*, 1963) and Ernest Gordon (*Through the Valley of the Kwai*, 1962). Such writings have established themselves as a distinctive sub-genre within the wider war literature that was written in English.

Although their memories may have become less vivid, for some writers, their war experiences were too hard to forget. As TAG Hungerford in his foreword to *A Knockabout with a Slouch Hat* (1985) puts it: 'I was surprised by the ease with which [the war stories I was writing] plunged me back into a world which I thought I'd forgotten'. A 'shocked silence' immediately after the war was the reaction of some writers (as we saw in Chapter Three) and many war stories were rejected by publishers because Australian readers wanted to forget its horrors. Other writers needed more time to express their experiences in words. In his foreword to *At the End of His Tether* (1981) Geoffrey Bingham writes that 'many years have to pass before people can feel free to read war novels and books which describe prison-camp life' and that 'writers have had time to mature in their thinking, to develop rich and useful insights concerning those terrible—and yet wonderful—days'.

The shift in time and the changes in society have certainly had an influence on both writers and readers. In 1952 Eric Lambert criticised TAG Hungerford's *The Ridge and the River* for its lack of 'anger and hatred against war'[56], but it seems that Australians felt as ambivalent soon after the war as they did before the war. The issue of race, as seen in previous chapters, was both an 'official and private' reason given for Australia's war against Japan. However, in the 1960s when the civil rights movement rose to prominence and the daily influx of immigrants grew substantially, the issue of race became more and more subdued, if not altogether extinct. A change of government in 1972 and the official adoption of multiculturalism further influenced the way Australian society viewed itself and its past.

Perhaps the changes in the political, economic and diplomatic relationships between Australia and Japan were more significant than changes in the ordinary Australian's way of thinking., It was not until 1952, after the occupation, that the first Japanese war bride was admitted into Australia. But because of the Korean War (and later wars) and especially because of Japan's rapid industrial recovery and economic boom, Australia and Japan established a partner-like relationship under the United States umbrella. By 1957, Australia and Japan had signed a trade agreement on 'most-favoured-nation' terms and in 1966 Japan exceeded Britain in terms of the amount of trade conducted with Australia (Barker 1996:300). Interaction between the citizens of both countries, which started for economic reasons, quickly expanded into social and cultural fields, supported by official agreements like the Cultural Agreement between the Government of Australia and the Government of Japan in 1976 and the Basic Treaty of Friendship and Co-operation in 1977. The Australia–Japan Foundation was established in 1976. Such changes led to Australian writers and readers reassessing their views on Japan and the Japanese.

The shift in the nature of the relationship between Australia and Japan and the mood of the times also gave more latitude to the authors of war writing. As Australian war-writing became established as a genre, authors who did not have direct war experiences or who were from younger generations adopted the topic and retold the stories of the war between Australia and Japan in the form of both fiction and non-fiction. Such writings included more women's stories and stories of 'the other side'—the Japanese. This genre gave writers a setting other than Australia itself or Europe, especially as it became part of a broader field of literature concerning the relationship between Australia and Asia in general, which had also grown significantly in the postwar years.

In this chapter, some authors of the war-writing genre from the 1960s and later will be examined to see what aspects of their writing developed over time and which remained unchanged. Further, we shall look at how the authors had 'time to mature in their thinking, to develop rich and useful insights' (Bingham 1985) concerning the terrible reality of war. Finally, we will look at some authors new to this field and examine their work to see how they created a new phase in the cross-cultural theme of the war between Australia and Japan.

Memoirs

Memoirs by ex-soldiers, or based on ex-soldiers' accounts, especially those related to prisoner-of-war experiences, continued to be published well into the 1990s. Although their themes remain basically the same as those referred to in Chapter Four—that is, the physical and mental hardships of the POW camp, the atrocities committed by the Japanese and the friendships that sustained and enabled them to survive captivity—there were new aspects which emerged, mainly because of changing attitudes. There were still the one-sided war-diarists who described the Japanese in a collective manner, 'either as homicidal maniacs or as simian buffoons'.[57] On the other hand, there were also authors who did not exaggerate the notion of the 'Oriental villain'. The title of Kenneth Harrison's memoir is a good example of this—*The Brave Japanese*. Even in 1966, such a title must have been controversial in Australian society, or as Gerster puts it, 'inauspicious in postwar Australia' (Gerster 1992:238). In 1983, the book was republished under the new title *Road to Hiroshima*. Despite its original title, this book is far from a simple homage to Australia's old enemy; as the author reveals in his foreword, it is a story without a hero or a heroine, and 'to offset this literary lapse', there are as many villains as possible and 'all had yellow skins and slant eyes'. That is why some 'good' Japanese stand out 'at a time when kindness and gentleness were the rarest of jewels'. It is these 'jewels' that are recorded in his story. The principal virtue that Harrison finds in the Japanese is their bravery. Although Harrison could not believe that such 'short monkey-like men in their shoddy uniforms' were competent in the jungle battles, he states that 'good or bad, kind or sadistic...in the final analysis their Sun God imbued each and every one of them with a courage that I believe to be unequalled in our time' (Harrison 1966:93 &117).

When he wrote *The Veterans* (1954) and *The Dark Backward* (1958), Eric Lambert concentrated on the battlefield as the 'underworld', where both enemies and allies turned into killing machines. As we have seen in Chapter Three, he describes the Japanese as targets who 'look all the same...act the same, like puppets' (Lambert 1958:29). Revenge proves a fitting end to the war when Harding kills Colonel Higitura, a man who had tortured him and shattered his wish to be a pianist by breaking his fingers. In his later work, *MacDougal's Farm* (1965), based on stories in Changi Prison, Lambert looked at both good and bad in Australians and Japanese. His assertion is that true heroes of war are not found in the high ranks but among the Privates and NCO's. Such heroes include the protagonist Malcolm MacDougal, who was not classified fit to be a soldier because of a bullet wound in his leg, but instead helped out his mates during captivity. There were malingerers, collaborators with the Japanese and black-marketeers among the Australians in the camp and both the author and protagonist agree that not all the 'Nips were black-hearted to a man' and that it was not always true that the Australians 'were all spotless white and the Nips should be scorned and hated for ever after' (Lambert 1965:59). This agreement between Lambert and MacDougal was reached when the author was writing the book (1960–62) and the passing of time seemed to have enabled them to look back at their experience and see it from a more balanced viewpoint.

The atrocities committed by the Japanese on the prisoners is presented no less graphically than in former memoirs. Despite admitting that 'as a soldier, they were always—the brave Japanese', Harrison confirms that,

[the prisoners] could loathe everything [the Japanese] stood for, be disgusted at their cruelty, shake [their] heads incredulously at their stupidity, be scornful of their duplicity, laugh [themselves] sick at the thought of such men believing they descended from the Sun God (Harrison 1966:117).

Non-fiction writer Cornel Lumiere's *Kura!* (1966), which is based on the author's research and memoirs of those 'who were all "there"' seems to have a more single-minded and biased approach toward the Japanese. The title, 'kura', is a Japanese interjection, which is spelled more phonetically than the real phrase *kora*. It indicates strong anger and reprimand and thus characterises the image of the Japanese presented in the book. Some of the descriptions about the Japanese are generic, stereotypical insults; '[Lieutenant Naito takes] revenge as only an Oriental could', (Lumiere 1966:134) or '[i]n the Oriental mind...anything might be turned into an offence' (Lumiere 1966:143). Harrison reveals that, as the result of their loathing for their captors, some prisoners secretly unhooked the rear van of the train where one of the most hated guards at their camp in Thailand was travelling, causing it to roll back down the slope, and kill several Japanese and Koreans (Harrison 1966:197).

The incomprehensibility and unpredictability of the Japanese are still stressed in these 'later' memoirs. Harrison's first-hand accounts of their behaviours are repeated throughout his memoir. During the three years of slave labour, his constant efforts were aimed at outwitting the Japanese. Some Japanese are presented as evil, while others are soft enough to let the prisoners carry their guns while they are asleep. One even allows them to catch insects for the officer's pet canary, giving them rest as a reward. To Harrison, it becomes 'painfully apparent' that the Australians 'had little in common with their captors and that time was not bringing understanding and mutual respect' (Harrison 1966:142). Japanese cruelty, in Lambert's *MacDougal's Farm*, is shown on one occasion when the Japanese pluck a live pigeon before they cook it for their meal. MacDougal then resigns himself to the Japanese way of life, thinking '[he] could not concern [himself] too often with their cruelty to animals when Changi itself was one enormous exposition of man's inhumanity to man' (Lambert 1965:99–101).

Hugh Clarke describes how he was punished and beaten with a piece of timber across his back for damaging a circular saw by making it 'look like an egg' at one of the POW camps in Nagasaki. He further wonders:

> ...you never could explain their actions: after a terrible thumping [the Japanese who owned the saw] gave me a bowl of rice and a drink of sake and showed me how to do the job—I was 'number one' with him after that (Clarke 1985:48).

In *The Tub* (1963), fiction that was based on his POW experiences, Clarke also notes the groundless Japanese presumption that 'anyone with red hair or freckles was not considered healthy and therefore excluded from the party' to be sent to Japan;. stereotypes and misapprehensions based on appearance obviously existed on both sides of the racial divide during the war.

Change in attitudes

Time and the forces of social transition brought about certain changes in the attitudes of some authors. In later memoirs and novels, these authors not only retraced their own 'passage of thorns' but tried to show the perspective of the 'Other' as well. After his prisoner-of-war experiences in Changi, on the Burma–Thailand Railway and finally in Japan, Hugh Clarke admitted that the cause of the constant clash between Australians and the Japanese may be of 'differing cultures as much as natural antagonism between captor and captive', and:

> [the captives'] attitude to [their] captors had, at all times, been defiant and arrogant...[They] must surely have been an infuriating embarrassment to [their] captors...[The Japanese] on their part had been indoctrinated from childhood to regard the white nations as oppressors and themselves as descendants from the sons of heaven (Clarke 1984:65).

As Braddon explains in his production note to *Naked Island: A Play* (1981), Anglo-Saxon prisoners may have learnt early 'to understand the mentality, habits and language of their Japanese captors very well indeed' if only for the purpose of survival, while their captors were successfully defied because 'they never understood the Anglo-Saxon mentality and therefore never looked for the low and outrageous kind of animal cunning exercised against them by their prisoners'. The prisoners' behaviour was aimed at day-to-day survival and so the fundamental gap in understanding between the two groups was not really reflected upon before and during actual contact between the two groups, but only after the war was over.

Stan Arneil, who kept a diary of his captivity in Changi, Thailand and Johore from 15 February 1942 to 9 October 1945, published it in 1981 (with little editing) as *One Man's War*. Arneil's contemporary observations of his surroundings as well as his own state of mind, together with explanatory notes (added later), are balanced and restrained. The book was honoured with a PEN award in 1981 for 'a non-fiction book of literary excellence best dispelling racial, religious and cultural class bigotry'. Such an example suggests that both 'time and tide' are needed in order for the portrayal of a more comprehensive and tolerant perspective on the violent, cross-cultural clash that occurred between Australia and Japan. Arneil does not flatter or idealise the Japanese. Rather, he is honest in describing the captors and captives as incompatible and reveals that he could never fraternise with them. It is easier for the author and other prisoners in Changi than in other POW camps because they saw less of the Japanese. As Manning Clark comments in the preface to the book, the importance of *One Man's War* perhaps lies not only in its objectivity in describing the cross-cultural contact, but in its integrated observation of 'what war does to human beings'. Captivity and slave labour in Thailand is 'a time when all artificiality disappeared and men saw themselves and others as they really were', captor and captive alike (in Arneil 1980:93). The environment surrounding them also becomes a test for each: '[t]he dense bamboo jungle with its cruel thorns crowded [them] into the narrow strips on which [they] were working. The sun rarely ever shone during that wet season; [and he] never heard a bird sing' (1980:93).

A greater effort to try and understand the differences between Australians and Japanese by Australian writers seems to be a major characteristic of some later memoirs and novels. In *The Brave Japanese*, Kenneth Harrison recognises several characteristics in the Japanese, which helps him to understand, maybe not completely, but at least partly, his captors' behaviour. He discovers that the Japanese despise their captives for surrendering and have mentally relegated them 'to the status of work animals', and yet the prisoners themselves, to the captors' surprise and anger, are never humble (Harrison 1966:142).

Few of them understood the Japanese obsession with 'face', which caused needless friction. As is described in Harrison's *The Brave Japanese*, they cannot understand why the Japanese can break promises without shame, where loss of face means more to the Japanese than not telling the truth (1966:143). They have to learn Japanese customs and superstitions through trial and error, by getting hit and by other forms of punishment. An example is the need to remember to pronounce the numeral 'four' as '*yon*', not '*shi*' (an alternative pronunciation which also means 'death'). This is a simple and impolite 'faux pas' (Harrison 1966:143). However strange the prisoners considered the Japanese way of life, it was also true that those ways of doing things were the 'right' ones at that time and place, and the author realises the importance of learning these protocols for the prisoners' own survival.

In *The Tub*, Clarke lets one of his characters use the Japanese as a way of reflecting on his own behaviour and conduct. When appalled at the sight of a brutality committed by one of the Japanese towards his lower ranks, the protagonist Steve wonders if the British were:

> much more humane a hundred years ago, when the British army spread-eagled its own men on gun wheels and flogged them; when keel-hauling British sailors was standard discipline? You want to read about our own convict days, especially Norfolk Island (Clarke 1963:103).

MacDougal, in Lambert's *MacDougal's Farm*, also reveals that the surrender to the Japanese and enslavement by its army disclosed the weak side of Australians: 'too many officers sought only to retain their status as officers... never has the absurd snobbery and class distinction of the army been so clearly demonstrated'; and '[d]uring the war there was a widespread myth in the British Army that the Australian Army was a democratic army...On the Death Railway that myth died once and for all' (1965:63). Such self-reflective observations may also have needed time to be voiced.

In *MacDougal's Farm*, MacDougal and the author try to find the answer to the very basic question: why did the Japanese behave as they did? On the one hand they talk about the Japanese having the 'hugest inferiority complex in all human history' towards the Western world. But they conclude that the inclination of the Japanese towards monkey-like imitation of the West is not because the Japanese are less human than Europeans, but rather it is because of their national doctrine, the most pernicious force in human history. This may show the protagonists' shift of viewpoint as well as the notion of their indoctrination about war (1965:59-61).

The author of *MacDougal's Farm* also recognises the Japanese obsession with ritual and ceremony, 'with an inherited *mystique* a thousand years old', which is typical in their 'ridiculous ceremonials in the arrangements of flowers and the serving of tea'. When the Australians come to realise such obsessions, they understand and take it in as part of the system, rightly or wrongly (Lambert 1965:86). For example the insistence on saluting by the Japanese is accepted as 'not an attempt to degrade but merely an instance of their obsession with ceremonial'. Understanding their actions, if not necessarily justifying the reasons for Japanese behaviour in terms of their background, seems to be a significant characteristic of Australian writing about the Japanese some two decades or more after the war.

Language of the 'Other'

One of the remarkable features of the memoirs and non-fiction of later war-writing is the perceived importance for Australians of understanding the enemy's language as a first priority for survival, followed by a better cultural understanding of their strange captors. When communication is successful, even with a few simple words, it leads to a quite different outcome for the prisoners and in turn influences their impression of the Japanese. In one of Ray Parkin's episodes in his memoir, he and the supervising Japanese guard share a little Malay, English and Japanese, as well as 'arms to wave in international semaphore', and also Bing Crosby songs. Their communication is not sophisticated, but it is enough to invite a degree of harmonious interaction (Parkin 1993:120). In another episode, Parkin observes the Australian prisoners cursing the Tamils as 'obscene boongs', 'only because they were talking a tongue the men did not understand and it jangled their nerves' (Parkin 1993:169–170). Thus the potential role of language is emphasised either as a bond or a barrier between different groups.

Cornel Lumiere's protagonist in *Kura!*, which is based on a true story, is an interpreter between the captors and captives: the interpreter himself thus represents the function of language in interactive behaviour. Erik Leeuwenburg, the protagonist, is a Dutch Private, who because of his multi-racial background and ability to speak several languages, is appointed as the interpreter for the AIF 8th Division under the administration of Australian senior officers on the Burma–Thailand Railway. Although his immediate senior, a Dutch officer, does not like Erik to 'fraternise' with the enemy by speaking Japanese, he is inevitably drawn to the task of go-between for both sides. Being only a civilian turned Private second-class, Erik becomes the representative of the whole group of the oppressed. Initially it was only his:

> personal load—the load every prisoner carried, the burden of hunger and hardship, disease and fear, the nearness of death [before]…Now he must carry the burden of the entire group with him. Whatever their rank, their nationality, their number, he, with his absurdly small vocabulary of Japanese words, had become their spokesman (Lumiere 1966:7).

In the beginning, Erik knows only about 200 Japanese words, but 'with a beating for every mistake', he has to master the language quickly.

By making his protagonist an interpreter, Lumiere shows how communication itself and the will and patience to master it, are necessary for different groups to co-exist. Erik 'sadly lacked' patience and tact, not only for communication between captor and captive but also between Australians and Dutch, higher ranks and other ranks, the punisher and the victim. Erik has to struggle to establish a form of communication for the whole camp, for Australian, American and Dutch prisoners. The bare necessity of understanding the oppressor's language for survival is well emphasised in Erik's chronicle. When he is accused by other prisoners of higher ranks of 'fraternising' with the Japanese, he retorts that he is trying to learn the Japanese language so that he can prevent them from being hit when 'a number of [them] are beaten up badly by the Japanese because [they] do not understand their orders' (Lumiere 1966:63). Despite his senior officers' warning, Erik continues to learn the language, even on the ship from Sumatra to the camp in Burma, by befriending four Japanese fishermen-turned-soldiers. He later wonders who would throw the first stone at him regarding fraternising with the Japanese (Lumiere 1966:64).

An interpreter, as seen in Chapter Three, is a middleperson, a mediator and he (or she) has to please both parties, especially when it is a matter of life or death as during the war. The task of being an interpreter takes a heavy toll on Erik's health and 'on several occasions, it very nearly [takes] his life' (Lumiere 1966:8). His job demands him 'to learn to be punished, beaten, insulted for the sake of a cause, for the sake of others' (Lumiere 1966:8). A Japanese colonel nick-named 'Butcher' and known for his brutality, spares Erik and lets him undergo surgery for appendicitis, but it is only because he does not want to lose this useful prisoner. Erik always has to 'barter and bargain' in dealing with the Japanese when the prisoners wish to make proposals, often at risk to his own life (Lumiere 1966:76).

Erik's attempts to save the prisoners' lives whenever he can are not always successful. When the prisoners sign the notorious paper prepared by the captors that stipulate escape under pain of death, some still attempt to break free. When they are captured, Erik tries his hardest, with as much power as his limited language allows, to persuade the camp commander to spare their lives. Although he tries to explain, plead and appeal to the vanity of the commander, he is faced with the limited capacity of his language skills. The cost is their lives. In this case, however, it is doubtful that even the most fluent translator could have prevented the execution of these men.

Erik's position as the interpreter is an ambivalent one. Being technically under Dutch command, Erik is also under the command of an Australian brigadier who is responsible for the whole camp and so he often faces a conflict between these two allied groups. The gap between captor and captive, however, is immense. Erik learns quickly that it is important 'seemingly first to agree with the Japs, to reduce their antagonism. One could then try to make the captors see matters from the prisoners' point of view' (Lumiere 1966:42). However, the interpreter's role is not to make any statements but only to translate them from left to right or vice versa and he has to '[fight] his lonely battle of wits, often [has] to take chances and hope for the best' (Lumiere 1966:43).

As a non-fiction writer, the author interpolated many episodes from the prisoner-of-war camp days. These episodes again reveal the author's sense of the incomprehensible Japanese, with their strange carrot-and-stick policy and their harsh behaviour directed towards prisoners and their own lower ranks. The author makes some rather generalised and biased statements about the enemy that highlight what Edward Said in a different context called 'Orientalist' prejudice: '[the Japanese and Koreans] hated as only the oriental can hate, with pathological strength of feeling, combined with the brutality of the primitive' (Lumiere 1966:28). The camp commandant, who 'hated with intensity all that was Western and white,' is a strange 'mixture of an inherent Oriental inferiority complex and a powerful victor's superiority complex' (Lumiere 1966:68).

Throughout Lumiere's narrative, readers are led to realise that to overcome the serious cross-cultural gaps faced in the prison camp, one has to understand the workings of the mind of the interpreter and those around him, and not just continuously be reminded of the atrocities and danger caused by the Japanese. By nature, Erik was an 'individualist' and for him there was 'no enemy, basically, all races, colours, creeds were the same' (Lumiere 1966:3). Thanks to his naturally fair disposition and his own cosmopolitan background, he may originally have found it easier than other prisoners to interact with the 'Other.' After three and a half years as a prisoner on the Burma–Thailand railway, he learns how to deal with the ultimate 'Other'—the enemy on whom he depends.

In Lumiere's story, some Australian senior ranks in the camp eventually come to realise the importance and advantage of knowing the Japanese language, despite their pride and prejudice. Subsequently their own bias against Erik as a fraterniser with the enemy dissipates. However, such a change of heart in the Australian officers, invites criticism by some of the Dutch and British senior officers who are less conscious of the importance of language. Friction within the same interest group then eventuates (Lumiere 1966:185).

Observations of the Japanese as individuals

A Japanese phrase becomes a key for speculation for Russell Braddon. In *The Naked Island* (1952), Braddon recounts an episode in which a Japanese interpreter called Terai stubbornly insists 'the war will last for a hundred years', which was a Japanese slogan used often during the war, indicating Japan's determination to win. This fanatically one-sided conviction seems to stay in the author's mind as significant for understanding the Japanese mind. Braddon again mentions the phrase in *End of a Hate* (1958), which was written as a 'factual' account of his

POW days when he was held by 'justly hated captors'. When Braddon finished *The Naked Island*, the war had 'only stopped', it had 'not ended'. Then in *End of a Hate*, he reveals that having published *The Naked Island*, he was able to 'end' the war and his 'prisonerhood'. This sense of closure allowed him to look at the former enemy in terms of their own background (1958:ch10). He further suggests that in order to understand and predict how the Japanese may act, one must look at their culture. By the end of the book, Braddon eventually reaches a stage where he could write 'not from hatred but from fact...not forget and forgive but remember and understand' (Braddon 1958:179).

In a later version, *The Naked Island: A Play* (1961), Braddon lets a Japanese guard use the phrase, 'the war will last for a hundred years', to the Australian prisoners, and during a rather comical conversation, presents the notion that Japanese soldiers believe they are destined to fight against the enemy until they die, even if it takes a hundred years. In his production note to the play, Braddon explains that the Japanese character should not be taken as a 'half-wit,' however silly and fanatical his interpretation of the slogan might sound.

As mentioned above, Japanese guards are defied by the prisoners only because they never understood the Anglo-Saxon mentality and therefore never looked for the low and outrageous kind of animal cunning exercised against them by their prisoners. Because the Japanese are the captors, they do not have to make the effort to understand. It is the captive prisoners who have to understand the 'Other's' mentality, a bit like the experience of Jesuits and traders from Portugal and Spain in Japan in the 16th century; as the first white men in Japan, they had contact with the Japanese at the risk of their own lives.

Braddon further uses the phrase, 'the war will last for a hundred years', as the title of his book *The Other Hundred Years War: Japan's Bid for Supremacy 1942–2041* (Braddon 1983).[58] After his memoirs and play, Braddon now tries to understand Japan in a different light, lamenting the scant knowledge about the Japanese that his seniors—especially his Intelligence Officer—had provided him. Based on his own experiences with the Japanese during the war and his later research from various economic, industrial, diplomatic, political and cultural sources, Braddon warns readers to 'beware of the Japanese'. The purpose of this book seems to be to 'let us know them', even if we cannot 'tolerate or accept them', thus suggesting the importance of the very first step of cross-cultural contact. McQueen also observes apparent changes in the author's attitude, as he shows in his comments that Braddon's 1952 book *The Naked Island* is hatred-filled, while the 1961 play version shows more careful observation of the Japanese. Once again, it's evident that time and detachment are necessary for objective descriptions of the former enemy (McQueen 1991:229).

Kenneth Harrison also admits that his hatred dissipated as time passed, and that he started to see the Japanese in more measured terms. He notes surprisingly, in *The Brave Japanese*, that:

> ...try as I might, I could find no hatred whatever for them. Instead I remembered more and more their basic virtues of loyalty, cleanliness, and courage, and the more I read, the more I became convinced that they were soldiers of tremendous bravery (Harrison 1966:279).

When some criticised his portrayal of the Japanese as mere fanatics, the author replied by saying that:

> the Japanese soldiers were men of flesh and blood—human beings with very human emotions of fear and foreboding...I had no doubt a Japanese in a position where he was fighting for his country and his Emperor would fight till he died (Harrison 1966:279).

Compared to other Australian memoirists, his conclusion is perhaps one of the most favourable towards the Japanese. A much later visitor to Japan, Humphrey McQueen, admits that his ideas were similar to those of millions of other Australians; however, with his random reading about the country, starting with Harrison's *The Brave Japanese*, he moved to a clearer recognition of Japan and the Japanese (McQueen 1991:268). This is an example of how writings can influence the formation of ideas about the 'Other'. As in Harrison's case, time for further reflection and contemplation seems to be needed to reach a stage where one can present experiences in a more considered and balanced manner.

Descriptions of individual Japanese in later memoirs and stories by Australian writers published from the 1960s also tend to present a calmer and clearer approach to the Japanese collectively. In Eric Lambert's *MacDougal's Farm* (1965), a very young Japanese soldier called Ono, shows how individuals of both sides can become close in war. Ono has admiration for 'the English-speaking peoples', influenced by his communist father who taught him Western ideas and who was later killed because of his beliefs. MacDougal becomes a mentor figure to young Ono at Changi and teaches him about the Australian way of life as well as the Christian faith. Ono tries to absorb everything he is told with the eagerness of one who has missed the chance to learn because he'd joined the army. Almost like a premonition, MacDougal wonders if Ono's seriousness is a form of obsession. When the war is over, Ono kills himself, following the Japanese tradition or code for the defeated. Here is another tragic example of what may happen to those 'in-between' cultures. By forcing people into oppositional roles, war destroys the normal complexity of human interactions, which even in the aftermath of war can have terrible consequences.

In some of his short stories, Geoffrey Bingham portrays not only the Japanese but also his own people in a vivid and frank way. Bingham himself was taken prisoner at Changi and his experience of prisoner-of-war life and observation of the Japanese become the main topic of his short stories. As one of the titles of his collected stories shows, a person begins to discover his 'true self' and 'become[s] genuine in living' when 'at the end of his tether' (Bingham 1985:xii). The characters of Bingham's short stories seem to re-define themselves through their POW experiences. In 'Three Rice Cakes', for example, the protagonist tests himself by picking up the smallest of rice cakes offered to him not out of desire for approval or fear of disapproval, but more as a test to prove his own courage. One prisoner in 'The Power Within' trains his mind to just survive through captivity, believing that the captives are fighting for the best, the British way of life and therefore should never surrender to the Japanese. He survives with strong self-righteousness, stoicism, and pride intact until the very day Japan capitulates and then unable to sustain himself any longer he dies. Here the Japanese as captors are presented as a means for some prisoners to discover their true selves. Ironically, however, the strain of this kind of stoicism and self-preservation is too great.

In his short stories, Bingham tries to look at the Japanese, even those who seem evil, not simply as 'captor-figures' but more as individuals, with unique characteristics. One such story is 'Killa t'Pig, George' from *To Command the Cats and Other Stories* (1981), where three captives and a Javanese native are psychologically punished by a Japanese guard. Out of sheer hunger, they kill a pig to make a stew and are found by Takahashi, one of the camp guards. When he discovers their cooking, Takahashi squats and takes his share from the pot as if enjoying the feast and then leaves them wondering what will happen next. Their fear of being punished, the unpredictability of their near future and the inscrutability of Takahashi gives readers an idea of the tense living conditions experienced by prisoners in a tragic-comic fashion.

Another example is 'The Mind of Matsuoko' from *To Command the Cats and Other Stories* (Bingham 1980). Matsuoko, responsible for mass murder during the war, pretends to be somebody else. He wants to avoid being judged as guilty by his enemy and to die an honourable death with his own hand. For Matsuoko, it is shameful to admit that what he did was a crime. It is 'too personal' for him to admit why he killed. An Australian soldier, Conn Webster, has to hunt Matsuoko till the end, motivated in part by his own incapability of being a 'real soldier' (Webster ran away when the Japanese landed and was later taunted by other fellow Australians for lacking the instinct of a 'born-soldier'). Webster also regards Matsuoko as a representive of the Japanese as a whole and therefore responsible 'for those little Japs who made him run' (Bingham

1980:53). In this episode of a defeated Japanese and his war crime, Bingham has raised more complicated issues resulting from the war than those usually found in previous literature about Japan.

Some authors of this period have tried to examine a more humane side of the Japanese, perhaps with greater clarity and interest than in memoirs and stories written during the 1940s and 50s. Time seems to have allowed both writers and readers to focus not only on suffering and hatred but also on other facets, such as the nature of their enemy. Kenneth Harrison is one such writer, as we have seen earlier in this chapter. In *The Brave Japanese*, he describes acts of kindness and consideration by the Japanese, however subtle and small, like the giving of extra water or protection from the more brutal soldiers, both precious acts during those hard days. It occurs to Harrison that 'kindness, like wildflowers, blooms in the most unlikely places, even in the heart of a pock-marked, bullet-headed Japanese guard' (Harrison 1966:130). Although most of the Japanese described in Harrison's memoir were 'villains…[who] came in all sizes and shapes and most were barbaric and sadistic; all had yellow skins and slant eyes'; there are 'others who were kind at a time when kindness and gentleness were the rarest of jewels'.

Harrison also observes the Japanese eagerness for polite behaviour; examples include their hatred of the use of swear words among prisoners or their habit of employing courtesy titles when addressing others (1966:143). The author also finds that despite their apparent savagery and indifference to human life, some Japanese have a 'sincere love of family life'. Discovering that the Japanese are 'much more lenient towards family men', Harrison takes a photo of a three-year-old boy from a dead man's possession and adopts him as his 'son'. Over the years he shows 'the photo of Teddy Harrison to hundreds of Japanese and invariably gained their attention and hisses of admiration. Many replied by producing photos of little black-eyed, round-faced, solemn Japanese children who were quite delightful' (1966:144–5).

Sharing the same feelings for certain things like family and sport seem to ease the antipathy between captor and captive. In one episode in Ray Parkin's diary, when prisoners are bathing in the river in the jungle of Thailand on a rest afternoon, they are found by the Japanese and believe they are about to be punished. Instead, to their surprise, the Japanese bring some tools and make them a springboard (Parkin 1993:256). Although the roles are reversed, this is similar to an episode in TAG Hungerford's novel *The Ridge and the River*, where Australian soldiers find the Japanese bathing in the river and observe their human side for the first time, as seen in Chapter Four (Hungerford 1971:92).

As Russel Ward mentions in his foreword to the book, *One Man's War*, Stan Arneil's diary of his captivity is free from racism and gives a fair description of the Japanese. He notices that unlike most Australians, the Japanese have deep respect for hierarchy in the army, in particular for the higher ranks. Unfortunately for the author and other ORs (Other Ranks), this respect for hierarchy is also evidenced in Japanese dealings with prisoners. As Harrison also mentions, beatings are a usual means to enforce discipline, from the highest to the lowest ranks (1966:144). When some prisoners, including the author, are assigned to dig tunnels in Johore, they fear that they may be digging their own graves, but the Japanese in charge, (officers, soldiers and engineers), turn out to be fair and treat the prisoners humanely. Apparently, small acts by the Japanese, such as knowing the prisoners' names, promising to build chairs and desks for them and treating them as ordinary human beings, enable the prisoners to look at the 'Other' from a different perspective (Arneil 1980:228).

Ray Parkin, who is cited by critics as one of the more balanced and objective memoirists[59], not only describes the Japanese as individuals but also reflects upon Australians and on human beings in general. The first book of his war-trilogy on the Second World War, *Out of the Smoke* (1960), is memoir-based 'faction', in which the author tells how his protagonist, John, fights the war at sea on the Australian cruiser *Perth* in the Sunda Strait. John survives after the boat goes down and eventually falls into the enemy's hands. *Into the Smother* (1963), the second book, depicts his prisoner-of-war experiences on the Burma–Thailand Railway, based on the diary the author secretly kept during his captivity. In the third and final book, *The Sword and the Blossom* (1968), the protagonist, John, appears again and talks about his captivity in Japan until the end of the war.

What is remarkable about Parkin's memoirs is a certain detachment in observing both the Japanese as captors and the Australians as captives. The author thinks he should be at a 'stage when [he] can observe things outside [himself]' with interest and without 'self-preservative selfishness' (Parkin 1993:250). Parkin is also an artist and his drawings of his surroundings decorate the diary in *Into the Smother*. Although he has to refrain from publicising his artistic ability in the prison camps to avoid being asked for 'dirty pictures for purpose of sex', (1993:55) he continues to exercise his artistic vision not only on the tangible natural surroundings but also on the intangible aspects of human nature. One of his mottos for survival during captivity is to try not to hate—'*[i]t is no good hating at all* [Parkin's emphasis]. That could kill you' (Parkin 1993:31). The author tries hard to be consistent in his attitudes, however difficult this may be, and to observe the enemy with stability and objectivity.

In Parkin's diary, nevertheless, the Japanese are portrayed as cruel and incomprehensible oppressors. One time, as he watches a Japanese troop of about 200 men pass by, their silence and uniformity makes him think of 'mass-thinking (or unthinking) Martians or Gammas from Aldous Huxley's *Brave New World*' (Parkin1993:88). The prisoners do not care about knowing the proper names of any of the Japanese,; they just give them various nicknames based on the individual's temper, as well as the degree of his cruelty.

And yet the author's unbiased observations are still brought to bear on the Japanese and this attitude is extended to his fellow prisoners too. Some of his own mates are condemned because of their low morale and 'laziness with an affected patriotism that they will do as little as possible for the enemy' (Parkin 1993:79). They are people who do not care what will happen to their mates. Parkin once compares the physical condition of prisoners to that of the unfortunates who were living in 'Happy Valley' in Australia during the depression in the 1930s. He then concludes that it is the consequence of the prisoners' decision to fight and be captured by 'an enemy with no cause to love [them]', whereas those who were in poverty in Happy Valley in the depression were put into that situation by their own country, for which they are now fighting (Parkin 1993:144–5). Parkin also criticises some of the officers and the better conditions they received compared to some of their subordinates; however, his diary is written from the 'point of view of the men' and so 'it is bound to be partial'. There are some prisoners in the higher ranks who:

> are thoroughly organised for their own preservation, who are as heartless as the Japs about the fate of the ordinary man here...At least the Japs have the excuse that they are our enemies, and they come into the open with their cruelty (Parkin 1993:187–8).

This remark perhaps underlies later comments made about senior officer-prisoners by McQueen: 'there was more than one value system at work in determining Japanese behaviour'. Within the prisoners too, there were differences in looking at the 'Other' according to their own positions, circumstances and environments (McQueen 1991:332).

It may be Parkin's ability to observe, draw and write that enabled him to be more balanced and composed than many others in such adverse circumstances. He even seems to have a gentle regard for the difficult natural conditions in the tropics when he expresses 'a sensuous pleasure walking in the rain', or manages to retain a sense of humour by regarding himself and his fellow prisoners as being like baboons in a zoo. To possess such an ability, even in the presence of an enemy, shows an extraordinary degree of tolerance and freedom of mind, untainted by bitterness. His balanced account is appreciated by readers in the years to come.

Prisoners-of-war in Japan

Some memoirists were also held in Japan in the latter years of their captivity and became the first Australians who had direct contact with the Japanese in Japan, both military and civilians, before official contact by the occupation forces. Some of their experiences were published from the 1960s onwards. These memoirs and memoir-based novels, some of which have already been referred to, include Ray Parkin's *The Sword and the Blossom* (1968), Kenneth Harrison's *The Brave Japanese* (1966) and Hugh Clarke's *The Tub* (1961), *Last Stop Nagasaki!* (1984) and *Twilight Liberation: Australian Prisoners of War between Hiroshima and Home* (1985). Although these men were in the enemy's hands in the enemy's land, as the war drew closer to an end, the destiny of these prisoners became more uncertain. It was these prisoners who had the first, if somewhat limited, opportunity to witness what it was like at the end of the war in Japan.

Clarke's *The Tub* is a novel based on the author's experiences, which tells a story of two prisoners from Changi who are sent to the Burma–Thailand Railway and finally to Fukuoka, Japan. One of them, Tony, carries a large iron tub, which symbolises the burden of POW life as well as being a reminder of civilised life. Tony becomes attached to this object as if it were his charm for survival. When the war is over, the tub is smashed and flattened by a drum container filled with relief goods airdropped from an American plane and Tony is finally set free, from both the tub and from 'prisonerhood'.

The memoirs mentioned above contain episodes of direct contact between the authors and the Japanese and the prisoners realise that they encounter less hostility than they expected when they arrive in Japan. When Clarke arrives in Nagasaki, people there seem to show more astonishment than animosity towards the prisoners (Clarke 1984:2). Prisoners also witness that the status of Japanese civilians is no better than theirs. In *The Tub*, Clarke says that only after losing it, do people come to know what freedom means. However, he learns the Japanese themselves 'were little better than slaves' (1963:165). The Japanese civilians working at the dockyard in Nagasaki, women and children alike, are given as hard a task as the prisoners, with no better clothes and food. It seems to Clarke that 'captors and captives [are] in the same boat' (Clarke 1984:30). It was a time when Japan had very little strength left to continue the war, something evidenced in the prisoners' encounters with the local Japanese.

In Southeast Asia and Papua New Guinea, living conditions were as abnormal and difficult for the Japanese as they were for their Australian prisoners. In Japan, prisoners were given the basic living standards of the time, even if it was a kind of living that was unfamiliar to them. Prisoners recall with astonishment sharing a tiny sized room, sleeping on a *tatami* floor with a bedspread, eating with chopsticks and drinking from cups without handles.

When the war finishes, their status among the Japanese becomes ambivalent. Clarke describes the situation in *Twilight Liberation* as 'those tense, bewildering days between slavery and liberation.' The men are uncertain of their fate should the US Army invade the major islands after Okinawa, for they know the 'lack of choice' faced by the Japanese. The prisoners themselves know that there is no 'surrender' for the Japanese, but only 'death' (Clarke 1985:54). It is an uneasy peace 'which could be blown away at any time by a mad resurgence of Japanese patriotism' (Clarke 1985:61). Harrison also reveals that 'they [are] neither freemen nor captives', and the balance of power between prisoners and the Japanese remains delicate (Harrison 1966:253). He further states that most prisoners do not want revenge or retribution after the war, although some individual cases of vengeance are described.

When news of the end of war reaches the camp, there are different reactions between each national group of allied prisoners—'Americans cheered, Dutch sang their national anthem, and Australians and English just stood silent' (Clarke 1985:80). Such differences in mood and behaviour among the nationalities made it difficult to command the prisoners after the war, because the majority of officers had been sent to Manchuria. Prisoners only wanted to obey officers of the same nationality. Even in the same interest group integration was difficult (Clarke 1985:93).

Having had direct contact with the Japanese and seen their ways, each author has a certain insight into their cross-cultural encounters. With hindsight, Clarke starts to think that their 'constant clash with the Japanese might be one of differing cultures as much as the natural antagonism between captor and captive'. He admits his generation had been raised under the influence of the White Australia Policy, and grew up considering themselves superior. He further admits that their attitude to the Japanese is at all times 'defiant and arrogant', while the Japanese thought of themselves as the 'descendants from the sons of heaven'. In such a situation it was difficult to find common ground (Clarke 1984:65). This recognition of the lack of common ground seems to be easier for later generations to recognise, an important change from the generations before and during the war. Clarke confesses that he weeps like a baby to see a white nurse on the ship back home and that although his hatred towards the Japanese starts to ebb away, after three and a half years captivity he does not want to see another 'Nip' as long as he lives. However, as his writings show, he continues to go back to Japan, not only in his head but by actually revisiting the country, to resurrect the past and to examine Australia's relationship with the Japanese. This includes the Cowra event (see Chapter Five). Such recognition of difference and similarity echoes Braddon's comment to 'not forgive and forget but remember and understand', an appraisal, which in turn will eventually foster cross-cultural understanding with the 'Other'.

Many prisoners-of-war witnessed the tragedies in Hiroshima and Nagasaki caused by the atomic bombs and this seems to have had a huge impact on their perception of their captors. When the Japanese are thrust into such a devastating state, the prisoners' sympathy for their enemy-captor, seen for the first time as suffering people, seems to emerge. After being liberated, Harrison goes to Hiroshima and witnesses the aftermath, unable to believe that 'one bomb had been responsible for this holocaust' (Harrison 1966:265). He mourns that it is:

> easy, painfully easy, to visualise the fate that had overtaken them as the countless fires joined hands with glee and danced high in the air, almost as if seeking to touch the evil mushroom cloud above./But that was imagination./The reality was the girl with scarred features who passed with averted face. And the listless people who went by so dully; the scarred people; the burnt people; the apathetic people. And the people who even now showed not the slightest sign of hostility or resentment (Harrison 1966:265–266).

These ex-prisoners of war are there to witness a major part, if not the whole of the event from the insider's point of view and their utterance, 'poor, poor, bastards,' expresses their feelings for their enemy. They had 'an odd pity for this strange race', and 'their hatred of the Japanese was swept away by the enormity of what [they] had seen' (Harrison 1966:267). Wilfred Burchett went to Hiroshima as a journalist, saw the immediate aftermath of the bomb and reported it to the world. The tone of Burchett's report is said to have been 'totally against everything else being written from Japan at that time, the "they-had-it-coming-to-them" and "I-saw-the-arrogant-Japs-humbled" type of story', thus revealing how different people observed and interpreted the events around them (Knightley 1986:10).

Harrison may also be one of the few writers, like Burchett, who 'felt no sense of either history or triumph...Our brother Man went by crippled and burned and we knew only shame and guilt' (Harrison 1966:15). Many prisoners believed that the bomb was inevitable as a means to end the war, otherwise they felt there would be more victims on both sides. Clarke was one such person. He had left Nagasaki before the bomb was dropped and did not know about the disaster until the end of war. On his way back home on a US plane, he sees from the air the remains of the city. He feels that:

> no matter how much [they have] suffered no people on earth could have deserved such a fate...at the same time,...without the atomic bomb halting the war as it

did the loss of Japanese and Allied lives which would have resulted from an invasion would have been incalculable (Clarke 1984:123–124).

In his recollection, cited by Clarke, Bert Donaldson also mentions the 'inevitability' of the atomic bomb which 'probably saved many lives, including service personnel, POWs and Japanese, because it prevented the expected landing on Japan with all its consequences', but he can only hope it will never happen again (Clarke 1985:144).

Soon after the Allied prisoners-of-war in Japan were liberated, more direct contact with the Japanese started, though the positions of both sides were still ambivalent and transitional. Before the occupation forces came, some prisoners started to enjoy their new status as captors in a lawless and undisciplined way and memoirists have recorded episodes of some ransacking premises as well as the soaring venereal disease rate (Harrison 1966:ch25). Then the occupation forces arrived and took over. As seen in Chapter Five, these newly arrived Australians were thrown into Japanese society, developing a unique relationship with its people from a very different background to that of the former prisoners-of-war and thus forming very different notions of the Japanese.

TAG Hungerford's early publication of this occupation force experience, *Sowers of the Wind*, revealed many crude aspects of the relationship between the two groups. As mentioned in Chapter Five, despite the fact it won a literary prize in 1949, this novel's publication was postponed until 1954. Later still, Hungerford returned to this experience in his memoir-short story in *A Knockabout with a Slouch Hat* (1985), one of his three autobiographical volumes. After the initial dismay experienced on their arrival in Kure, a place not very different from Fremantle, Hungerford and others set out to explore Japan. The author recalls his outrage at local wharf labourers who assumed 'cheerful, un-conquered attitudes' and who bustled around 'shouting and smiling and spitting as if they had never heard of the Coral Sea or...the Kokoda Trail...' (Hungerford 1985:64). He had expected Japan to be 'a bit more exotic' and is shocked 'almost to resentment by the rosy peaches-and-cream complexions of the Japanese when [they have been] led to expect the leathery yellow hides of reptiles' (Hungerford 1985:64).

Although the non-fraternisation policy had been introduced, what the town Kure was able to offer to the occupation forces most was 'women'. This aspect of the relationship between the conquerors and the conquered is one that Hungerford tackles candidly and unsentimentally in his memoirs.

His observation of the local Japanese leads him to understand how ordinary people live. The scarcity of food, hard labour and the struggle for postwar recovery are thus recorded. He meets by chance a Japanese civilian, an ex-

English teacher and his wife. They lost their four sons in the war, but do not show any hostility towards their ex-enemy. This Japanese man shows Hungerford the Japanese ways of life by inviting him to his house, taking him to the public bath-house and introducing him to his 'favourite' brothel, where Hungerford wonders whether he should offer a 'shout' of a girl to his Japanese friend or not. In the lounge of the brothel Hungerford talks with the madam and the local customers with the help of his 'phrase-book'. It is a 'pleasant, somewhat fractured, gossip' and the people there are 'ordinary, respectable-seeming folk, rather like any Australian group you'd join at the local pub after tea, for a few noggins and whatever scandal might be knocking around'. He then ponders that these are 'the sort of people the brass [has] forbidden [them] to meet or even talk to'. Such occasions with the civilian 'Other' thus make the author realise the importance of sharing common ground, and putting aside the moral question of right or wrong concerning the circumstances that have brought them together (Hungerford 1985:75–76).

Hungerford's new Japanese friend introduces him to haiku, which turns out to be an important factor for him in understanding the cultural side of Japan. He is at first amazed by this traditional poetry form—seventeen syllables in three lines of five, seven and five—and thinks it sounds 'so bloody Japanese'. However, when his friend recites one of Matsuo Basho's poems—*The stillness of a summer day...it pierces the very rocks...the locust cry*, written about 300 years before, he instantly feels as if he is immersed in the natural environment of the Darling Range in Perth. Beyond the differences of time and place, nationality and cultural background, the words in their Japanese form offer Hungerford and his friend a moment of shared understanding. Through haiku, he is reminded of what his poetry teacher had once taught him—'a poem always had to be a *statement of fact*'. He also discovers that what is important is not the words one uses but the picture one paints with them.

Civilian writers and their stories of the war

Besides the memoirists who write about their war experiences, other writers have emerged who have dealt with various aspects of the war between Australia and Japan. The themes of war-writing, which were dominated by masculine and often highly partial, biased views based on wartime experiences or propaganda, started to develop new dimensions with the emergence of the perspectives of women, most of whom had remained in Australia during the war. Younger generations who did not have a direct experience of the war also offered their viewpoints. This literature in turn eventually expanded to become part of a more multicultural pattern of writing on Asia in Australian literature in the 1970s and 1980s.

The experience of female prisoners-of-war, of nurses and civilians, continues to be the subject of research and publication by non-fiction writers, including Shirley Fenton Huie's *The Forgotten Ones: Women and Children under Nippon* (1992), Alice Bowman's *Not Now Tomorrow—ima nai ashita—: Australian Civilian and Army Nurses—Prisoners of the Japanese in New Guinea and Japan 1942–1945* (1996), Norman Manners' *The True Story of Vivian Bullwinkel, a Young Army Nursing Sister Who Was the Sole Survivor of a World War Two Massacre by the Japanese* (1999). The hardship encountered by those who were waiting back home for captured family members has also been written about in Margaret Reeson's *Whereabouts Unknown* (1993).

Stories about Japanese war brides, one of the consequences of the Australian occupation forces in Japan, have so far not received much attention, although they were a major factor in the breaking of the White Australia policy. The story of the first Japanese bride, Cherry Parker, has been written about in 'faction' form by Isobel Carter and published as *Alien Blossom: A Japanese–Australian Love Story* (1965). This book reveals the hardship encountered by the first officially admitted couple—Don Parker, a sapper of the Regimental Aid Post and Nobuko Sakuramoto, his house girl in Kure. It traces how Don, who was prepared to see the Japanese as 'inhuman', especially after his training in Cowra when he heard about the 'fanatic and lunatic courage of the breakout' (Carter 1965:10–11), meets Nobuko in Hiroshima and decides to bring her back to Australia against tremendous odds. With his family's strong support and encouragement and after six years' struggle, the family—they already have two children—are reunited in Australia. Carter's story is not only about the fulfilment of the love of two people, it is about the changes in feelings for the Japanese held by Don, his family and finally Australia.

As a certain stigma was still attached to their status, both in Japan and Australia, some Japanese brides did not wish to discuss their personal histories. However, in later years they reached a stage where they could reflect on their own journey and tell their stories. Recently, research by writers and memoirs of the women themselves have started to be published. Two such authors, Julie Easton (1995) and Keiko Tamura (2001), saw the 40th anniversary of the first arrival of a Japanese war-bride, which was held in 1993, as the beginning of this change. The number of these brides may be small—altogether about 650; however, as one of them commented at the 1993 anniversary event, they have helped to play a major role in breaking the stereotype of the Japanese held by Australians as well as promoting mutual understanding between the two countries (Easton 1995:31).

Some novelists who were in the war started to use their experience as the background for their own fictional works. Two of Jon Cleary's popular novels, *A Very Private War* (1980) and *The Phoenix Tree* (1983), are examples of this. Both employ Japanese characters with the latter book set mainly in Japan with mostly Japanese characters. In *A Very Private War*, the protagonist is an American coast-watcher in New Britain called Mullane, who with the help of a young Australian, uncovers the camouflaged airstrip of a Japanese base. Mullane had once stayed in Japan and was married to a Japanese. As he was considered a suspicious foreigner in pre-war Japan, she was later killed because of her relationship with him,. It is thus his 'private war' to avenge his dead wife, as well as to complete their mission. During the course of their undercover mission, they pick up a wounded Japanese lieutenant general called Nara. This character is a rather simplified embodiment of Japanese militarism; however, he is depicted more as a 'human' villain, thus creating both the readers' enmity towards a fanatical enemy and at the same time inviting their sympathy for the defeated. Japan is not a total enemy in Cleary's novel and the image of vice-ridden characters seen in pre-war novels on Japan is not evident.

The Phoenix Tree (Cleary 1983*)*, according to the author himself, is 'not a spy novel but a novel about spies', who are American-born Japanese. It is set in Japan during the closing months of the Second World War and the two young spies are Minato and Okada. Minato is for traditional Japan and Okada against it; both are assigned to identify the members of the 'Peace Faction' in Japan. It is a story of these young men's self-discovery while being torn between two cultures. Through them one sees the war both won and lost: with the pro-American spy surviving while the pro-traditional Japan supporter dies.

Eric Lambert also employs Japanese characters to describe a more personal war between West and East in *Hiroshima Reef* (1968). Like Cleary, Lambert uses an American medical missionary called M'Glennon, who once worked in Japan and learnt the language. M'Glennon has organised a leper colony for the native people on one of the Gilbert and Ellice Islands in Polynesia, where a Japanese contingent invades. M'Glennon assumes, against his wish, the role of a spy for the Australian military forces. Among the Japanese is Colonel Hakanate, an aloof, cold and harsh officer, who forbids his subordinates to fraternise with the villagers. Eventually, Hakanate himself becomes attached to a half-caste local girl Taluni, and is faced with a dilemma. Despite his arrogance and violence, Hakanate is depicted as a lonely man, not understood by either side. With Taluni as the only one who knows his human side, he eventually decides to hide and remain deep in the jungle with her after the American Forces invade the island.

The Japanese figure is again depicted not as a complete villain but rather as a helpless figure who tries to find his own role in a situation beyond his control.

These novels by Cleary and Lambert may indicate the authors' uncertainty about how to include Japanese characters in their fiction, for both fall back on allegorical national types. But they also tackle some complex issues of race—for example, the close relationship of the American M'Glennon and the Japanese language and people; Polynesians and Japanese; Polynesians and American; and the different Polynesian groups. The standpoint of the 'Other' seems to become important in these novels. These authors seem to feel freer than many of their predecessors to employ Japanese characters and settings in their adventure novels. Although there continues to be a degree of simplification and fixed character definition, these novels continued to push some of the boundaries of Australian writing.

Despite these new approaches, old archetypes remained. Invasion scare novels, which were discussed in Chapter Two, were still being written in the 1970s and 1980s, with realistic plots of Australia being invaded by the Japanese. One example is John Vader's *Battle of Sydney* (1971). In this novel the main characters are fictitious, while real military figures are interpolated here and there in the story, thus giving it a sense of credibility. Like previous invasion novels, Vader's story fails to give any clear description of individual Japanese. Admirals and Generals are mentioned, but the main Japanese character is 'the army' as a group. Their advance into Australia proves its vulnerability and without the victory of the Americans in the Midway or natural disasters such as heavy rain and floods that hampered the Japanese movement southward, the author insists Australia could have been conquered.

Another example, John Hooker's *The Bush Soldiers* (1984), is about a group of Australians who are assigned to destroy the infrastructure of each town to 'delay and deny the enemy' who has already landed in Australia. They are convinced that the Japanese cannot handle the bush, whereas they can and so they try to outwit them. However, their march into the outback turns out to be like that of the explorers of the past against whom nature turned its back. Here the Japanese are just heard and talked about but hardly seen. They are like an imaginary enemy and the group is forced to chase that image. Besides nature, their fatal enemy turns out to be not the Japanese but the 'Australian blackfellows', about whom they have shown little concern and have in fact killed some along the way. Similar to the march of Patrick White's *Voss*, the white Australians perish surrounded by hostile nature, natives and their supposed enemy. These invasion novels again provide little description of the Japanese, the 'Other' who generates so much fear in the Australians, but they do provide Australians with an opportunity to reflect upon themselves.

As we have seen in this chapter, since the 1960s there have been many different themes in a variety of novels which reflect on the Pacific War and examine the relationship between Australians and the Japanese. Many ex-soldier-writers continue to write about their experiences, while others with no war experience have found the theme important enough to adopt for their own works. As mentioned at the beginning of this chapter, time and circumstances have allowed certain changes in thinking and expression for both authors and readers, and as a result, many works in the 1960s and later show multicultural and cosmopolitan aspects. In particular, the use by some authors of Japanese culture—language, proverbs, poetry, and so on—to describe 'the enemy' in their stories seems to be innovative when we compare them with pre-war writing in Australia.

In examining John Romeril's play *The Floating World*, Brisbane comments that the protagonist Les Harding, who suffers from his traumatic memories of having been a Japanese prisoner-of-war, has not learned anything from the war. Brisbane argues that the war 'only reconsecrated the myth of mateship, confirmed a century's conditioning in fear and gave us fuel for another fifty years of anti-Japanese prejudice' (Brisbane 1994:xxxii). Les, presented as the typical Australian ex-serviceman who suffered from the war against the Japanese, is depicted as being obsessed by notions of his own identity as white, Australian and male. When his identity is under crisis he goes insane, only to find happiness in a solitary state in the asylum. Here thus is, as Webby puts it, the 'human tendency to escape into dream worlds and hide behind facades' (Webby 1990:43). Romeril seems to show in his play how for some, beliefs hardly change, especially where one's own identity and prejudice against the 'Other' are concerned.

And yet, such notions can change, too. As mentioned above, Clarke recalls his hatred for the Japanese seemed to ebb away, but he strongly hoped never to see 'another Nip' as long as he lived (Clarke 1984:124). However, as years passed, his ideas and attitudes changed and he went back to Japan to trace his own path and become reconciled, however partially, with the Japanese. If the battle against Japan and the prisoner-of-war experiences of Australians mark the beginning of an understanding of the 'Other' instead of a period of shame and anger, it can be regarded as an important step towards the tolerance of Australians toward different members of its increasingly multicultural society. If this is the case, then Japan may have unwittingly provided a 'test match' for this step. As Stan Arneil's title, *One Man's War*, shows, a war is fought and experienced by each soldier on an individual level. However, using literature as a means, these individual experiences can be recreated, reflected upon and shared widely among those who were not there or who came later.

chapter eight

Writing in a multicultural context since the 1980s and the 1990s

The lifting of the White Australia policy and the shift towards a more multicultural society from the 1970s encouraged different writers to air their opinions in the 1980s. Exchanges between Australia and Japan, mainly for economic reasons, became more varied, with organisations such as the Australia–Japan Foundation, (founded in 1976) beginning to co-ordinate cultural and educational interchanges. Japan's international economic expansion generated a huge interest in promoting the learning of the English language, which resulted in the invitation of English teachers from outside Japan and the encouragement of its students to go overseas to study. Australia became one of the key suppliers of language instructors as well as a destination for Japanese students wanting to study abroad. Such interactions between its citizens were a new phenomenon in the history of the relationship between the two countries, thus offering new opportunities for Australian writers to experience and observe the Japanese in both countries.

Multicultural policies were introduced by the Whitlam Labor Government between 1972 and 1974 and the notion of multiculturalism seemed to seep into the national psyche, gradually affecting both authors and readers in their identification with and perception of their country, society and themselves. Hage maintains that even though multiculturalism 'cannot operate with a "soft" notion of culture which excludes, for instance, political and legal traditions, [it] has opened up a space which permits the articulation of diverse cultural forms, as well as facilitating the interaction between them' (Hage 1998:83). In the postmodern, postcolonial environment of the last two decades of the 20th century, the universality of Eurocentric values and criticism was being questioned, while the values of minority groups were recognised, not only as legitimate, but also as something to be noticed and even appreciated. Such changes in Australian society and thinking had an impact on Australian literature, with the emergence of many writers from different ethnic backgrounds.

Since Australia's colonisation by Britain, Australians have often tried to 'define' or 'invent' their sense of uniqueness, especially in terms of their culture and literature. However, this definition was usually along the lines of its Anglo-Celtic, European heritage. In the 1980s, this orientation broadened to include not only the North Western hemisphere but also the North Eastern hemisphere. Although the Anglo-Celtic heritage was still dominant and those of so-called ethnic minorities were on the periphery, the situation was no longer that of a 'dominant centre' versus 'minor other'. It was, as Turner points out, a time when, with the development of multiculturalism as a stimulus, 'literary theory and government social policy appear to have been more or less in step' (Turner 1998:353), thus opening the way for people to look at the 'Other' in a serious way. In this period (since the 1980s) the 'Other' becomes a less fixed and oppositional entity and more shifting and problematic, as both Australian and Japanese societies adapt to a globalising environment (with much influence from the United States) and their own internal pressures. With changes going on outside Australia, especially in North America with its ethnically diverse society and minority-based political movements, and changes happening inside Australia, with new patterns of immigration and the increase of population from the Asia-Pacific region, literature in Australia inevitably started to be seen from different perspectives.

In such an atmosphere, Japan again provided a source for unique literary experiments. In post-colonial literature, where the formerly-colonised re-examined themselves as well as their coloniser, so-called 'mainstream' writers in Australia—Anglo-Celtic, white, and often male—tried to reflect upon their dual roles of both coloniser and as part of the British colonised. Japan had been an incomprehensible ally, then a possible enemy, then a real military enemy. Now Japan became an economic ally and potential friend of Australia. The master-subordinate relationship during and after the war, with fear, suspicion and misunderstanding on both sides, remained a characteristic of the relationship between Australia and Japan, especially among the older generation. However, it was different from other post-colonial relationships and this difference seems to be uniquely reflected in some literary works of the period.

The environment of the time accelerated the emergence of various authors in Australia writing on Japan, from professional to amateur, from experienced to superficial. The genres of their writings also varied from fiction to non-fiction, from crime to romance, from observation to hearsay. As Australian society became more ethnically plural and the presence of the Japanese was no longer unusual, the use of Japanese characters, even as protagonists, became less extraordinary in Australian writings. In such a context, authors writing about Japan can be categorised in groups according to their themes or positions: those who visited Japan on business or as travellers; those who stayed for a while as journalists, teachers and academics; those who chose to stay and work in Japan; and those who adopted the Japanese just as 'ordinary' characters, whether in Australia, in Japan or elsewhere.

In this chapter, the different types of authors in the 1980s and 1990s are examined according to the above groupings. Would these authors present totally new images of the Japanese? Or, would they still be affected by old biases held by their predecessors in earlier writings? What 'types' of Japanese are dominant as characters? When they employ Japanese figures, how confident and sure are their characterisations? Are the Japanese characters 'authentic' when described in fictitious stories? Looking at what is new and what remains the same in the present multicultural environment of Australian literature may help in understanding, however partially, the nature of late 20th century Australian (and perhaps Japanese) society.

Visiting Australian authors in Japan

With the rapid development of technology, interactions between Australia and Japan became more active than before. This was especially so in the business field, with the rapid postwar recovery of both countries. Despite the antagonism caused by the Pacific War, Japan developed into one of Australia's largest trading partners and the relationship became smooth and controlled, with any pre-existing personal and private feelings pushed below the surface. As Gerster puts it, businessmen became 'the most visible of contemporary Western travellers in Asia' (1995:410). From soon after the war, businessmen from both countries were at the front line of this increased interaction. Each had the opportunity to observe and directly interact with the other.

Among those Australians visiting Japan on business, some are presented as potential conquerors. They may not be described in as crudely conquistadorial terms as in those stories written about the Western occupation of Japan in Chapter Five; however, behind the official talk and business negotiations, such figures take the opportunity as visitors in Japan to present themselves as victors. John Bryson and Robert Allen are among those Australian writers who present critical and satiric pictures of such businessmen from Australia.

Bryson's 'Whoring Around', a story from the book bearing the same title (1981), depicts how the protagonist looks for sexual adventures while in Japan on business. Japan again becomes the place where magical affairs could, or should happen and where Westerners can live in a fantasy world of double standards. Humphrey, the protagonist, now an Honorary Treasurer of an exclusive tennis club, recollects his business trip to Japan. Even before his arrival, he tries to put his fantasies about women into practice at the first stop in Hong Kong. For Humphrey, to achieve sexual conquest is a way to show his virility, a form of revenge against his dominant and sarcastic wife as well as a reward for all his hard work.

Humphrey's obsession comically diverts to various mishaps, including an old masseuse, with 'a wash-house authority' just like his aunt, and an American prostitute who takes him around in Tokyo, from a casino to a strip show. Such infatuation can be fatal to some and Humphrey hears of the tragi-comical death of an Australian man who accompanied young football players in their sexual orgies in Japan. Humphrey's 'ambition' in Japan does not amount to anything significant. Instead, he experiences 'merely fragments of decay that made him apprehensive and wary', and eventually he realises that his place is not next to a prostitute who is known to doormen and card-sharps and whose body is known to the businessmen of 30 countries, but back in Australia (Bryson 1981:153). The author Bryson is a lawyer-turned writer and perhaps through his observations of the Australian businessmen, he tries to portray satirically some of the negative aspects of Western businessmen, with Japan providing the backdrop.

Robert Allen, on the other hand, writes about such businessmen's opportunities more sympathetically from his own observations and experiences, thus giving a realistic feel to the encounters between Australians and the Japanese. In his *Tokyo no Hana* (1990), he depicts the education of an Australian called Andrew Paton into Japanese society, mainly on the topic of *hana*—the 'flowers'—of the floating world. Paton's instructor is a plump old Japanese lady in kimono called Nakajima-*sensei*, his Japanese teacher. Through their comical interactions, he learns about both Japanese customs and Japanese society. Although Paton is an outsider who does not try to become one of the locals, being a rather adaptable man in 'exotic places', he does not intend to be totally outside, either. He finds himself 'starting again from the bottom of the cultural ladder in a society' (Allen 1990:1), a typical position for most outsiders from overseas in a seemingly homogeneous Japanese society. Paton's interest seems to lie in determining how to maintain a balance between committing oneself and distancing oneself to take as much advantage as possible of the status of outsider. While being guided by his instructor in various places and situations, Paton seizes whatever opportunities present themselves.

Paton observes many other foreigners in Japan, single and married, businessmen and their families. For many, Japan still remains somewhere far from home where the rules are different and especially, an 'Illicit Space where serial sex with unequal partners was what a Western man could expect' (Allen 1990:188). Like Bryson's presentation, Allen's Australian businessmen are here described not as keen partners in business itself but rather as opportunists who are determined to take whatever they can from this different social context. This theme is not very different from what we have seen in earlier authors such as Dawe about a hundred years earlier (Chapter One), although Dawe's strong West-over-East power-relationship is no longer apparent.

In works of this time, Japanese business stories also begin to appear: examples include John Brown's *Zaibatsu* (1983) and Peter Corris's crime novel *The Japanese Job* (1992). Japanese businessmen in these novels are depicted mainly as 'invaders' of Australia and its nearby neighbours, again themes similar to the invasion scare novels early in the 20th century mentioned in Chapter Two, but without the dire consequences envisaged in the earlier works. These novels will be discussed later in this chapter.

Businessmen are not the only examples of characters depicted as viewing Japan as a land of fantasy. The tendency to regard Japan as a place where extraordinary things can happen, where different standards can apply and where one can move beyond one's ordinary self back home, can be observed in other writings. Ross Davy, in his novel *Kenzo: A Tokyo Story* (1985), tells the story of free attitudes towards homo-and hetero-sexuality among both Japanese and Europeans (Australian and American). As Broinowski points out, *Kenzo* may perhaps be among the first novels in Australian literature to describe homosexual lovers (1992:184). Because his characters do not belong to the 'normal' elements of society and their associated codes of behaviour in Japan, the author is able to let his characters behave more freely. However, at the same time it appears that the author does not feel completely comfortable in describing Japanese homosexuality as the title character, Kenzo, dies in the middle of the novel, leaving behind his homosexual lover. The central character is then taken by an Australian language teacher called Linda.

Linda comes under scrutiny as one of the many foreigners who go to Japan 'to get away from modern narcissism', where one has to have reasons and explanation for everything and with everyone trying to psychoanalyse themselves or become members of fanatic cults, therapy or self-help groups (Davy 1985:23). In Zen, Linda thinks she finds her answer, but Kenzo sees it as 'just a long or short passing phase' for her. Foreigners in Japan seek novelty as an alternative to their own meaningless existence. *Kenzo* thus depicts 'freelance' foreigners, escapees of Western society in Japan in the 1980s, as looking for the answer or solution for their fantasies, only to find that they cannot belong to either side.

Another author who chooses Japan as a place for self-discovery is Geraldine Hall. In her *Talking to Strangers* (1982) the protagonist Ebba, who is at her prime at the age of 49 and who is torn between family claims, both from her husband

and her mother, finds an opportunity to explore her true self alone in Japan. With English and American seducers providing the cue, she is able to step out of her old self, gain new insight and start to become an independent person. Japan here provides the female protagonist with the latitude and atmosphere to discover herself, something she cannot do in her own society in Australia.

The author, Hall, travelled widely in Europe and Asia, as did her predecessor Rosa Praed. Both of their protagonists are critical of Australia and Western society in general, including complaints about the Australian male who is described as 'a drunk, a snob, and a lout, having no idea beyond racing and the stock exchange and treating women like chattels' (Hall 1982:82). Unlike Praed, however, Hall does not extensively explore the Japanese in her story. Her novel is set in special places of symbolic importance such as the area near the Imperial Palace in Tokyo and the exquisite resort of Hakone, places which are described by Ebba as 'quiet charming, polite, silent, neat and clean'. They are not usual places for 'ordinary' Japanese, either. Hall's aim evidently does not lie in observing and describing what is different, but rather, Japan is simply adopted as a unique place, where despite the modern age, a Western woman can feel and act in a way free of the social codes of Australia, where men are still dominant.

Besides the temporary visitors, there are those who stay in Japan for an extended period of time, observing the differences between people and society here and back at home and in the process rediscover themselves. One such author, Ann Nakano, was a British journalist for the *Mainichi Daily News* in Japan for ten years before becoming a writer in Australia. Nakano tells a life-story in *Bit Parts* (1985) of a Western woman in Japan, of how she, as the 'Other' in an alien country, copes with both work and private life. In this epistolary novel, in which a great deal seems to be autobiographical, Nakano's protagonist Katherine undergoes several difficult phases—her brief and unsuccessful marriage to a Japanese man, unstable employment in journalism, a fragile relationship with another foreign correspondent and a subsequent unwanted pregnancy. Her Catholic faith causes her internal conflict about the idea of abortion, which eventually leads to the birth of her son and single-motherhood.

Through these events, Nakano's protagonist reveals fundamental changes in human relationships in the modern era—such as casual affairs between men and women, the tendency to avoid or be reluctant to have a family, the 'capitalistic indifference' (Nakano 1985:42) of so-called friends to one another, and so on. Japan as the background, and especially its capital city, Tokyo, may have helped to emphasise these events and their consequences. Katherine admits that things are exceptional in Japan: 'Japan is a haven for illusionists. We foreigners living on the periphery of Japanese society may be what we please' (Nakano 1985:4). They are away from normal Western codes and they are able to act more spontaneously and freely. Tokyo, as Katherine puts it, 'destratifies' them and makes them equal. She is thus enabled to do things she would not normally do, such as go out with Steve, who is from a different social class (he belongs to the propertied, upper-middle class) and therefore someone whom she probably would not have met back home.

Katherine's attitudes towards Japan and the Japanese may be typical of those who come and stay in Japan. She thinks English-speaking foreigners are valued, even though they may have no other qualification or reasons to be there, simply because they are able to sell their language (Nakano 1985:46). This belief leads to her cynical comment about the Japanese when she concludes that Japan is 'the land of cultural transvestites, dressing up as Westerners when really beneath it all they are good old scrutible Orientals' (Nakano 1985:8–9). She regards Japan as 'a culturally unstable and spiritually poor country', as, according to the author, Mother Theresa has put it (Nakano 1985:9). Katherine's initial motive for staying in Japan was to get away from the class-system and her unhappy family background in Derby, England. However, without any real effort to immerse herself in the new society, Katherine finds she is still alone and trapped by what she thinks she has left behind.

As the title shows, Katherine has to 'pick up the shattered parts of her personality' (cover blurb) while Japan again provides a setting. However, unlike Kata's story, *Someone Will Conquer Them*, as we saw in Chapter Six, Katherine's story is self-centred, more like a story of a woman's battles with herself, with scant interest in the 'Other'. Nakano does not allow Katherine to observe or understand Japan and the Japanese. The easier it becomes (with increasingly fluid travel and borders) to live in countries very culturally different from ones own, the less individuals seem to appreciate the opportunities they have to experience and understand those countries. Katherine's character highlights this phenomenon. The aim of this novel is not substantial descriptions of cross-cultural contact but rather of the friction between the central character and everyone else, with Japan simply providing a unique backdrop.

Another woman's story in the 'struggle with self' genre, set in an earlier period, is *Sayonara My Friend Love Annie* (1994) by Charlotte Manessen Mori. This is the author's memoir about her friend Annie; both are of Dutch origin and both lived in Indonesia before and during the Second World War. In the form of correspondence consisting mainly of letters written over 13 years by Annie to the author, the book describes how Annie meets Osamu, a civilian Japanese engineer working for the war-time Japanese government in Indonesia, how they form a relationship and then secretly marry. When the war is over, Annie accompanies Osamu to Japan and there her second battle for life begins in a totally alien atmosphere.

The difficulties experienced by Annie are well chronicled throughout the book, from living in Japan as a female foreigner married to a Japanese in the turmoil of the war's aftermath, with scarce food and goods, to being troubled by ill-health due to tuberculosis. In the closed Japanese society, she often experiences 'culture shock' and Japanese notions about abortion provide one such example. As seen in Kata's and Nakano's stories, the author reflects on the more practical and less guilt-filled attitudes towards abortion in Japan, an urgent issue to these female authors, which in turn leads them to reflect on their own culture's social and religious morality as well as their own feelings.

Annie's children, with half-Japanese and half-European heritage, cause anxiety and worry for her, as it is not yet a time when Japan is ready to accept such crossbreeds. Both Annie and her children suffer from alienation even from Osamu's own family, while Osamu himself is too busy supporting a big family to concern himself with their feelings.

Annie's observations of Japan and the Japanese are often bitter and penetrating. Their sense of humour is very different from hers—her jokes are not appreciated and the Japanese become 'either offended or puzzled, sometimes bewildered' (Manessen Mori 1994:187). The Japanese people around her are all private, formal and reserved. They are so group-oriented that it seems to her that such deeds as *seppuku/harakiri* (ritual disembowelment) or their excessive drinking may represent forms of 'self-denial' that are fundamental in this society (Manessen Mori 1994:84). A Japanese phrase, '*shikata-ga-nai*' (cannot be helped by oneself), strikes Annie as typical, something that is also noted by other authors—Nakano, Kata and Porter, for example, who also lived among the Japanese for extended periods of time.

Before she and her family can migrate to Australia, Annie dies. Her wish is denied because of the Australian government's immigration policy at the time. The author decided to make Annie's story public in 1973, although it was not published until 1994, almost 30 years after Annie's death. Like certain war memoirs, stories that touch sensitive nerves like this one are sometimes delayed for many years before they become known to a wider reading audience.

In 1947, at about the same period as Annie's story, an Anglican priest and pacifist called Frank Coaldrake went to Japan with his wife as 'the first Australian civilians to enter Japan after the War' (Coaldrake 2003:cover blurb). They opened a Christian mission in Odawara and during this period kept rare documents of their observations of Japan and the Japanese soon after the war—newsletters, letters and articles together with photographs. It was not until 2003 that these materials were published as *Japan from War to Peace: The Coaldrake Records 1939–1956* by their son who had been born in Japan. Such stories reveal rare glimpses of cross-cultural contacts at the grass-roots level soon after the war.

Elizabeth Kata again took Japan as the setting for her stories after *Someone Will Conquer Them* (1962), in which she described what it was like to live with the Japanese during and postwar with the master–subordinate relationship reversed. If *Someone Will Conquer Them* is a direct evocation of Kata's own experience, her later work was more detached and controlled. A long novel called *Kagami* (1989) depicts three generations of a scholar's family of the Samurai clan, before and after the Meiji Restoration (1868). The author's aim in the novel seems to be to show how a person, family, clan or whole society, despite being caught within the old traditions, is forced to change as the tide turns in Japan and new knowledge and abundant goods and materials are introduced from the West. While they may still worship mythical Mt Fuji and value the continuation of the family name, there emerges a new breed of Japanese who try to break out of the old mould. Examples in the story include a young man who tries to cut across a feudal lord's procession and is put to the sword, an ex-samurai who sees the limit of the power of such swords and who starts a business, a young woman of the higher class who tries to escape the ancient system by mixing with European visitors and a nouveau riche man who buys the title of nobility after the class system of the Edo period collapses. *Kagami* may be the first novel by an Australian author where only Japanese characters appear. Based on her own experiences among the Japanese, Kata seems confident in dealing with them as a people during one of the most dramatic and dynamic periods of their history, from the 19th to 20th century, when Japan opened itself to the world.

One of Kata's short stories on Japan, published earlier than *Kagami*, also reflects on Japan in the early 20th century. This was a time when scholars such as James Murdoch were actively involved in educating Japanese students and Japanese society was more open and eager for foreign influence than the period just before the Second World War. The characters of Kata's story, 'The House on the Hill', from *With Kisses on Both Cheeks* (1981), nostalgically depicts a family's life in Yokohama. The story follows an English man and his Japanese wife living with their son, his Russian wife and her parents from Manchuria, as well as their grandchildren, a Chinese cook and a Japanese assistant. This embodiment of the harmony of East–West relationships simply collapses during the earthquake of 1923, which is then followed by a period when Japan starts to look inward.

A more recent resident in Japan, Roger Pulvers, writes about Japan and the Japanese from a different point of view, a difference that may derive from his own culturally rich experiences. Born in the United States into a Jewish family, educated both in the United States and Poland and fluent in both Polish and Russian, Pulvers eventually became an Australian citizen. Pulvers taught in Japan and Australia and wrote novels and plays and directed them. As a frequent resident in Japan for over 20 years after 1967, Pulvers had the chance to observe all kinds of Japanese, and as an outsider, he was able to analyse them and their behaviour, and use them in his stories.

In *The Death of Urashima Taro* (1980), Pulvers uses the Cowra breakout during the Pacific War and its consequences in present Japanese society to describe a particular group of Japanese who express a strong degree of racial prejudice and have not fully accepted that Japan was defeated during the war. Here Pulvers proceeds to raise the problematic issue concerning the responsibility of the Showa Emperor for the Pacific War. The protagonist, Ron, a correspondent from the Australian Broadcasting Corporation, tries to solve the murders that occurred during the Cowra uprising and discovers a plot concerning how the war should be ended to protect Japanese society. As an outsider trying to adopt an insider's view, Ron's observations of the Japanese system, reveal how difficult it is to do such a thing. For Westerners including Ron, 'everything is logic, thinking, the mind'. For the Japanese, however, 'everything is felt... [e]ven the mind is felt,' and Ron is denied access to the people he wants to interview because no matter how long he stays in Japan, he 'will never be a Japanese or understand [their] *nasake* (compassion, kindness, mercy)' (Pulvers 1980:44). This denial of outsiders by the Japanese is often noted by other authors too, including Kata, Nakano, and Caroline Shaw who will be discussed later in this chapter.

This belief by the Japanese that they cannot be understood by outsiders, nor can they understand the outsiders themselves, is apparent when outsiders try to become 'insiders'. However, at the same time, many authors note Japan's desire to be seen as equal to Western society. This may be one of the reasons why criticism of Japan by outsiders is widely read in Japan, as Pulvers points out in his *General Yamashita's Treasure* (1994:15).

When Ron's attempt to uncover information about the murder cases, past and present, reaches the sensitive question about Japanese motives for the war, his attempt meets all kinds of obstacles. He realises that '[t]he Japanese must never be confronted with the truth. If they are they will withdraw to the periphery, leaving nothing at the centre where all cause and responsibility reside' (Pulvers 1980:96). As Broinowski points out, Pulvers's novel is like a 'surrealistic masked drama' (Broinowski 1992:71) and Ron's fear is not caused by certain objects, but rather by some ambiguous and vague entity—a mixture of Japanese tradition, history and ethos, which seems to withold truth from the outsiders. He is lost and left for 'dead' as an outsider who wanted to know too much.

Pulvers's *General Yamashita's Treasure* (1994), written soon after *The Death of Urashima Taro*, was first translated and published in Japan in 1986. This novel, again comically narrated, also adopts a war-related topic, this time a feud between an Australian and a Japanese from the time of the occupation of Japan. Using a form of slapstick comedy, the author allows his Japanese protagonist Hirose to reflect on the war and its aftermath.

Hirose was an interpreter, a go-between for those in control and their subordinates during and after the war—for Japan in the prisoner-of-war camp and for the allied forces during the occupation of Japan and the Korean War. He regards himself as a tool of the perpetrator, presenting himself as 'a victim, used by one side against another...[a] man dies, the executioner vanishes, and I alone, the interpreter, retain the memory' (Pulvers 1994:170).

Having been tormented by this burden of being the middleman, Hirose takes his revenge on Major Stick who prides himself on being an expert on Japanese culture after the war, profiting from the Japanese appetite for self-criticism and from ex-lieutenant-colonel Kakuta, who in war-time Manila, hides treasure that he confiscated in the Philippines. By killing both of them, Hirose is finally able to end the war within himself. In this novel, Pulvers examines the Pacific War from the Japanese point of view; his attempt to gain an inside perspective is now welcomed in Australia, where a multicultural viewpoint had by the 1980s become politically and socially accepted.

Another group of people who stayed in Japan for a period of time and who wrote about their impressions of the country and its people were university academics. Such descendants of James Murdoch include Humphrey McQueen, David Myers and Robin Gerster. Apart from their own academic education and research, these authors are able to write about their honest views of Japanese universities as institutions and as working places, and the people working and studying there. McQueen's detailed and insightful observation of Japan, based on his conscientious diary of almost every day in the record of his two years' stay as a visiting Professor at Tokyo University, was published as *Tokyo World: An Australian Diary* (1991). Myers's experiences during his occasional visits to Japan are turned into two collections of comical stories, *Cornucopia Country: Satiric Tales* (1991) and *Storms in a Japanese Teacup: Satirical Tales* (1996).

In his *Legless in Ginza: Orientating Japan* (1999), the most recent of the above books, Gerster sets out to give an 'idiosyncratic picture of Japan', thus making the book 'part travel, part personal and professional memoir, cultural study' (cover blurb) as well as a study of the travel experience itself. As an invited professor at Tokyo University from 1996 to 1998, Gerster's description of Japan ranges from the tiny apartment for public servants in Chiba prefecture in which he resided, to the overcrowded commuter trains and drinking places in the middle of Tokyo.

Gerster's reason to be in Japan as an academic was not for 'fun and profit', for such a motive would easily 'fall prey to Orientalist fancies of the gorgeous East'; rather, his observations show how Japan, 'that paradigm of the 'politically incorrect', continues to stump even the most zealous post-colonialist' (Gerster 1999:12). Gerster has travelled to Japan simply for 'a change as well as a challenge'. Like McQueen, whose reason for his visit was 'to see Australia better' (McQueen 1991:12), Gerster finds himself confronting his 'Australianness' when he wants to get away from it. Like anyone in a foreign country, he becomes a representative for his own country. He becomes concerned about how the news on Australia (almost always bad while he is there, including the massacre at Port Arthur in Tasmania, the 'stolen generation' story and Prime Minister John Howard's reaction to the Wik judgment) is presented from only one perspective (Gerster 1999:13). But he notes too, how the same is true for Australian news about Japan, as 'Australian journalists have been prominent in promoting a gloomy picture of Japan...beset by a succession of calamities, natural and ecological, economic, social and political' (Gerster 1999:106). Both countries are forced to look mainly at negative images of each other as portrayed by journalists, because such stories offer sensational and eye-catching journalism. This is similar to the image of Japan as scary enemy-invader portrayed in the early 20th century. Eventually, 'some things become clearer when seen from a distance' and his stay in Japan becomes a 'ritual of reassurance' of Australia, as well as of Japan (Gerster 1999:232).

Gerster makes it clear that he is not an insider and cannot even dream of becoming one. Also, without speaking Japanese, he finds it hard and agrees with Harold Stewart when he says 'expatriates in Japan exist in a "kind of social vacuum"' (Gerster 1999:221). However, again as Stewart notes, Gerster becomes an 'onlooker from the sidelines...but the observer sees most of the game' (Gerster 1999:221); and despite his lack of the Japanese language, Gerster observes Japan and tries to define it as an outsider who has worked for a time within the Japanese institutional system.

Gerster seems to reach a conclusion that the image of Japan is an elusive, ever-changing one. He cites Marilyn Ivy's opinion on Japan, that it 'appears ubiquitous, nomadic, transnational by virtue of the nation's global economic presence...[but] Japan's economic expansiveness is countered by a "national inwardness", so that the country often seems to reinscribe old distinctions between "East" and "West"' (Gerster 1999:83). However, he refuses to delineate the country this easily. For Gerster, Japan 'challenges the representational "hegemony" exercised by the Occidental imagination over the Oriental world... Its elusive character, by turns brazenly "Western" and inscrutably "Eastern", intrigues, perplexes and finally irritates the hell out of foreign observers' (Gerster 1999:84). Furthermore. he cites observations from people as varied as Basil Hall Chamberlain in the 19th century to the *Lonely Planet* guide books of the late 20th century to suggest that the West has difficulty in forgiving Japan for outgrowing its old and traditional image to become industrialised and financially successful. He suggests that the West has tried to impose its own favourite pictures on how it thinks Japan should be.

Japanese characters seen in Australian society

As Australian society becomes more ethnically diverse, more Japanese characters are included in Australian stories, as either major or minor figures. In past Australian writings, the Japanese were always a special topic, and such writing was often specially categorised. Later, in the 1980s and 1990s, a Japanese presence in Australian society gradually became a common phenomenon and it was not unusual to have Japanese characters appear in Australian writing.

There are some works which inevitably retain earlier images of Japan, for example, the Japanese as invaders of Australia, but by this time they are not physical or political invaders but economic invaders. Peter Carey's novel *Illywhacker* (1985), follows the saga of three generations in Australia and ends with the protagonist, Herbert Badgery's grandson Hisao becoming a worldwide salesman of Australian animals when a Japanese company takes over their pet shop. Carey here draws on patterns in Australian business history, when the first generation, typified in Herbert Badgery, tries to produce and sell nationally-made aeroplanes and cars, but Australians want to buy British or American products. The second generation is more practical, and Charles, Herbert's son, opens a pet shop selling exotic animals overseas, an enterprise supported by American capital. As representative of the third generation, Hisao is an efficient salesman, not only of animals but also of the human resources of Australia, with capital support from the Mitsubishi Company. The author himself was once an advertiser in the business community and so is able to describe Australian dependence on foreign capital realistically , especially on Japan in the postwar years. He is able to simplify and exaggerate for humorous and satirical effect.

The Japanese and their business dealings in Australia become the topic of other writers, too, including John Brown in his novel *Zaibatsu* (1983). Brown had 27 years of experience in Papua New Guinea, working initially with the Australian Administration and then with the PNG government, before becoming a full-time writer in Australia. He examines the Japanese passion and persistent interest in the island both during and after the war. Although Japanese characters are presented as 'evil' and with nefarious ambitions, while the Dutch and Australians are 'good', the issue becomes complicated because of the local Papua New Guinean unrest over the annexation of West Papua (Irian Jaya) to Indonesia. Australia, as well as Japan, is partly responsible for the unrest, as both countries had their own political and economic agendas in mind, as shown by their reluctance to intervene. In *Zaibatsu* (meaning a conglomerate), Japan's military power in the Asia–Pacific region is emphasised and while the Japanese characters are not given full character descriptions, they still play an important role in the story.

A more direct invasion by the Japanese in Australia is depicted in John Lynch's novel *The Proposal* (1995). Lynch was a senior public servant, and later a consultant whose speciality was tourism and trade for many years. The author uses his knowledge of the relationship between Australia and Japan as a resource for his story. In the novel, a place called Acacia Point has been targeted by the Japanese to be 'developed' into a big resort. The Japanese side, again a big company with cold-blooded entrepreneurs, tries to take over the place. On the Australian side, Lynch presents an assortment of people with a variety of motives, including a stubborn ex-prisoner-of-war parish priest who is against any development, Aborigines who worship the place as sacred, an eco-conscious artist who wants publicity for herself, a real-estate developer hoping for as much profit as possible, a Chinese resident who believes the opposition is based on racism, bureaucrats in Canberra who need the investment and a journalist who wants a sensational scoop to further her own career.

The Japanese in *The Proposal* are described generally as being one-dimensional; their role is principally that of economic invaders. However, the Japanese sub-protagonist called Kurosawa, the head of the entrepreneurs, goes beyond ordinary negotiation and talks with opposing Australians as an individual. In the end, after becoming acquainted with the local residents, Kurosawa decides to leave and Acacia Point is saved from being a Japanese resort. This novel was published at the time of the unsuccessfully planned multifunction-polis in Adelaide and a number of other proposed resorts, thus revealing a degree of anxiety about Japanese development in Australia at the time.

Peter Corris's crime novel *The Japanese Job* (1992), one of the Pokerface series with Ray Crawley as the detective, also adopts the theme of Japanese ambition in Australia. The Japanese plan to build a skyscraper in Brisbane is halted with the murder of the head of the Japanese company by a group called 'the Diggers'. Crawley investigates the case, experiencing interference from both Canberra and from the Japanese. He is aided by a Japanese–American woman called Kurosawa, typically young, beautiful and fluent in English, just like the Japanese woman helping the secret agent in *Little Blue Pigeon* almost a hundred years earlier (Chapter One). Although the Japanese characters are once again described from a one-sided perspective and conveniently named after internationally famous real figures (like Kurosawa or Ohira), they start to interact with Australians, thus offering more fully-rounded, informed images to Australian readers, even if they are still seen as villains. At the end of the story, Crawley solves the murder, but he is unable to uncover the whole affair, for both he and his enemies are puppets of the higher ranks and victims of the company, the governments and the nations.

The Pacific War still casts a shadow over the story of the relationship between Australia and Japan. The 'Diggers' in Corris's novel, for example, feel very bitter about a second wave of 'invasion' by the Japanese after the war and suspicion and antagonism remain regarding the former enemy. In David Malouf's *The Great World* (1990) two protagonists, Digger Keen and Vic Curran go to war, become acquainted with each other and form a strong bond of mateship. Nourished by their experience as prisoners of war, their relationship lasts into the 1980s. As a result of the harshness of Japanese camp life, their bond remains strong even though their paths take very different directions in the postwar period. In describing the POW camp, the author acknowledges that he owes much to such memoirists and writers as Stan Arneil, Hank Nelson and Edward Dunlop. He has incorporated several episodes from their stories into his own to give a vivid picture of two Australian men during the war.

Malouf himself had no war experience. Despite the vivid descriptions of the hard life and suffering in Malaya, Thailand and Burma during the war, he retains a balanced view and does not portray all the Japanese characters as villains. The prisoner-of-war experience seems to offer a chance for both protagonists to recognise and develop their own ideas and goals, which eventually affect their life after the war. Vic, who was young and dependent on Digger, becomes a tough survivor and tries against all odds to climb up the social ladder, while Digger tries to suppress his feelings and live quietly, with the only consolation being from his deceased soldier-mate's sister-in-law. While Japan and the Japanese are not the main topics in Malouf's novel, they provide a place and time in the story for the characters to develop, again against a background of suffering and deprivation.

Steven Carroll writes about a relationship between an Australian interpreter and a Japanese woman during the occupation of Japan in *Momoko: A Novel of Betrayal* (1994). In the story a naïve young Australian called Spin, once dressed in the uniform of authority as a member of the occupation force, tries to conquer everything including the Japanese girl's full attention. He has 'never known the onset of defeat, is full of enthusiasm and liveliness and feeling they have moral superiority and an odd sense of power' against the occupied (Carroll 1994:49–50).

Momoko, educated in pre-war London, has returned to Japan and is overwhelmed by the bombing of Tokyo by 'B-29' American bombers, which burned 40% of Tokyo and claimed almost 100,000 people's lives. She retains detached, cynical views of both enemy and ally, West and East, as well as old traditions and the new system. The young man and woman form a relationship, which for Momoko is an act of liberation, but Spin's obsessive and possessive attitudes soon invite disillusionment and disappointment. Spin, despite his role as an interpreter who should be able to understand both sides and become a go-between, is unable to see the other side clearly. When Momoko leaves him he believes he has been betrayed, when in fact it is Spin who has betrayed her trust in him by failing to answer to Momoko's expectations. A complex power relationship is evident here; however it does not simply work at the individual level. Carroll's story shows the difficulty of forming a relationship without knowing the 'Other' well.

During the 1980s and 1990s, more writings featuring Japanese characters, which were not necessarily war-related, started to appear. Authors such as Brian Castro, Nancy Corbett, Don'o Kim and Clive James tried to use Japanese as leading or subsidiary characters in their novels. Among them, Kim, originally from North Korea, is one of the very few Asian writers writing in English in Australia from the 1970s, while Castro has a complex and 'hybrid' family background (1995:6–7).

Kim's earlier novel called *Password* (1974) was about a Chinese intellectual who, after the fall of Nanking, finds himself in a dilemma when he comes under the Japanese military's command. It is one of few novels published in English in Australia, alongside Kata's *Kagami*, which deals exclusively with Asians. In *The Chinaman* (1983), Kim tells the story of a Japanese student in Australia and the physical and emotional hardship he experiences during a voyage on a yacht with other Australians. Jo-bu, the protagonist, is nicknamed Joe because Dean, an Australian taking Japanese lessons from Joe, maintains: 'in this fair country of ours, we've got to have fair sounding names, don't we?' (Kim 1983:12). As this is also a time when Japanese investment in Australia is high, Joe is forced to listen to crude comments about Japan and the Japanese by the other Australian crew. Furthermore, he finds it very uncomfortable to hear the crew's cry 'kill the chinaman' when a fish called 'Chinaman', the most poisonous one in the reef, appears (this incident provides the reason for the novel's title—a novel whose protagonist is actually Japanese.)

Eventually Joe realises several things: 'that not shared but separate realities make living together possible, and that not sharing but the destiny of that march itself is the primary question' (Kim 1983:71). He further realises that his predecessor, Lee, who wrote about his experiences as an early Asian in Australia, is right about what it is like for Asians in Australia: 'a revolution can change a government overnight, but what revolution would change the soul of man, what could change the shape of [their] love?' In the book Joe is reading, Lee insists that 'the issue is not how not to be a racist but how to be a racist well,' because racism is part of the ability to discern differences that make the idea of an individual possible (Kim 1983:115). The idea challenges views about a bland convergence of cultures and personalities in an increasingly interactive world.

This story has double protagonists, with Lee's story incorporated into Joe's. Both tell their own tales about how they cope with the racism they experience and how they survive in mainstream Australian society with its predominantly Western influence. Lee, trapped in his own pessimism, can find no way to solve his dilemma and his attempt to 'undermine the Western culture' through his writing fails, resulting in his suicide. His reader, Joe, is still searching, but is far from finding the answer. In fact, the people around Joe are also in an ambiguous state of mind. They are vague about whether they are content being Australian and thus try to escape their reality by cruising on a boat in the reef or visiting a Buddhist congregation in the mountains behind Cairns. As the name of the yacht 'Quovadis'—whither goest thou?—shows, the novel seems to suggest that people both of the mainstream and of the periphery keep asking for guidance, to find their own place in the contemporary world.

Problematic relations between East and West are a major topic of Brian Castro's novel *Stepper* (1997). His story is based on a real spy called Richard Sorge from Germany who served as a secret agent for the Soviet Union in Japan in the 1930s and was eventually caught and executed in 1944. In Castro's novel, Stepper believes that the East–West relationship can be best formed in the relationship between man and woman and he practises and uses his inter-personal and seductive skills in this mission. Without claiming any concrete nationality and identity (although he does his job for communism's sake), Stepper is always on the border, coming and going between East and West, Japan and Germany and the USSR. He is solitary and even when the only woman in whom he finds a kindred spirit wants a child, he refuses because it 'will be a hybrid. Won't belong anywhere; like [him]. Look damned funny...The world's not right for that yet' (Castro 1997:147). As a spy operating in and between cultures, Stepper does not belong fully to either side, nor does he claim any identity, trying to deceive both sides for his own survival. Set in Japan before and during the war and using Japanese and other nationalities as characters, *Stepper* offers another example of the diversity, both in themes and settings, in contemporary Australian literature.

Clive James's novel *Brrm! Brrm!* (1991) is set in England, with a young Japanese man as its main character. Suzuki is the butt of many jokes because of both his name, (which is the same as the motorbike company) as well as his inadequacy with the English language. James portrays Suzuki as a person of contradictions: as a graduate of Tokyo University he is an intellectual, but he looks 'dumb' because of his slowness in spoken English. He has pride in Japan and the East but wants to become Western. He is polite and patient with English people but ignorant of history, such as the atrocities committed by the Japanese during the war. Through his martial arts skills he is strong, but he is always picked upon and bullied because he is a foreigner. He seems to gain favours easily from girls but ends up becoming obedient to them. In these ways, James tries to portray the incomprehensible Japanese from many different angles.

While this novel is a comedy, behind the comic scenes James seems to raise serious subjects, such as the continuing racism in England, including that by police officers against Asians, as well as by the Japanese character's own prejudices as revealed in his comments about Europeans. James's father, like Robin Gerster's, had battle experiences with the Japanese. James's father was a prisoner-of-war in Changi. Nevertheless, James, like Gerster, tries to keep a sense of humour and a fair and balanced attitude towards his characters, partly because of his 'fondness for Japan' and his ability to use his imagination to record the impact of the fire raids and bombs over Japanese towns and cities.[60] As with Malouf and Pulvers, we see the shadow of war cast over James's novel. However, James, as a well-travelled member of the postwar generation, also seems able to maintain a humorous and sympathetic attitude towards the Japanese.

Japanese characters are sometimes employed with less restraint and hesitation by female authors. One such writer is Nancy Corbett. Iin her 'boldly imaginative' (Wilde, Hooton & Andrews 1994:192) novel called *Floating* (1986), two female characters, Australian and Japanese, are destined to meet because of their former lives during the Edo Period (from 17th to mid-19th century) in Japan. Hannah, an Australian dancer, realises she is a reincarnation of a *Tayu*, the highest ranked courtesan with great dancing skills, while Hanako, a Japanese model, has also inherited a *Tayu*'s talents. Hannah's name sounds like *hana*, the Japanese name for flower, while Hanako's name means 'flower' thus symbolically linking them both to the 'floating world'. They inevitably fall in love with the same man and during the tug-of-war in their triangular relationship, they eventually realise that they share the same fate and recognise that they belong to each other.

Corbett juxtaposes the *Tayu's* episodes with contemporary ones, thus showing that women face difficulties in oppressive societies, be they in the 18th or the late 20th century. Examples include the refusal of Hanako's immigration application to Australia by the authorities because of her sex and age and the difficulty the *Tayu* faced at the '*Sekisho*'—a checkpoint designed to check female travellers in Japan two centuries earlier. This novel is a romance with Japanese tradition and history as its spice. It creates an exotic atmosphere of a fantasy world, into which an ordinary Australian woman enters. Although ideas of reincarnation and destiny may sound unrealistic in mainstream 21st century Australian society, the fact that a novel where Japanese characters—both past and present—are main characters, indicate dramatic changes in Australian society.

Another female writer who introduces a Japanese as a key character, is Caroline Shaw. In her Lenny Aaron crime series, *Cat Catcher* (1999) and *Eye to Eye* (2000), Dr Sakuno, Lenny's psychiatrist and Zen instructor, plays an important role in maintaining her mental stability as a detective. Lenny is a cat-catcher-detective in Melbourne and also an ex-police officer. She suffers from the effect of a traumatic attack by a criminal, in which her arm was injured. To relieve the trauma she takes a number of different drugs, mainly aspirin and other analgesics, a habit which is just on the verge of being illegal. In order to make herself less dependent on such drugs, she seeks guidance from the Japanese instructor.

This rather comical doctor–instructor Sakuno, who believes that 'to be the Japanese is the highest form of life on this planet', tries to teach Lenny how to become Japanese: by growing bonsai, drinking Japanese tea and meditating on *tatami* mats. The reason Lenny is attracted to Sakuno is because of his 'difference'. Sakuno values action more than discussion and does not give Lenny sympathy. A loner with a complicated background, including an abusive family, Lenny needs Sakuno's apparent indifference and honesty. Lenny's other neighbours include a hairdresser from Russia and a porn shop owner with a strong northern English accent. Sakuno fits easily into Melbourne city life, where many people like Lenny lose their orientation and seek guidance from other religions, thoughts and cultures.

Shaw visited Japan several times, with one of her visits subsidised by Asialink from Melbourne University. Travel grants like this seem to help authors such as Shaw who wish to experience the 'Other' and enable them to make the 'Other' part of their own culture and society.

Short stories and plays

As well as novels, there emerged a number of short stories and plays by Australian writers during the 1980s and 1990s which included Japan and the Japanese as their subject. These works show various authors' experiences in Japan and/or their contact with the Japanese, as well as their interest in things Japanese. Plays, being a physical art, produced for an audience, attract a different kind of attention from that of books. With the direct interaction of producers, directors and actors between Australia and Japan, supported by both public and private funds, Australian plays on Japan started to be performed in both countries, which often resulted in the publication of play scripts in book form.

As Bennett points out, against a backdrop of dramatic change caused by globalisation, advances in computer technology and the presence of more visual methods for mass audiences, writers in the 1980s and 1990s seem to try to 'dig deeply into their personal and communal experience to show continuities as well as discontinuities of contemporary living', by asking how one's sense of belonging and alienation is affected or how one's sense of identity becomes dislocated' (Bennett 2002:225). In such an atmosphere, some writers use Japanese places and people to help examine their own self and society in the concise form of short stories.

In a story called 'The Bonsai Nursery' (1989:1-6), Alison Dell sees rows of bonsai as the symbol of conformity in Japanese society and then superimposes her own childhood on this image. Bonsai is the art of restricting a plant's growth to a certain form that is supposed to represent a minimal and complete world in itself. She compares herself, an unconventional child, to bonsai which are thrown away because they outgrow such forms. Bonsai, an alien object different from her cultural background, is used as a means to recall the author's negative memories of herself growing up in Australia.

The word or concept of 'bonsai' is often used to represent a miniature image of Japan in short stories and Dianne Highbridge's 'A Bonsai Christmas on a Tokyo Tatami' is one such story. Her main character, Janet, is an English teacher in Japan, presumably in a big city like Tokyo or Osaka. She decides to give a Christmas party in her tiny apartment for her Japanese students and her non-Japanese friends who live in Japan. As a Christmas party held on *tatami* mats seems ill-fitting, so do the foreigners, including Janet, appear in Japan. Being a divorcee, Janet does not wish to return to Australia and yet finds it hard to become part of Japanese society. In Highbridge's story, feelings of the excluded 'Other' held by Australians and other Westerners in Japan, are emphasised.

Christmas in such an exotic setting as Japan is used in Chris Doran's story, 'Christmas Cake', too (1993:90–101). Doran's protagonist, a young Australian man, expresses his uneasy and helpless feelings in meeting an English-teaching Japanese woman. She considers herself an outcast in Japanese society, because she is too old to be married and feels left on the shelf like a Christmas-cake after Christmas Day. The protagonist himself is acutely aware that he does not belong there, that he is a kind of outcast, too, although that is where he has ended up.

Moya Ellis's 'Feathers' (1982:5–6) describes the decadent and destructive life of foreign girls working at bars in Japan. They are drifters in Japan, where they can earn easy money by selling their 'Otherness' as different sexual commodities. Pam Harvey writes about a woman's search for her lost brother, supposedly living like a hermit in Kyoto in 'Searching Kyoto' (1996:72–74). She is a photographer but realises the pictures of her brother do not convey what he really thinks and feels. She knows that away from home her brother might reveal his truer self, a person unknown to her and her family in Australia. These stories are narrated by expatriates, who are more interested in finding themselves than exploring the psyche of the Japanese. Their own 'Otherness' in Japan seems to provide the characters with the chance to look within themselves. But the more they try to find out, the less they become certain of who they are.

Sexual encounters between a person and his or her exotic 'Other' are still favoured topics. In 'Tatsuma-san' (1990:44–47), Bruce Grant, in a comical conversation between a professional Australian woman and a Japanese customer over the telephone, shows a new form of sexual conquest of East by West. The Japanese man is desperate for sympathy from the woman to fill the void in his family life, trying in vain to talk to her in his clumsy English. Although he is the customer, the professional woman dominates their brief liaison over the telephone line. In a comical setting, Grant's story seems to show the difficulty of forming a relationship in contemporary life between East and West, even between customers and professionals.

In Robert Drewe's 'Life of a Barbarian' (1989:147–167), the situation is reversed when a businessman from Sydney tries to recover from the disappointment of his shattered family life. Pond, the protagonist, is discouraged as he recalls his only son's decision to become a member of the Hare Krishna movement and his wife's associated bitterness. He seeks comfort from prostitutes when he goes to Japan on business, but is never given any sympathy, nor even pseudo-love. Japan was always the enemy to his father, even after the war and

Pond realises the same is true for the Japanese with regards to Westerners. Enmity does not end when war finishes. Although the geographical distance between Japan and Australia becomes shorter with rapid air travel, the mental distance between their inhabitants is not easily overcome.

The form of the short story seems to provide these travellers or expatriate writers with a chance to explore not only the Japanese but also themselves, or versions of themselves, in cross-cultural encounters. Such short stories record both the impact and impressions of the 'Other' as well as the reflection and redefinition of themselves.

Plays work in a similar way. Plays such as Pulvers's *Yamashita* (1981) and Thérèse Radic's *The Emperor Regrets* (1992) deal with recollections of the war between Australia and Japan, thus confirming that it is still an important subject in the Australia–Japan relationship. Radic employs the Showa Emperor Hirohito as one of her two main characters, with the other an Australian private. She lets them reflect on the Pacific War to examine the nature of 'honour, guilt and responsibility' (1992:foreword). The sensitive subject matter make such plays very difficult to produce in Japan. Judging by the reticence of Japan to explore parts of its war history, an apology for its actions remains but a distant possibility, much to the chagrin of some Australians, especially ex-prisoners-of war

A number of other plays with diverse topics have also appeared, ranging from a remake of Madame Butterfly by Daniel Keene in his *Cho Cho San* (1987) to a new type of play based on the contemporary relationship of Australia and Japan in tourism. As mentioned, Anna Broinowski describes the cultural gap between Australia and Japan in her play about an Australian guide for Japanese tourists in *The Gap* (1995). Being the daughter of Alison Broinowski, Anna Broinowski spent some time in Japan as a young woman when her mother was a diplomat at the Australian Embassy in Japan. The Australian guide, Alex, is annoyed by her Japanese boss (also female) of the travel agency and her demand for punctuality and accuracy, which to Alex seems to be typical of the Japanese. Eventually she realises that being a tour guide is delicate work and that she needs to be a 'buffer' for the Japanese tourists who encounter Australian ways for the first time. The 'middleman's burden' falls on such occupations in this period of globalisation.

After showing the mental wounds of his ex-prisoner-of-war experiences in *The Floating World* (see Chapter Seven), John Romeril has more recently revived the 18th century text of Monzaemon Chikamatsu, a playwright for Kabuki and Joruri—dramatic narratives—in the modern Australian environment. Romeril's play, *Love suicides*, being rather illogical and dreamlike in a way similar to Nancy Corbett's *Floating*, draws the protagonists together: a bankrupt Australian businessman and a Japanese bride-to-be engaged to the wrong man. Fate brings them together and leads them inexorably to their own end. A double suicide for love is not a popular subject in Western literature and this experimental play by Romeril, which was first produced in 1997 in Canberra, provides a stark new dimension in Australian drama.

The diversity of Australian authors, both visitors to Japan and recipients of Japanese visitors, as well as the diversity of genres, has given Australian literature many different ways to describe and imagine Japan and the Japanese. Political, economic, demographic and cultural changes in Australian society have allowed such diversity to grow and have encouraged more experimental works to be written. Short stories have given many writers a chance to test and tell their own experiences. Autobiographical writings have become more common during the 1980s and 1990s. Examples include Cynthia Menadue, the wife of a former Ambassador to Japan and her *Ambassador's Wife—Minshuku Tour*, which was translated and published both in Japan and in Australia in 1983. *Encounters with Japan: Twenty Extraordinary Stories* which was published in Japan and in Australia in 1994, shows multifarious experiences and responses to encounters with Japan. It provides relatively straight-forward ideas and opinions about Japan and its people.

Caroline Shaw admits to drawing on her experiences during her stay in Japan to create Dr Sakuno, one of the important characters in her novels. She further maintains that there are already Japanese in various occupations living in Australia and a Japanese Zen-instructor-psychiatrist does not look unnatural.[61] But Shaw does not believe that Dr Sakuno necessarily represents the Japanese as a whole.

Despite being few in number, since the 1980s the various experiences of and responses to Japan and the Japanese by Australian writers have resulted in the 'Other' being represented in more plural, complicated and inclusive ways. While certain stereotypes of the Japanese are still favoured in many stories, some authors seem to be confident in employing the Japanese as their main characters, thus breaking the power of repetition which is observed, as Said suggests, in typical Orientalist discourse. New pictures are now possible of the 'Other' (see Introduction). Australian writers have thus become cultural 'mediators' themselves and responding to contemporary situations and the atmosphere of the times, they represent Japan and the Japanese in their writings.

conclusion

The focus of this book has been on the nature and course of change in the description and portrayal of Japan and the Japanese in Australian literature from the beginning of the relationship between these countries in the late 19th century to the end of the 20th century. I have adopted Edward Said's Orientalist notion of the 'Other' and examined a range of stereotypes and patterns of ideas and images of the Japanese 'other' held by Australian writers. By examining the development and changes in these patterns and stereotypes in published literary texts over time, I have attempted to articulate the inter-related roles of Australia's literary, historical, political and social environments in the formation of such ideas and images. Through this process, this book has argued, authors play two roles. They are responsible for creating images of the 'Other', catering to their contemporary readers' interests and tendencies according to the contemporary social and ideological environment. At the same time, they can play a vital part in breaking down stereotypes, by showing novel and unexpected sides of the 'Other'. This book highlights the importance of the roles of literary authors and readers in the representation, formation and changing nature of Australian society.

My general aim of this book is to advance our understanding of how both general and specific literary images and representations of the Japanese, this particular 'Other', as expressed in various literary works, has changed over the course of the relationship between the two countries. Understanding how a nation of generally strange and 'unknown people' is perceived and interpreted in writings by Australians, can, in turn, shed some light on the way Australians see themselves and their place in the world.

This book has concentrated principally on prose narratives, especially novels, short stories and 'life stories' in the form of biographies, autobiographies and travelogues, but with the inclusion of some poems and plays when they have particular relevance. Fiction published since the turn of the 21st century, as well as poems and plays from the 19th century to the 21st century, provide a rich source of Australian images and ideas of Japan and the Japanese. The novel, with its wide scope for representing character, setting and plot, is of particular importance and this genre receives special attention.

One of the general conclusions that can be drawn is that the pattern of representation of the Japanese 'Other', initially developed at the beginning of contact between Australia and Japan at the end of the 19th century to the beginning of the 20th century, survived in a relatively intact form for many years, with significant elements continuing to be found in literature today. Early patterns of representation include the apparently contradictory figures of a young, exotic and vulnerable woman—like Madame Butterfly—and a demon-like masculine enemy. Phrases which have been used to describe traditional Australian notions of Japan, such as 'fears and phobias' (Meaney) and 'far east fallacy' (Broinowski), suggest extreme images of the 'Other', further suggesting that such simple and dichotomised images perhaps originate from ignorance, prejudice or convenience. The remarkable thing is that certain Australian authors, both women and men, have resisted the simplistic Madame Butterfly image of Japanese women and drawn more complex and interesting characters. Such writers identified in this book include Rosa Praed, Hal Porter, Don'o Kim, Roger Pulvers and Brian Castro.

These vivid and persistent images of the Japanese portrayed in Australian literature reveal how certain deeply implanted ideas about the 'Other' can become part of a nation's psyche. Such images and ideas formed in the mid-to-late 19th century, when colonial Australians tended to see Japan through transplanted 'British' eyes, set certain patterns and formulae which can be seen, with some variations, in later stories. The pre-Second World War works examined in Chapters One and Two, which contributed to the development of such patterns, often offer strong, deeply felt and uni-dimensional perceptions, written with a sense of confidence and authority. On the other hand, some of the works discussed in later chapters, (eg Chapters Six and Eight), are sometimes accompanied by a certain awkwardness in their attempts to portray the 'Other', resulting in rather unstable and less confident impressions. This is despite the fact that the environment in which they were written was more multicultural and flexible and their seemingly varied themes and subjects involving Japanese characters. This may be evidence that Australian authors in the late 20th century were still in a transitional stage where their writings were striving to extend beyond the boundary of the previously unknown to describe a more completely understood nation and people.

In an age of easier and more rapid communication, with greater opportunities for public and private interaction and physical and intellectual exchanges to learn about the customs and cultures of other parts of the world, there is room for Australian authors to narrate the 'Other' with more confidence. At the same time, it is also true that earlier authors, with direct contact and first-hand experiences of the often feared 'Other' enhanced their Australian narratives with some complex and comprehensive descriptions of the Japanese, which did not always depend on public preconceptions and prejudices. The only fallback is that these earlier authors used stereotypes to embellish their narratives.

As has often been said, Australia and Japan have very different origins, histories and cultures. The two nations are often seen as opposites. Both countries and their peoples are uniquely different and yet among these seemingly disparate characteristics, there can be observed some areas of commonality, some shared values. Literature has shown that many elements of human nature, expressed in variations of fear, hatred, passion, ambition, compassion or love, are shared by both sides.

Japan's exclusiveness, often pointed out in Australian literary works, has tended to keep external interest and knowledge at bay, thus hampering the opportunity to share experiences of 'commonness'. The myth of Japan's cultural 'homogeneity', held by its people, 'becomes the still centre into which cultural difference is continuously absorbed, consumed, and transformed' (Morris-Suzuki 1998:95). It is important to note that Australia also tried something similar through its pre-Second World War 'White Australia' policies, when it tried to establish a culturally exclusive nation. National or personal identity was often regarded as something simple and plain, each of which was compared and differentiated from opposites, or perceived enemies, during this period. However in the 21st century, as Morris-Suzuki has pointed out, such identities 'do not exist in isolation from one another. The present wave of globalisation is not simply a phase of shifting identity debates, but also an era in which many individuals find it more than ever necessary to live with multiple identities' (Morris-Suzuki 1998:184). More inclusive perspectives, both of what is classified as 'inside' and of 'outside' can lead to variety, and can help to diversify a nation's identity. Writings about the 'Other' will eventually become more multi-layered, too. In Australian writings on the Japanese, ideas of the 'Other' have also tended to be dominated by collective thinking. When this uniformity of views started to be undermined on both sides, individual writers gave their writings more complex delineations and contexts.

One of the most dramatic changes regarding Australians' quest for a distinctive identity may be seen in the country's geographical re-location of itself since the 1980s in the Asia–Pacific region. Although its strategic and mental ties with Europe and North America are still strong—especially with the USA in the early 21st century—since the official introduction of multiculturalism in the 1970s and the influx of more Asian migrants, economic and diplomatic ties have become closer with countries of the Asia–Pacific. Despite changes in governments, the notion of Australia as a nation in the Asia–Pacific has remained. This new orientation has been recognised in the publication of books such as the report produced by the Asian Studies Association of Australia (ASAA) called *Maximizing Australia's Asian Knowledge* (2002), Broinowski's *About Face: Asian Accounts of Australia* (2003) and the special edition of the journal *Meanjin* on the writings of Asian-Australians called 'Australasian' (2004).

In such an atmosphere, has the 'mapping' of Japan and the Japanese in the Australian psyche changed? Meaney's book on the relationships between Australia and Japan at the turn of the century, *Towards a New Vision: Australia and Japan through 100 Years*, shows how this 'odd couple', so different in cultural origin and so far apart geographically, can have a 'shared vision'; how both countries could 'take the initiative themselves, in co-operation with their neighbours, to produce a new regional order' (1999:140). After all their experiences, both negative and positive, Meaney insists that 'Australia's cultivation of the Japanese relationship is altogether novel and it has much to suggest generally about Australia's problems and possibilities in learning to live with Asia' (1999:140). In this 'cultivation', literature seems to reflect how much effort certain Australian writers and thinkers have put into paying attention to, observing and understanding the Japanese.

Chapters Three and Four documented the negative experiences between Australia and Japan, especially during their actual violent confrontation in wartime, as the first major opportunity—though a catastrophe for many on both sides—for Australians to really face the Japanese, the long-imagined foe. In what may seem like a contradictory statement, this also becomes the first time that many authors could write about the human side of the 'Other', thus providing a breakthrough in some previous firmly-set stereotypes of Australian literary convention. The tragic experience of the Pacific War remains strong in the collective memory, a fact that is still noted in many publications on the subject in the 21st century. Recent examples include: McKernan's *This War Never Ends: The Pain of Separation and Return* (2001), Probert and Probert's *Prisoners of Two Wars: An Australian Soldier's Story* (2001), Kelly's *The Flamboya Tree: Memories of a Mother's War-time Courage* (2002), Bullard and Tamura, eds., *From a Hostile Shore: Australia and Japan at War in New Guinea*, (2004) and Bullard's *Blankets on the Wire: The Cowra Breakout and its Aftermath* (2006).

While war is an extraordinary event, which can affect normal thinking and being, it has served as an opportunity for Australian writers to go beyond many clichéd descriptions of the 'Other'. It is ironic that the first major opportunity to have direct cross-cultural contact, to experience the 'unknown' and to attempt to understand the Japanese at the level of the ordinary person was through military confrontation. As Johnston points out, Australians discovered that '[the Japanese] are human just as we are' at the very moment they tried to destroy each other (Johnston 2004:ch6). As was discussed in Chapter Seven, ex-prisoner-of-war memoirists such as Ray Parkin and Russell Braddon, despite the hardship they experienced during the war, kept writing their stories after the war and eventually came to terms with their former enemy. Some of the titles show how these and later authors have reached reconciliation with their former feelings about the Japanese. Examples include Braddon's *End of a Hate* and Harrison's *The Brave Japanese*. In the last volume of his war-trilogy, *The Sword and the Blossom*, Parkin cites a *haiku* at the beginning of each part in order to describe his state of mind, thus acknowledging his former enemy's literature. As Sir Edward Dunlop suggests, a negative part of the shared history between Australia and Japan, such as the prisoner-of-war experience, should be discussed more freely, because 'until then [Australians] will remain prisoners of [their] own propaganda' (Dunlop cited in McQueen 1991:321).

Even after the economic 'bubble' in Asia burst and Japan as an economic lure had lost its former charm in the later years of the 20th century, books on Japan still continued to be published. The Japanese language was the most studied Asian language at tertiary level in 2001, with enrolments more than double those in 1988 (ASAA 2002:35). However, the first grass-roots level efforts in learning Japanese were probably made by the prisoners-of-war (cf. Chapters Four and Seven). Almost all memoirists cite the master-enemy's names, words and phrases, incorrect uses of the language included.[62] Despite occasional errors, it was new in Australian writings to include such alien phrases from the 'Other's language', and it provided another dimension to Australian literature.

Language is a crucial component of culture and the strangeness and incomprehensibility of the Japanese language can give Australian authors a novel view of their own first language, English. In works of the late 19th and early 20th century (cf. Chapters One and Two), Japanese characters, when they are 'eligible' to be given names and faces, almost always speak English in order to be 'promoted' in the narrative. Encountering a foreign 'Other' who happens to speak English can be an enormous relief and release, especially during tense times when survival depends on communication, as occurred on a day-to-day basis during the war. Harding in Lambert's *The Dark Backward* clearly describes how he could not help feeling released when he was able to speak with a Japanese interpreter-interrogator. Under the guise of 'gentle requests with an air of understanding' spoken by the Japanese in his own language, however, Harding later realises this is an introduction to hard questioning and eventual torture (Lambert 1958:53–54). Australian writings about the Japanese reveal that language issues are crucial in cross-cultural encounters of all kinds.

Although Australian society continues to look towards the Asia–Pacific, an increase in the development in Australian writings on the Japanese does not seem to be keeping pace, partly because there are still very few authors of Japanese origin who raise their own voices within Australian society. As Broinowski suggests in *About Face,* there are many 'insiders'—hyphenated 'Asian-Australians' who, by producing Asian-Australian fiction, show the diversity and dynamism of present Australian society. However, such writers are mostly Chinese, Indians or from other parts of Asia rather than Japan. In the Asian issue of the journal *Meanjin* (v.63 no.2 2004), out of 44 contributors only three authors took up Japan-related topics—an article on film, another on video games and a poem with a Japanese setting—and all of them were written by non-Japanese.

The question thus remains—in Australia, who will write about Japan and how? In the multicultural society of Australia, the number of 'hyphenated' Japanese-Australians is small, and the number of Japanese-Australian fiction writers is much smaller again. It is true that Japanese studies and research have continued to develop, with several conferences and meetings organised and publications encouraged, a recent important example being Oliver's *Allies, Enemies and Trading Partners: Records on Australia and the Japanese*, the 20th volume of the Research Guide series of the National Archives of Australia (2004). A general observation arising from this book is that non-Japanese Australian writers are still responsible for most of the writing about Japan and the Japanese and so their explanations and descriptions will possibly continue to produce most of the general and collective Australian representations of the Japanese.

If there are borderlines where different cultures meet within a 'multicultural' society such as Australia's, there are many spaces—'cultures in-between', in Bhabha's terms—where 'culture-sympathy and culture-clash appear' that provide opportunities for people to recognise the enrichment of their cultures and society (Bhabha 1998:30). Similarly, Longley suggests that immigrants in Australia form a 'Fifth World', thus gaining both a sense of being and space to express their transplanted cultures in society (Longley 1992:19–28). The number of Japanese authors seems to be very few to provide such 'interstitial experience' in Australian writings and narratives on Japan and the Japanese written by non-Japanese Australians are still assigned the role of 'speaking for' the Japanese. Castro compares writing with a migratory process, 'birds of passage', or 'shooting of arrows', in which 'the writer stands a little to the side, with an expression of alarmed uncertainty as the traces disappear into the eternal roar of society's unconscious' (Castro 1992:8).

When the then Japanese Prime Minister Koizumi visited Australia in 2002, including a tour of the Australian War Memorial in Canberra, Australian Prime Minister Howard commented on 'the great benefits and merits of the long-standing close ties and co-operation between Australia and Japan' (cited in Bullard and Tamura 2004:4–5). However, such 'ties and co-operation' seem at this juncture to be mostly political, economic and strategic, which are easily affected by the changing tides in international economic, diplomatic and military affairs, as we have seen in propaganda-filled stories mentioned in this book. John Menadue, former Australian Ambassador to Japan, articulates this in his comment that during his term in Japan in the late 1970s 'it was hard to get away from tonnes and dollars…The relationship seemed overwhelmingly about trade and investment. If the business relationship declined, there was a real risk that the relationship as a whole would be undermined' (Meaney 1999:foreword).

The necessity of creating 'new Asianists' in Australia has been raised by Altman, who says that in order to understand another society we need to have an 'intimate knowledge of its history, culture and language' (Altman in ASAA 2002:8). Sheridan also maintains that 'skilled, informed people are essential for Australia's survival in its globalised region' (Sheridan in ASAA 2002:12). Through an intimate knowledge of another culture, such as Japan's, a dimension can be cultivated in writings that work for mutual benefit, rather than for one-sided gain.

During the eight and a half years (from 1996 to 2005) that I spent researching this topic, several major events occurred, including the 11 September 2001 attacks on the United States, the Bali bombing in 2002, the bombing of the United Nations office in Iraq in 2003 and the bombing of the Australian Embassy in Jakarta in 2004. All these events involved Australia and Japan in the international arena. In this context, the Australian government's decision in 2005 to send troops to defend Japanese construction work in Iraq has a powerful political symbolism.[63] Living in such times of tense international relationships, it is clearly necessary to better understand the long-term, in-depth cultural relationships between countries that have a history of misunderstanding, partial knowledge and direct conflict, such as Australia and Japan. Can such a project contribute to the understanding of different cultures? Again, I would argue that through such analysis we are better able to understand how cultural and ethnic stereotypes can arise between nations. Given the significant role and growing importance of the media in today's world, understanding the effect of writing on the reader is essential. Understanding the way 'Others' are portrayed, and why, becomes critical as we navigate the current unknowns of international relations. Such analyses are probably even more important now than ever before in this 'global' society.

As we have seen, it took a major war for Australia to begin to develop a clearer and deeper understanding of the 'Other'. It seems times have not changed that much. As Lieutenant General Cosgrove, after the East Timor affair in 1999, put it, the Australian Defence Force 'needs to prepare and anticipate a requirement to be more politically and culturally sophisticated in the conduct of "good neighbour" operations in the future', including the speaking of each other's languages. Furthermore, it 'must increase its investment in civil affairs capabilities as well as languages and cultural training' (Cosgrove in ASAA 2002:66). For both internal and external reasons, it is critical that we consciously perceive, understand and tolerate the 'Other' in our literature as well as in our practical daily life. For many of us, it may be through various literary forms that we can better understand the 'Other' in practice. The identification, description and analysis of Australian literature about Japan which has been carried out here reveals changing attitudes, values and structures of feeling ranging from ignorance, bitterness and enmity, to appreciation and relaxed good-humoured acceptance. Peter Carey's *Wrong About Japan* (2004), which describes his journey to Japan with his young son Charley, reveals that one's hard-set notions of the 'Real Japan' may actually hamper one from giving unbiased and direct observations of the country and its people. Charley's spontaneous liking of Japanese comics and cartoons—*manga*—and his natural attitude in taking the country as he finds it, allows him to interact with Japan in easier, smoother and more accepting ways than his father. Such approaches in observing different cultures and peoples, without pretension and bias, may enable us to have closer views of them.

While it is true that this book draws some conclusions that might support potentially trite statements, such as 'old habits die hard' and 'once established stereotypes remain', one of the major conclusions must also be that among such stereotypes and conventions, one can also find new and different insights or perceptions which, although based on some past context, move beyond the cliché, break the confinement of public emotions and bias and push the limits of Australian literature. As the theme 'Witness Literature' at the centennial anniversary in 2001 of the first Nobel Prize for literature suggests, literature can be seen as a testimony of the time in which it is written. The ways in which Australian authors have depicted the 'Other', the Japanese, from a mysterious and unknown people to a military opponent, neighbour, visitor, customer and even fellow countryman or woman, reveal the way Australian society and the nation itself has changed over the past hundred and more years.

Endnotes

1. Sources include Endo (1993; 2000) and Sekine (2006:8–10).
2. The terminology of 'otherness' is used in this book both in its common meaning of different or diverse and also in its more specific, capitalised form to suggest that which is distinct from, different from, or opposite to something or oneself, as in 'fear of the Other' (see Said 1985; Bhabha 1994). While such uses of postcolonial theory are adapted to the present argument from time to time, this book recognises that Australians, as colonial dependents on Britain for much of their history, can never speak of an 'other' with the full force of imperial authority and have developed a variety of perspectives on the Japanese 'Other'.
3. Information highlighted by Gerster (1997).
4. Because of Murdoch's advice, William Hughes, then Minister of External Affairs, decided at the imperial conference to agree to maintain the Anglo–Japanese Alliance (Hirakawa 1984:136–8).
5. Hepburn, an American missionary and doctor (1815–1911), originated the method of writing Japanese in Roman characters; Clark, an American scientist, professor and military officer (1826–86), helped establish the former National University of Hokkaido; Fenollosa, an American professor of art and philosophy (1852–1908), who was invited to teach at the University of Tokyo, helped establish the Tokyo University of Art, and introduced Japanese art to the West.
6. This word originally meant a young girl before marriage, or a virgin; however, since Loti, Western writers have given it a more multi-sided meaning to suit their own purposes. For example, for James Murdoch (1892b:173), 'musume' means a 'cha-ya' (tea-house) girl who waits at table and often serves as a courtesan as well.
7. This anthropological, sociological and literary interest can be seen in such works as *Glimpses of Unfamiliar Japan* (1894), *Out of the East* (1895), *Japan: An Attempt of Interpretation* (1904), and the collection of short stories *Kwaidan : Stories and Studies of Strange Things* (1904).
8. See Basil Hall Chamberlain's criticism on Hearn in *Things Japanese*, 1939.
9. Despite Sladen's claim, Isabella Lucy Bird's *Unbeaten tracks in Japan* had been published in Britain in 1880. This was written about her three month journey in the northern part of Japan during her eight month stay in 1878.

10　It was actually conventional for her to do this as the Japanese word 'Goshujin-sama' means lord as well as husband.

11　Sadler (1935:116) argues that it was a misunderstanding for Europeans of the time to think of Japan as simply pretty and bizarre, and that it should not have been a surprise for the West to discover Japan's expansionist ambitions. While closed, Sadler says, Japan developed in its own way, and became 'a very highly organized and severely beautiful civilization', and its hidden 'strong and flexible but unyielding quality underlay the elegant and odd exterior, thus providing "an excellent camouflage"'.

12　Murdoch taught at several places in Japan, including Otsu and Kagoshima on Kyushu Island, Kanagawa and Tokyo on the main island at Ichi-Ko (The First High School), which eventually became part of the Imperial University. One of his students there was Soseki Natsume. Natsume later published some articles on Murdoch and his *A history of Japan* in the newspaper *Tokyo Asahi Shimbun*.

13　Uchimura, a Christian scholar, was accused of lese-majesty for not saluting the 'Imperial Rescript of Education' in 1891; he was also against the Russo–Japanese war in 1902.

14　Stewart is discussed in chapter six. William Lane may have been in Murdoch's mind. Lane, who was an acquaintance of Murdoch, went to Paraguay after his ideas for the labour movement in Australia were not realised. Asked by Lane to be one of the tutors there, Murdoch joined him for a while, before returning to Japan via the United States and Australia.

15　Ouyang's Chinese stereotypes in *The Bulletin* include: the sensual Chinaman, the money-grabbing Chinaman, the vindictive Chinaman, the comic Chinaman (see also Ouyang 1994).

16　Murdoch died in 1921, before the publication of *A history of Japan* volume 3, revised and edited by JH Longford, who introduces him in the preface (Murdoch 1926:vii).

17　Murdoch's importance as an authority and informant on Japan is also apparent in the government's support of his promotion to a professorship in Oriental Studies at the University of Sydney, with funds to conduct research on Japan. He also consulted with the foreign intelligence service and military intelligence (see Meaney 1996a; Sadler 1935:102).

18　Praed might have borrowed this name from Kencho Suematsu (1855–1920), who represented Japan as a diplomat in Britain for eight years from 1878. Suematsu translated and published *The tale of Genji* in England in 1882 (see Inoue 1999:20).

19　For example, the number of fiction titles published in the decade of the 1890s is almost equal to the total number of fiction titles that were published before then. From 'Table one: number of titles of verse and of fiction published in each decade of the nineteenth century', based on a count of titles listed in E Morris Miller and FJ McCartney's *Australian Literature: A Bibliography* cited in Ken Stewart, (ed) *The 1890s* (1986:27).

20　At the time the *Immigration Restriction Act* was introduced, there were about 3,500 Japanese in Australia. See Yuriko Nagata, *Unwanted Aliens* (1996).

21 For example in volume 8, Jan.2; Feb 2; Mar 1; Apr 1; volume 9, May 1, 1911.
22 See, for example, Michael Schaper's 'The Broome Race Riots of 1920', in Jan Gothard, *Asian Orientations* (1995:112).
23 Around the same time as Idriess, Xavier Herbert also published some short stories based on his experience with Japanese pearl divers in the pearling industry. Herbert's stories will be discussed in chapter six.
24 Most Japanese women who arrived in Australia before 1901 were either wives or prostitutes. Prostitution is said to be the third most common occupation, after pearling and sugar. See Yuriko Nagata, *Unwanted Aliens* (1996:22).
25 Gayatri Spivak cited by Drusilla Modjeska in the introduction to KS Prichard's *Coonardoo* (1990:xii).
26 Japan's aim of creating a navy 'more than equal to the combined Pacific squadrons of Britain, Russia, France, Germany and Yankeeland' had been mentioned in the 1890s. An example is a column in *The Bulletin* 2.5.1896.
27 Found in *The Lone Hand*, v.3 Oct.1 (1908). Neville Meaney concludes that Kirmess was a pseudonym for Frank Fox, the editor of *The Lone Hand* at the time of the publication and one of the chief members of the National Defence League. See *The 1890s*, Notes, 347. The interpolation appears only in the first serialised version.
28 Examples include 'The Deliverer' by Aldridge Evelyn, July 1, 1910; 'The Command of the Air' by Lawrence Zeal, 1 March, 1911; 'First Blood' by Boyd Cable, May 1 1911.
29 Hughes, with his firm belief in racial disparity, advocated strengthening Australia's defence to guard the White Australia policy. Neville Meaney (1996:45–47) suggests this was an example of over-reaction to the concept of the yellow peril in Australia, which he believes might have affected Japan's national sentiment over racial issues.
30 In fact, the novel itself has a certain manual-like tone of how-to-counterattack-when-invaded; the author GD Mitchell was originally a military officer, a Major of the AIF who won a MC and a DCM.
31 An American equivalent to Australians' experience in the Pacific War against the Japanese.
32 *Fires on the Plain* was originally entitled *Nobi* in Japanese and published in 1952. An observation of cannibalism on the part of the Japanese also appears in Eric Lambert's *The Veterans*, (1954:142).
33 There is also such cruelty in him that he spontaneously kills one of the prisoners after pretending to show him mercy.
34 This was originally a concluding short story to the novel in the first edition published in 1958, and was placed at the beginning of the Pan edition in 1960.
35 John Coast, in the introduction to his *Railroad of Death*, 1946, notes that his book is 'the personal narrative of a Subaltern taken prisoner' from 1942 to 1945 and he apologises to 'the Other Ranks…[who] had a worse time than the Officers'.

36 Examples include such characters described by Pulvers as Ron in *The Death of Urashima Taro*, to be discussed in chapter five, and Hirose in *General Yamashita's Treasure*, to be discussed in chapter eight.
37 For example, words like 'Yasmae' would be written with Roman letters as 'Yasume'. The title of Cornel Lumiere's book, which is discussed in chapter seven, may be written *Kora!* rather than *Kura!*
38 Examples can be found in Braddon, *The Naked Island*, 109 or *End of a Hate*, 31; or the title of Alice M Bowman's book, *Not Now Tomorrow: Ima Nai Ashita*.
39 The casualties numbered 234 in other sources, which include those who died after being recaptured.
40 For example see Harry Gordon's *Die Like the Carp!* 1978:ch 21.
41 Such as Alison Broinowski in *The Yellow Lady* and Wilde, Hooton, and Andrews (eds), in *The Oxford Companion to Australian Literature* (1994:224).
42 Author's words cited by Diana Davis in the Introduction in Angus & Robertson 1975 Classics edition.
43 Examples include Japanese soldiers' comments in Gordon's *Die Like the Carp!*.
44 Clarke's publications on his experiences include *The Tub* (1963), *Last Stop Nagasaki!* (1984), *Twilight Liberation* (1985), and *When the Balloon Went Up* (1990), which will be discussed in chapter seven.
45 Roger Pulvers uses one such case in *The Death of Urashima Taro*, which will be discussed later in chapter eight. In 2005, the NHK documentary *Cowra no Dai Dasso* (Mass Breakout in Cowra) was aired in Japan in which some of the survivors probably for the first time spoke about the event in public.
46 Examples include a British author Ted Willis who wrote about the outbreak in *The Naked Sun* (1980) with both good and bad Japanese characters having their own voices.
47 This becomes such a strong archetype again that Porter later uses another 'butterfly' in his play *The Professor*, although the Japanese woman in the play sacrifices herself not for 'Pinkerton' but for a Japanese man infected with 'Westernisation'.
48 On Porter's disillusionment with Japan see Alison Broinowski's *The Yellow Lady* 1992:103–104.
49 'Living Dangerously', first published in *Wide World*, London, 1931; 'Sounding Brass', first published in *Australian Journal*, 1933; 'Sailor Bring Joy', first published in *Australian Journal*, 1933; 'Miss Tanaka', first published in *Australian Journal*, 1933.
50 See the author's note in *A Town Like Alice* 1956:333.
51 It would have been more interesting to this reader, although not relevant to the plot, if the author had included the nature of the relationship and the perception of the Japanese towards the Australians as compared to the Americans.
52 Staged in London in 1965 and published in 1966.
53 Mary Lord cites Porter from *The Actors, Hal Porter: Man of Many Parts*, 51.

54 Tipping 1987, 'Harold Stewart: Interviewed by Richard Kelly Tipping', *Westerly* no.4 December p. 32.
55 ibid, p. 26.
56 Eric Lambert, from the book review of TAG Hungerford's *The Ridge and the River*, *Meanjin*, 1952:415–6. Lambert's criticism does not seem to apply to Hungerford's stance as a writer, for Hungerford also wrote the more anti-war oriented stories such as 'Last Entry in Red' or 'Letter' early in 1950s as seen in Chapter 3.
57 Examples include Henry 'Jo' Gullett and his *Not As A Duty Only* (1976); Robin Gerster, *Big-Noting* 1992:233.
58 Braddon's *The Other Hundred Years War* was also published in the same year under another title *Japan Against the World 1941–2041: The 100-Year War for Supremacy* by Stein and Day in New York.
59 Examples include Gerster, *Big-Noting*, 1992:230–233; Wilde, Hooton, & Andrews (eds), *The Oxford Companion to Australian Literature*, 1994:606.
60 Robin Gerster on Clive James, *Australian Book Review* January (1997): 17.
61 Personal correspondence between Shaw and the author, dated 16 June 2004.
62 Examples include Lumiere's title Kura! or the name of the long-established Japanese brewery in Lambert's Hiroshima Reef.
63 See, for example, 'Reinforcing the Bond', The Australian, 21.3.2005:15.

Chronology

1831	The crew of the *Lady Rowena* land on Hokkaido
1853	Commodore Perry arrives from the United States and Japan 'opens its door to the world'
1868	The Meiji Restoration
1874	First Japanese contract pearl divers come to Australia
	New South Wales wool traded with Japan for the first time
1879	James Hingston, *The Australian Abroad*
1880	Japan has entries in the Melbourne International Exhibition
1888	Centenary of the British landing
	Chinese Exclusion Bill passed by NSW parliament
1890	Fusajiro Kanematsu opens a branch of his trading company in Sydney
	James Murdoch, *Don Juan's Grandson in Japan*
1892	Ownership of pearling boats prohibited to non-white people in Western Australia
	James Murdoch, *Tales of Australia and Japan*, *Ayame-San*
	Douglas Sladen, *The Japs at Home*
1895	Carlton Dawe, *Kakemonos, Yellow and White*
1896	First Japanese Consulate opens in Townsville
1897	Japanese Consulate in Sydney opens
1898	Carlton Dawe, *A Bride of Japan*
	John Luther Long, 'Madame Butterfly'
1899	Rosa Praed, *Madame Izàn*
1900	Carlton Dawe, *Rose and Chrysanthemum*
1901	Australian Federation
1902	British-Japanese alliance (which is renewed for further ten years in 1911)

	AB Paterson, 'The Pearl Diver'; CN, 'The Vigilance at Coolaba'
	The premiere of 'Madama Butterfly' by Puccini at La Scala, Milan
1904	Douglas Sladen, *A Japanese Marriage*
1905	Victory of Japan over Russia
	Australian National Defence League formed in NSW
	Albert Dorrington, 'The Baltic Man'
	AG Hales, *Little Blue Pigeon*
	Britain's capital ships withdrawn after the renewal of the alliance in the Pacific
1908	Consulate in Townsville closed
	CH Kirmess, 'The Commonwealth Crisis' (-09)
1909	Federal decision to introduce compulsory military training in Australia
	Arthur Adams, 'The Day the Big Shells Came'
1910	Edith Graham, 'Roses and Grey Mist'
1911	Randolph Bedford, 'The Mates of Torres'
	'A Gypsy Girl', 'Purple Wisteria'
1913	S Efari, 'These I Have Known'
1914	First World War begins (–1918)
1916	First conscription referendum rejected by a narrow margin
1917	Second conscription referendum rejected
	James Murdoch appointed Professor of Oriental Studies at Sydney University
1919	Paris Conference; WM Hughes defeats Japan's insertion of racial equality clause
1921	Washington disarmament conference
1931	Japan invades Manchuria
1933	Japan secedes from the League of Nations
1936	Japan's retaliation against Australia's trade diversion policy by cessation of wool and wheat imports
	Henrietta Drake-Brockman, *Sheba Lane*
1937	Ion Idriess, *Forty Fathoms Deep*; G.D. Mitchell, *The Awakening*
1938	Australia's cessation of iron ore exports to Japan
1939	Erle Cox, *Fool's Harvest*

1941	Japan bombs Pearl Harbour
	Prime Minister Curtin declares war on Japan
	Katharine Susannah Prichard, *Moon of Desire*
1942	Singapore surrenders to Japanese
	Japan's bombing of Darwin and Broome
	Japan defeated in the Battle of the Coral Sea
	Japan's midget submarines enter Sydney Harbour
	Australians win the battle of Kokoda Trail
1943	George Johnston, *New Guinea Diary*
1944	Breakout by Japanese prisoners of war in Cowra
1945	Atom bomb attacks on Hiroshima and Nagasaki
	Japan surrenders and the Pacific War ends
1946	British Commonwealth Occupation Force starts its operation in Japan
	Francis Webb appointed Chief Justice of the Tokyo War Crimes Trial
	W Kent-Huges, *Slaves of the Sun of Heaven*
	Graeme McCabe, *Pacific Sunset*
	Walter Summons, *Twice Their Prisoner*
1947	Australian trade with Japan re-commenced
	Rohan Rivett, *Behind Bamboo*
1950	Korean War (–1953)
	Frank Clune, *Ashes of Hiroshima*
1951	ANZUS Treaty signed in San Francisco
	Treaty of Peace between Allied Powers and Japan signed in San Francisco
	Australia's occupation force in Japan ceases operations
	Colombo Plan inaugurated
	Kenneth Mackenzie, *Dead Men Rising*
	Roy Whitecross, *Slaves of the Sun of Heaven*
1952	Australia's first post-war Ambassador to Japan arrives in Tokyo
	First Japanese war bride arrives in Australia
	Russell Braddon, *The Naked Island*
	TAG Hungerford, *The Ridge and the River*

1953	Japan's first post-war ambassador to Australia arrives in Sydney
	Japanese Embassy opened in Canberra
1954	Jon Cleary, *The Climate of Courage*
	LH Evers, *Pattern of Conquest*
	TAG Hungerford, *Sowers of the Wind*
	Betty Jeffrey, *White Coolies*
	Eric Lambert, *The Veterans*
1955	Norman Bartlett, *Island Victory*
1956	Melbourne Olympic Games held and 118 Japanese athletes participate
	Neville Shute, *A Town Like Alice*
1957	Australia-Japan sign a trade agreement on most-favoured nation terms
1958	Russell Braddon, *End of a Hate*
	Eric Lambert, *The Dark Backward*
	Hal Porter, *A Handful of Pennies*
	Tom Ronan, *The Pearling Master*
1959	David Forrest, *The Last Blue Sea*
	Peter Ryan, *Fear Drive My Feet*
1960	Ray Parkin, *Out of the Smoke*
	Harold Stewart, *Net of Fireflies*
1962	Elizabeth Kata, *Someone Will Conquer Them*
1963	Hugh Clarke, *The Tub*
	Ray Parkin, *Into the Smother*
1965	Australian troops sent to Vietnam War
	Isobel Carter, *Alien Blossom*
	Hugh Clarke, *Break-Out!*
	Stephen Kelen, *Goshu*
	Thomas Keneally, *The Fear*
	Eric Lambert, *MacDougal's Farm*
	Morris West, *The Ambassador*
	Randolph Stow, *The Merry-Go-Round in the Sea*
1966	Japan replaces Britain as Australia's largest customer

	Kenneth Harrison, *The Brave Japanese*
	Cornel Lumiere, *Kura!*
1967	Eric Lambert, *Hiroshima Reef*
1968	Russell Braddon, *When the Enemy is Tired*
	Ray Parkin, *The Sword and the Blossom*
	Hal Porter, *The Actors*
1969	Japanese school opened in Sydney
1970	Hal Porter, *Mr Butterfry and Other Tales of New Japan*
1971	John Vader, *Battle of Sydney*
1973	Alison Broinowski, *Take One Ambassador*
1974	Restriction of immigration of non-Europeans abolished
1975	John Romeril, *The Floating World*
1976	Australia and Japan sign the Basic Treaty of Friendship and Co-operation
	Australia-Japan Foundation established
1978	Harry Gordon, *Die Like the Carp!*
	Japanese Garden and Cultural Centre established in Cowra
1980	Stan Arneil, *One Man's War*
	Geoffrey Bingham, *To Command the Cats and Other Stories*
	John Brown, *Zaibatsu*
	Jon Cleary, *A Very Private War*
1981	John Bryson, *Whoring Around*
	Elizabeth Kata, *With Kisses on Both Cheeks*
	Roger Pulvers, *The Death of Urashima Taro; Yamashita*
	Harold Stewart, *By the Old Wall of Kyoto*
1982	Geraldine Hall, *Talking to Strangers*
1983	Russell Braddon, *The Other Hundred Years War*
	Stephen Kelen, *I Remember Hiroshima*
1984	Geoffrey Blainey's criticism of the rate of Asian immigration
	Hugh Clarke, *Last Stop Nagasaki!*
	Jon Cleary, *The Phoenix Tree*
	John Hooker, *The Bush Soldiers*
	Daniel Keene, *Cho Cho San*

	Don'o Kim, *The Chinaman*
1985	Geoffrey Bingham, *At the End of His Tether*
	Peter Carey, *Illywhacker*
	Hugh Clarke, *Twilight Liberation*
	Ross Davy, *Kenzo*
	TAG Hungerford, *A Knockabout with a Slouch Hat*
	Ann Nakano, *Bit Parts*
1986	Nancy Corbett, *Floating*
1988	Bicentenary of the British landing
1989	First meeting of APEC held in Canberra
	Elizabeth Kata, *Kagami*
	Jill Shearer, *Shimada*
1990	Robert Allen, *Tokyo no Hana*
	Hugh Clarke, *When the Balloon Went Up*
	Brian Williams, *Blood Oath*
1991	The Gulf War
1992	Geoffrey Bingham, *Laughing Gunner and Selected War Stories*
	Peter Corris, *The Japanese Job*
	Clive James, *Brrm! Brrm!*
	Thérèse Radic, *The Emperor Regrets*
1993	Japan Foundation opens its branch office in Sydney
1994	Stephen Carroll, *Momoko*
	Charlotte Manassen Mori, *Sayonara My Friend: Love Annie*
	Roger Pulvers, *General Yamashita's Treasure*
1995	John Lynch, *The Proposal*
1996	The word 'peace' withdrawn from the name of the Canberra-Nara sister city park
1997	Brian Castro, *Stepper*
	John Romeril, *Love Suicides*
1998	Iraq War
1999	Referendum results in rejection of Australian republic
	Robin Gerster, *Legless in Ginza*
	Caroline Shaw, *Cat Catcher*

2000	Sydney Olympic Games held and 268 Japanese athletes participate
	Caroline Shaw, *Eye to Eye*
2001	Keiko Tamura, *Michi's Memories*
2003	Australian troops sent to second Iraq war
2004	Peter Carey, *Wrong About Japan*
2005	Australian force posted to protect Japanese aid operations in Iraq
2006	Australia-Japan Year of Exchange (30th Anniversary of the 1976 Basic Treaty of Friendship and Co-operation)

glossary

Ashita	tomorrow
BCOF	British Commonwealth Occupation Force
Bon-Odori	a dance to welcome the soul of the deceased at *Obon* (see *Obon*)
cha-ya	a teahouse
go	a Japanese board game
Goshujin-sama	lord, husband
hana	flowers
harakiri	ritual suicide
Hina	baby bird, chick, traditional Japanese doll
kakemono	scroll-painting
kendo	Japanese fencing
Kashira Migi	Military command for 'Eyes right'
Kiwotsuke	Military command for 'Attention'
manga	Japanese comics
mentsu	face (as in to lose face)
mousumee (musume, musme)	literally daughter, or a young girl before marriage, a virgin
Naore	Military command for 'As you were'
nasake	compassion, kindness, mercy
nisei	second generation Japanese-American
Obon	period of every year when the souls of the dead visit the world of the living

sake	Japanese rice wine
samisen or shamisen	a Japanese string instrument
Sekisho	a checkpoint designed to check travellers and collect tax since ancient times, especially to check female travellers during the Edo period
Senjinkun	Japan's Military Code, issued by Hideki Toj
sensei	teacher
shyogi	Japanese chess
tatami	traditional Japanese flooring made of woven straw
Tayu	highest ranked courtesan
tenko	rollcall
yakuza	Japanese mafia
Yasmae	Military command for 'At ease'
zaibatsu	a conglomerate

bibliography

'A Gypsy Girl' 1911, 'Purple wisteria', the *Australian Town and Country Journal*, 14 June.

Ackland, Michael 2000, 'Beyond 'Darkest Oz: the diverse stations of Harold Stewart's road to Kyoto', *Southerly* 60(3).

—— 2001, *Damaged men: the precarious lives of James McAuley and Harold Stewart*, Allen & Unwin, Crows Nest.

Adam, Ian and Helen Tiffin (eds) 1991, *Past the last post: theorizing post-colonialism and post-modernism*, Harvester Wheatsheaf, New York and London.

Adams, Arthur 1909, 'The day the big shells came', the *Bulletin* 30(1509), 14 January.

Adam-Smith, Patsy 1992, *Prisoners of war: from Gallipoli to Korea*, Penguin Books, Ringwood.

Albinski & Ikin 1995a, 'Australian invention of Chinese invasion: a century of paranoia, 1888–1988', in Ouyang (ed) *Australian Literary Studies* 17(1).

Allen, Robert 1990, *Tokyo no Hana*, Angus & Robertson, North Ryde.

Alomes, Stephen and Catherine Jones 1991, *Australian nationalism: a documentary history*, Collins/Angus & Robertson, North Ryde.

—— 1904, 'Selling books', the *Bulletin* 25(1263).

—— 1910, the *Bulletin* 31(1601), 20 October.

Arneil, SF 1980, *One man's war*, second edition, Alternative Publishing Co-operative, Sydney.

Arthur, Richard, 1911 'The sham of our defence: our toy army and our tiny fleet', *The Lone Hand*, May 1 (1–6).

ASAA (Asian Studies Association of Australia) 2002, *Maximizing Australia's Asia knowledge: repositioning and renewal of a national asset*, report.

Asada, Teruhiko 1970, *The night of a thousand suicides: the Japanese outbreak at Cowra*, St Martin's Press, New York. Originally published as *Hiroku: Kaura no Bodo*, Kongo Shuppan, Tokyo, 1967.

Ashcroft, Bill, Gareth Griffiths and Helen Tiffin (eds) 1989, *The empire writes back*, Routledge, London.

—— 1995, *The post-colonial studies reader*, Routledge, London and New York.

Bader, Rudolf 1992, *The visible past: images of Europe in Anglo-Australian literature*, Peter Lang, Bern.

Ball, W Macmahon 1948, *Japan: enemy or ally?*, Cassell & Company, Melbourne.

—— 1969, *Australia and Japan: documents and readings in Australian history*, Thomas Nelson, Melbourne.

Barker, Anthony 1996, *What happened when: a chronology of Australia from 1788*, Allen & Unwin, Sydney.

Barnard, Marjorie 1987, cited in Robin Gerster's *Big Noting*, Melbourne University Press, Carlton.

Barrel, Tony and Rick Tanaka 1995, *Higher than heaven, war and everything*, Private Guy International, Strawberry Hills.

Bartlett, Norman 1954, *The pearl seekers*, Melrose, London.

—— 1955a, *Island victory: a novel*, Angus & Robertson, Sydney.

—— (ed) 1955b, *Australia at arms*, Australian War Memorial, Canberra.

BCOF (British Commonwealth Occupation Force), Unit and Operational Record #AWM114, Australian War Memorial, Canberra.

Beaumont, Joan (ed) 1996, *Australia's war, 1939–1945*, Allen & Unwin, St Leonards.

Bedford, Randolph 1911a, 'The mates of Torres', *The Lone Hand*, January–May.

—— 1911b, 'White yellow and brown: the present situation of white Australia in a Pacific that is rapidly becoming browner', *The Lone Hand*, 1 July.

Bennett, Bruce 1978, 'Australian perspectives on the near north: Hal Porter and Randolph Stow' in Tiffin, Chris (ed), *South Pacific images*, University of Queensland Press, St Lucia.

—— 1991, *An Australian compass: essays on place and direction in Australian literature*, Fremantle Arts Centre Press, Fremantle.

——1998 'Literary culture since Vietnam: a new dynamic', in Bennett, Bruce & Jennifer Strauss (eds), *The Oxford Literary History of Australia*, Oxford University Press, Melbourne.

—— 2002, *Australian short fiction: a history*, University of Queensland Press, St Lucia.

Bennett, Bruce and Jennifer Strauss (eds) 1998, *The Oxford literary history of Australia*, Oxford University Press, Melbourne.

Bennett, David (ed) 1998, *Multicultural states: rethinking difference and identity*, Routledge, London.

Bhabha, Homi K 1995, *The location of culture*, Routledge, London.

—— 1998, 'Culture's in between', in Bennett, David (ed), *Multicultural States* Routledge, London.

Bingham, Geoffrey C 1980, *To command the cats and other stories*, Angus & Robertson, London and Sydney.

—— 1985, *At the end of his tether*, New Creation Publications, Blackwood.

—— 1992, *Laughing gunner and selected war stories*, Troubadour Press, Blackwood.

Blainey, Geoffrey 1983 [1966], *The tyranny of distance: how distance shaped Australia's history*, revised edition, Sun Books, Melbourne.

—— 1994, *A shorter history of Australia*, William Heinemann, Melbourne.

Booth, Alan 1996, *Looking for the lost: journeys through a vanishing Japan*, Kodansha, New York and Tokyo.

Bourke, Roger 2003, 'The last subject in the world: fiction of the prisoner-of-war experience under the Japanese', PhD thesis, University of Western Australia.

Bowman, Alice M 1996, *Not now tomorrow—Ima Nai Ashita—Australian civilian and army nurses—prisoners of the Japanese in New Guinea and Japan 1942–1945*, Daisy Press, Bangalow.

Braddon, Russell 1952, *The naked island*, Werner Laurie, London.

—— 1958, *End of a hate*, Cassell, London.

—— 1961, *The naked island: a play in three acts*, Evans Brothers Ltd, London.

—— 1968, *When the enemy is tired*, Michael Joseph, London.

—— 1983, *The other hundred years war*, Collins, London.

Brisbane, Katherine 1994 'The Play in the Theatre' from *The Floating World* (play script,1975; revised and reprinted, Currency Press, Paddington).

Broinowski, Alison 1973, *Take one ambassador*, Macmillan, Melbourne.

—— 1992, *The yellow lady: Australian impressions of Asia*, Oxford University Press, Melbourne.

—— 2003, *About face: Asian accounts of Australia*, Scribe, Melbourne.

Broinowski, Anna 1995, *The gap*, Currency Press, Sydney.

Brown, John 1983, *Zaibatsu*, Walrus Books, Sydney.

Brydon, Diana and Helen Tiffin 1993, *Decolonising fictions*, Dangaroo Press, Sydney.

Bryson, John 1981, *Whoring around*, Penguin Books, Ringwood.

Bullard, Steven and Keiko Tamura (eds) 2004, *From a hostile shore: Australia and Japan at war in New Guinea*, Australian War Memorial, Canberra.

Burchett, Wilfred G 1969, *Passport: an autobiography*, Thomas Nelson, Sydney.

Caesar, Adrian 1998, 'National Myths of Manhood 1914–1939', in Bennett, Bruce and Jennifer Strauss eds, *The Oxford Literary History of Australia*, Oxford University Press, Melbourne.

Campbell, David 1955, 'Recco over Rabaul' in Bartlett, Norman (ed), *Australia at arms*, Australian War Memorial, Canberra.

Carey, Peter 1985, *Illywhacker*, University of Queensland Press, St Lucia; Japanese translation 1995, Hakusuisha, Tokyo.

Carr-Gregg, Charlotte 1978, *Japanese prisoners of war in revolt: the outbreaks at Featherston and Cowra during World War II*, University of Queensland Press, St Lucia.

Carroll, Steven 1994, *Momoko*, McPhee Gribble, Ringwood.

Carter, IR 1965, *Alien blossom: a Japanese–Australian love story*, Lansdowne, London.

Brian Castro, 1992 'Necessary idiocy and the idea of freedom' Longley, Kateryna and Sneja Gunew (eds) 1992, *Striking chords*, Allen & Unwin, North Sydney

—— 1995, *Writing Asia and Auto/biography: two lectures*, Australian Defence Force Academy, Canberra.

—— 1997, *Stepper*, Random House, Milsons Point.

—— 1999, *Looking for Estrellita*, University of Queensland Press, St Lucia.

Cavendish, Marshall (ed), *War diary 1939–1945*, Marshall Cavendish Books, London.

Chamberlain, Basil Hall 1939, Things Japanese, 6th edition, Kegan Paul, London.

Chapman, Ivan 1990, *Tokyo calling: the Charles Cousens case*, Hale & Iremonger, Sydney.

Clancy, Laurie 1992, *A reader's guide to Australian fiction*, Oxford University Press, Melbourne.

Clark, CMH 1955, *Select documents in Australian history 1851–1900*, Angus & Robertson, Sydney.

Clark, Manning 1980, *A short history of Australia*, revised edition, New American Library, New York.

Clark, Ross 1992, 'Japanese tourists at the Australian War Memorial', *Still waiting for the thunder*, Jacaranda Press, Milton.

Clarke, Hugh 1963, *The tub*, Jacaranda Press, Brisbane.

—— 1984, *Last stop Nagasaki!*, George Allen & Unwin, London and Sydney.

—— 1985, *Twilight liberation: Australian prisoners of war between Hiroshima and home*, George Allen & Unwin, Sydney.

—— 1986, *A life for every sleeper: a pictorial record of the Burma–Thailand railway*, Allen & Unwin, Sydney.

—— 1990, *When the balloon went up: short stories from a war*, Allen & Unwin, Sydney.

—— 1994, *Escape to death: the Japanese breakout at Cowra*, Random House, Milsons Point. Originally published as *Break-out!*, Horwitz, Sydney.

Clarke, Hugh and Colin Burgess 1992, *Barbed wire and bamboo: Australian POWs in Europe, North Africa, Singapore, Thailand and Japan*, Allen & Unwin, St Leonards.

Clarke, Hugh, Colin Burgess and Russell Braddon 1988, *Prisoners of war*, Time-Life Books and John Ferguson, Sydney.

Clarke, Patricia 1999, *Rosa! Rosa!: A life of Rosa Praed, novelist and spiritualist*, Melbourne University Press, Carlton South.

Cleary, Jon 1955, *The climate of courage*, Collins, London. Also published as *Naked in the night: a novel*, Popular Library, New York, 1955.

—— 1967, *The long pursuit*, Collins, London.

—— 1980, *A very private war*, William Collins Publishers, Sydney.

—— 1984, *The phoenix tree*, Collins, London.

Clune, Frank 1950, *Ashes of Hiroshima: a post-war trip to Japan and China*, Angus & Robertson, Sydney.

Clunies Ross I, (ed) 1935, *Australia and the Far East: diplomatic and trade relations*, Angus & Robertson and the Australian Institute of International Affairs, Sydney.

CN 1902, 'The vigilance at Coolaba', the *Bulletin* 23(1174), 16 August.

Coaldrake, William H (ed) 2003, *Japan from war to peace: the Coaldrake records 1939–1956*, RoutledgeCurzon, London.

Coast, John 1946, *Railroad of death*, The Commodore Press, London.

Coombs, Anne and Susan Varga 2001, *Broometime*, revised edition, Sceptre Books, Sydney.

Cooper, Leontine 1890, 'Another mysterious disappearance', *Centennial Magazine* 2(12).

Corbett, Nancy J 1986, *Floating*, Wild and Woolley, Sydney.

Corris, Peter 1992, *The Japanese job*, Collins/Angus & Robertson, Pymble.

Cowan, Peter 1983, 'Broome—A Fiction', *Westerly* 3.

Cowling, Anthony 1996, *My life with the samurai*, Kangaroo Press, Kenthurst.

Cox, Erle 1939, *Fool's harvest*, Robertson & Mullen, Melbourne.

Craven, Ian, M Gray and G Stoneham (eds) 1994, *Australian popular culture*, Cambridge University Press, Melbourne.

Dai, Yin 1994, 'The representation of Chinese people in Australian literature', PhD thesis, Murdoch University.

Davies, George 2001, *The Occupation of Japan: the rhetoric and the reality of Anglo–Australian relations 1939–1952*, University of Queensland Press, St Lucia.

Davies, Lloyd 1984, 'The ally' in Davis, Faye, Mary Dilworth and Jennifer Kemp (eds), *Laughing cry: an anthology of short fiction*, Gooseberry Hill Press, Kalamunda.

Davy, Ross 1985, *Kenzo: a Tokyo story*, Penguin Books, Ringwood.

Dawe, Carlton 1895, *Yellow and white*, Roberts Bros, Boston and John Lane, London.

—— 1897, *Kakemonos: tales of the Far East*, John Lane, London and The Bodley Head, New York.

—— 1898, *A bride of Japan*, Hutchinson, London.

—— 1900, *Rose and chrysanthemum*, Knight and Millet, Boston.

De Groen, Frances 1998, *Xavier Herbert: a biography*, University of Queensland Press, St Lucia.

de Lepervanche, Marie and Gillian Bottomley (eds) 1988, *The cultural construction of race*, Sydney Association for Studies in Society and Culture, Sydney.

Dell, Alison 1989, 'The bonsai nursery', *Redoubt*, 7/8 November.

Denoon, Donald, Mark Hudson, Gavan McCormack and Tessa Morris-Suzuki (eds) 1996, *Multicultural Japan: Palaeolithic to postmodern*, Cambridge University Press, Cambridge.

Dixon, Robert 1995, *Writing the colonial adventure: race, gender and nation in Anglo–Australian popular fiction 1875–1914*, Cambridge University Press, Cambridge.

Doran, Chris 1993, 'Christmas cake', *Westerly* 38 (4).

Dorrington, Albert 1905, 'The Baltic man', the *Bulletin* 25(1311), 8 June.

Dower, John 1993, *War without mercy: race and power in the Pacific War*, 7th edn, Pantheon Books, New York (first published in 1986).

—— 1993, *Japan in war and peace: selected essays*, New Press, New York.

—— 2000, *Embracing defeat: Japan in the aftermath of World War II*, Penguin Books, London.

Drake-Brockman, Henrietta 1936, *Sheba Lane*, Angus & Robertson, Sydney.

Drewe, Robert 1989, 'Life of a barbarian', *The bay of contented men*, Pan Books, Sydney.

Duffy, Jennifer and Gary Anson (eds) 1994, *Encounters with Japan*, Angus & Robertson, Sydney. Published in Japan as *Watashi ga deatta Nippon*, Simul Press, Tokyo, 1994.

Dunlop, Sir Edward 1990, *The war diaries of 'Weary' Dunlop: Java and the Burma–Thailand railway 1932–1945*, Penguin Books, Ringwood.

Dutton, Geoffrey (ed) 1982, *The literature of Australia*, revised edition, Penguin Books, Ringwood.

Easton, Julie 1995, 'Japanese War Brides in Western Australia: Immigration and Assimilation in the Nineteen Fifties', in Gothard, Jan (ed) *Asian Orientations: Studies in Western Australian History* v.16, University of Western Australia, Nedlands.

Efari, S 1913, 'These I have known', the *Bulletin* 34(1732), 24 April.

Ellis, Moya 1982, 'Feathers', *Westerly* 27(1).

Endo, Masako 1993, *Maboroshi no Sekihi* [*Pursuing an elusive epitaph: a tale of early Japan–Australia contact*], The Simul Press, Tokyo.

—— 2000, *Australia Monogatari: Rekishi to Nichi Go Koryu Jyuwa* [*A story of Australia: ten episodes from the Australia–Japan relationship*], Heibonsha, Tokyo.

Esson, Louis 1908, 'Japanese Imperialism', *The Lone Hand*, September 1.

Evans, Raymond, Clive Moore, Kay Saunders and Bryan Jamison 1997, *1901: our future's past: documentary Australia's federation*, Macmillan, Sydney.

Evers, LH 1954, *Pattern of conquest*, Currawong Publishing, Sydney.

Finkemeyer, Gunner 1994, *It happened to us: the unique experiences of 20 members of the 4th anti-tank regiment*, CE and DJ Finkemeyer, Melbourne.

—— 1998, *It Happened To Us: Mark II*, CE and DJ Finkemeyer, Cheltenham.

Fitchett, Rev WH 1912, *Deeds that won the Empire: historic battle scenes*, G Bell & Sons, London.

Foong, Ling Kong 1999, 'Bad subjects', review of *White nation* by Ghassan Hage, *Australian Book Review* 209, April.

Forrest, David 1985, *The last blue sea*, Penguin Books, Ringwood (first published 1959).

Foster, Kevin 1999, *Fighting fictions: war, narrative and national identity*, Pluto Press, London.

Frame, TR 1990, *The garden island*, Kangaroo Press, Kenthurst.

Frei, Henry P 1991, *Japan's southward advance and Australia: from the sixteenth century to World War II*, Melbourne University Press, Carlton.

Frow, John and Meaghan Morris (eds) 1993, *Australian cultural studies: a reader*, Allen & Unwin, St Leonards.

Fussell, Paul 1975, *The Great War and modern memory*, Oxford University Press, New York.

Ganter, Regina 1994, *The pearl-shellers of Torres Strait: resource use, development and decline, 1860s–1960s*, Melbourne University Press, Carlton.

Gerster, Robin 1992, *Big-noting: the heroic theme in Australian war writing*, revised edition, Melbourne University Press, Carlton.

—— (ed) 1995, *Hotel Asia*, Penguin Books, Ringwood.

—— 1997, 'Japanese images in Australian literature', seminar, Japan–Australia Seminar, Hachioji, Tokyo, 7 June.

—— 1999, *Legless in Ginza: orientating Japan*, Melbourne, University Press, Carlton South.

Gerster, Robin & Bassett, Jan 1991, *Seizure of Youth: the Sixties and Australia*, Hyland House, South Yarra, Victoria.

Gerster, Robin and Peter Pierce (eds) 2004, *On the war-path: an anthology of Australian military travel*, Melbourne University Press, Carlton.

Gibaldi, Joseph 2003, *MLA handbook for writers of research papers*, 6th edition, The Modern Language Association of America, New York.

Gordon, Harry 1978, *Die like the carp!: the story of the greatest prison escape ever*, Cassell, Stanmore.

Gordon, Harry 1994, *Voyage from shame: the Cowra breakout and afterwards* (expanded and updated version of *Die like the carp!)*, University of Queensland Press, St Lucia.

Gothard, Jan 1995, *Asian orientations*, University of Western Australia, Nedlands.

Graham, Edith 1910, 'Roses and grey mist', the *Australian Town and Country Journal* 81(1–4).v.81 no.2110 13 July 1910; no.2111 20 July 1910; no.2112 27 Jul 1910; no.2113 3 August 1910

Grant, Bruce 1990, 'Tatsuma-san', *Overland* 117.

Grant, Don and Graham Seal (eds) 1993, *Australia in the world: perceptions and possibilities*, Black Swan Press and Centre for Australian Studies, Curtin University, Perth.

Grassby, Al 1984, *The tyranny of prejudice*, Australian Education Press, Melbourne.

Griffiths-Marsh, Roland 1990, *The sixpenny soldier*, Collins/Angus & Robertson Publishers, North Ryde.

Gullet Henry 'Jo' 1976, *Not As A Duty Only: an infantryman's war*, Melbourne University Press, Melbourne.

Hage, Ghassan 1998, *White nation: fantasies of white supremacy in a multicultural society*, Pluto Press Australia, Annandale.

Hales, AG 1905, *Little blue pigeon: a story of Japan*, Hutchinson, London.

Hall, Geraldine 1982, *Talking to Strangers*, Constable, London.

Hamilton, Annette 1990, 'Fear and desire: Aborigines, Asians and the national imaginary', *Australian Cultural History* 9.

Hanson, GM 1994, 'See Nikko and die' in Rowe, Jennifer (ed), *Love lies bleeding: crimes for a summer Christmas*, Allen & Unwin, St Leonards.

Harrison, Kenneth 1966, *The brave Japanese*, Rigby, Adelaide. Also published as *Road to Hiroshima*, Rigby, Adelaide, 1983.

Harrison-Ford, Carl (ed) 1986, *Fighting words: Australian war writing*, Lothian, Melbourne.

Harvey, Pam 1996, 'Searching Kyoto', *Westerly* 1.

Hassall, Anthony J 1988, *The making of Xavier Herbert's 'Poor fellow my country'*, James Cook University, Douglas.

Herbert, Xavier 1963, *Larger than life: twenty short stories*, Angus & Robertson, Sydney.

—— 1990, *South of Capricornia: short stories 1925–1934*, edited by Russell McDougall, Oxford University Press, Melbourne.

Hergenhan, Laurie 1985, 'War in post-1960's fiction: Johnston, Stow, McDonald, Malouf and Les Murray', *Australian Literary Studies* 12(2).

Heseltine, Harry 1964, Ch. V, *The Literature of Australia*, Geoffrey Dutton (ed) Penguin Books, Ringwood; revised and reprinted, 1982.

Highbridge, Dianne 1987, 'A bonsai Christmas on a Tokyo tatami', *Times on Sunday*, 20 December.

Hills, Ben 1996, *Japan: behind the lines*, Hodder & Stoughton, Rydalmere.

Hingston, James 1879, *The Australian abroad: branches from the main routes round the world*, Sampson Low, Marston, Searle & Rivingston, London.

Hirakawa, Sukehiro 1984, *Soseki no Shi, Murdoch Sensei* [*Professor Murdoch, the mentor to Soseki*], Kodansha, Tokyo.

Hooker, John 1984, *The bush soldiers*, Collins, Sydney.

Hooton, Joy and Harry Heseltine 1992, *Annals of Australian literature*, Oxford University Press, Melbourne.

Hornadge, Bill 1976, *The yellow peril: a squint at some Australian attitudes towards Orientals*, second edition, Review Publications, Dubbo.

Horne, Donald 1998, *The lucky country*, fifth edition, Penguin Books, Ringwood.

Hosking, Rick 1985, 'The usable past: Australian war fiction of the 1950's', *Australian Literary Studies* 12(2).

Hughes, Kent WS 1946, *Slaves of the Samurai*, Ramsay Ware, Melbourne.

Huie, Shirley Fenton 1992, *The forgotten ones: women and children under Nippon*, Collins/Angus & Robertson, Pymble.

Hungerford, Thomas Arthur Guy, 1950, 'Last entry in red,' *The Bulletin*.

—— 1954, *Sowers of the wind: a novel of the Occupation of Japan*, Angus & Robertson, Sydney.

—— 1971 [1952], *The ridge and the river*, Pacific Books, Sydney.

—— 1985, *A knockabout with a slouch hat*, Fremantle Arts Centre Press, Fremantle.

—— 1989, *Hungerford: short fiction by TAG Hungerford*, selected and introduced by Peter Cowan, Fremantle Arts Centre Press, Fremantle.

Hutchinson, Garrie 1999, 'Travelling to war: three war graves', *Meanjin* 1.

Idriess, Ion L 1937, *Forty fathoms deep*, Angus & Robertson, Sydney.

Inglis, C et al (eds) 1992, *Asians in Australia: the dynamics of migration and settlement*, Institute of Southeast Asian Studies and Allen & Unwin, St Leonards.

Inoue, Eimei 1999, 'Suematsu Kencho in Lodnon', abstracts of papers of the 44th International Conference of Eastern Studies.

Jacobs, Lyn and Rick Hosking (eds) 1996, *A bibliography of Australian literary responses to Asia*, Flinders University Library, Bedford Park.

Jakbowicz, Andrew 1994, *Racism, ethnicity and the media*, Allen & Unwin, St Leonards.

James, Clive 1992, *Brrm! Brrm!*, Picador, Chippendale.

Jeffrey, Betty 1954, *White coolies: a graphic account of Australian nurses held captive during World War Two*, Angus & Robertson, Sydney.

Johnson, Chalmers 1996, *Japan: who governs? The rise of the developmental state*, WW Norton and Company, New York.

Johnson, Sheila 1975, *American attitudes toward Japan, 1945–1975*, AEI Policy Studies, Stanford University, Stanford.

Johnston, George 1943, *New Guinea diary*, Angus & Robertson, Sydney.

—— 1964, *My brother Jack*, Collins, London and Sydney.

Johnston, Grahame (ed) 1962, *Australian literary criticism*, Oxford University Press, Melbourne.

Johnston, Mark 2000, *Fighting the enemy: Australian soldiers and their adversaries in World War II*, Cambridge University Press, Cambridge.

—— 2004 'Yet they're human just as we are' in Steven Bullard and Keiko Tamura (eds), *From a Hostile Shore*, Australian War Memorial, Canberra.

Jones D and Andrews B , 1988 'Australian Humour', in Laurie Hergenhan, et al (eds), *The Penguin New Literary History of Australia*, Penguin Books, Ringwood.

Jones, Evan 1969, *Kenneth Mackenzie*, Oxford University Press, Melbourne.

Jose, Nicholas 1995, *Chinese whispers: cultural essays*, Wakefield Press, Kent Town.

Kata, Elizabeth 1962, *Someone will conquer them*, Michael Joseph, London.

—— 1981, *With kisses on both cheeks*, Child & Henry and Western Plains, Hornsby.

—— 1989, *Kagami: a novel*, Pan Books, Sydney.

Keene, Daniel 1987, *Cho Cho San*, Currency Press, Sydney.

Kelen, Stephen 1965, *Goshu*, Horwitz, Sydney.

—— 1983, *I remember Hiroshima*, Hale & Iremonger, Sydney.

Kelly, Clara Olink 2002, *The flamboya tree*, Random House, Milsons Point.

Keneally, Thomas 1965, *The fear*, Cassell, Melbourne. Revised edition published by Horwitz Grahame Books, Melbourne, 1980. Condensed version published as *By the line*, University of Queensland Press, St Lucia.

Kerr, Alex 1996, *Lost Japan*, Lonely Planet, Hawthorn. Originally published as *Utsukushiki Nippon no Zanzo*, Shinchosha, Tokyo, 1993.

Kiernan, Ben (ed) 1986, *Burchett reporting the other side of the world 1939–1983*, Quartet Books, London.

Kim, Don'o 1974, *Password: a political intrigue*, Angus & Robertson, Sydney.

—— 1984, *The Chinaman*, Hale and Iremonger, Sydney.

Kirmess, CH 1908–09, 'The Commonwealth crisis' in *The Lone Hand*, Lothian, Melbourne. Also published as *The Australian crisis*, George Robertson, Melbourne, 1909.

Knightley, Phillip 1986 'Cracking the Jap: Burchett on World War Two', in Kiernan Ben (ed) *Burchett Reporting the Other Side of the World 1939–1983*, Quartet Books, London.

Krauth, Nigel 1983, 'The Australian soldier's experience of the New Guinea jungle war in fiction', *New Literature Review* 12.

Lambert, Eric 1952, review of Peter Pinney's *Road in the wilderness* and TAG Hungerford's *The ridge and the river*, *Meanjin* 11(4).

—— 1953, 'Back from Gangaya' in Murray-Smith S (ed), *The tracks we travel: Australian short stories*, Australasian Book Society, Melbourne.

—— 1954, *The veterans*, Shakespeare Head, London.

—— 1958, *The dark backward*, Shakespeare Head Press, London.

—— 1965, *MacDougal's farm*, Frederick Muller, London.

—— 1967, *Hiroshima Reef*, Frederick Muller, London.

Lane, John 1987, *Summer will come again*, Fremantle Arts Centre Press, Fremantle.

Lane, William (as 'John Miller') 1948 [1892], *The workingman's paradise: an Australian labour novel*, Pinnacle Press, Sydney.

Levis, Ken 1950, 'The role of the *Bulletin* in indigenous short-story writing during the eighties and nineties', *Southerly* 11(4).

Lockwood, Douglas 1966, *Australia's Pearl Harbour: Darwin 1942*, Cassell, Melbourne.

Long, Gavin 1963, *The final campaign*, from *Australia in the war of 1939–1945*, Series 1 (Army) Australian War Memorial, Canberra.

—— 1973, *The six years war: a concise history of Australia in the 1939–45 war*, Australian War Memorial, Sydney.

Longley, Kateryna and Sneja Gunew (eds) 1992, *Striking chords*, Allen & Unwin, North Sydney.

Lord, Mary 1993, *Hal Porter: man of many parts*, Random House Australia, Milsons Point.

Lumiere, Cornel 1966, *Kura!*, Jacaranda, Brisbane.

Lynch, John 1995, *The proposal*, Wedgewing Books, Woden.

Mackay, Colonel Kenneth 1908, *Songs of a sunlit land*, Angus & Robertson, Sydney.

Mackenzie, Kenneth Seaforth 1951, *Dead men rising*, Jonathan Cape, London. First published in Australia by Angus & Robertson, Sydney 1969.

Mailer, Norman 1948, *The naked and the dead*, Rinehart & Company, New York.

Malcolm Janet 1999, in Kevin Foster's *Fighting Fictions: War, Narrative and National Identity*, Pluto Press, London.

Malouf, David 1991, *The great world*, Pan Macmillan edition, Sydney.

—— 1999, seminar, the Word Festival, Canberra, 19–22 March.

Manassen Mori, Charlotte 1994, *Sayonara my friend: love Annie*, Hill of Content, Melbourne.

Manners, Norman G 2000, *Bullwinkel: the true story of Vivian Bullwinkel, a young army nursing sister who was the sole survivor of a World War Two massacre by the Japanese*, revised edition, Hesperian Press, Carlisle.

Marks, E George 1933, *Pacific peril: menace of Japan's mandated islands*, Wynyard Book Arcade, Sydney.

Maximizing Australia's Asia Knowledge, 2002, a report by the Asian Studies Association of Australia, Inc (35).

McCabe, Graeme 1946, *Pacific sunset*, Oldham, Beddome & Meredith, Hobart.

McCarthy, John (ed) 1992, *Australia and the threat of Japan 1919–1945*, Australian Defence Studies Centre, Canberra.

McCooey, David 1996, *Artful histories: modern Australian autobiography*, Cambridge University Press, Cambridge.

McCormack, Gavan 1996, *The emptiness of Japanese affluence*, ME Sharpe, New York and Allen & Unwin, St Leonards.

McCormack, Gavan and Hank Nelson (eds), *The Burma–Thailand railway: memory and history*, Allen & Unwin, St Leonards.

McCormack, Gavan and Yoshio Sugimoto (eds) 1988, *The Japanese trajectory: modernization and beyond*, Cambridge University Press, Cambridge.

McCrae, Hugh 1930, 'The red page', the *Bulletin*, 20 August.

McDougall, Russell, 1980, *South of Capricornia: Short Stories 1925–1934 by Xavier Herbert*, Oxford University Press, Melbourne.

McGregor, Craig 1997, *Class in Australia*, Penguin Books, Ringwood.

McGregor, John 1980, *Blood on the Rising Sun*, Bencoolen, Sydney.

McGregor, Richard 1996, *Japan swings: politics, culture and sex in the new Japan*, Allen & Unwin, St Leonards.

McKernan, Michael 2001, *This war never ends: the pain of separation and return*, University of Queensland Press, St Lucia.

McQueen, Humphrey 1991a, *Japan to the rescue: Australian security around the Indonesian archipelago during the American century*, William Heinemann Australia, Port Melbourne.

—— 1991b, *Tokyo world: an Australian diary*, Heinemann, Port Melbourne.

Mead, Philip 1995, 'Cultural pathology: what Ern Malley means', *Australian Literary Studies* 17(1).

Meaney, Neville 1996a, *Fears and phobias: EL Piesse and the problem of Japan 1909–39*, National Library of Australia, Canberra.

—— 1996b, 'The yellow peril, invasion, scare novels and Australian political culture' in Stewart, Kenneth (ed), *The 1890's*, University of Queensland Press, St Lucia.

—— 1999, *Towards a new vision: Australia and Japan through 100 years*, Kangaroo Press, East Roseville

—— (ed) 1989, *Under new heavens: cultural transmission and the making of Australia*, Heinemann Educational Australia, Port Melbourne.

Meaney, Neville, Trevor Matthews and Sol Encel (eds) 1988, *The Japanese connection: survey of Australian leaders' attitudes towards Japan and the Australia–Japan relationship*, Longman Cheshire, Melbourne.

Menadue, Cynthia 1985, *Shadows on the Shoji: a personal view of Japan*, John Ferguson, Sydney. Originally published in Japanese with the English title *Ambassador's wife—Minshuku tour*, Simul Press, Tokyo.

Menikoff, Barry 1988, 'Color and culture in the short stories of Carlton Dawe', *La Nouvelle de Langue Anglaise, the short story: Rencontres Internationals*, Publication de la Sorbonne Nouvelle, Paris.

Mitchell, GD 1937, *The awakening*, Angus & Robertson, Sydney.

Mitchell, Jim (ed) 1995, *The moon seems upside down: letters of love and war: letters of Arthur Alan Mitchell 1939–45*, Allen & Unwin, St Leonards.

—— (ed) 1990, *The Burma–Thailand railway 1942–1945*, Penguin, Ringwood.

Modjeska, Drusilla 1990, 'Introduction' in Prichard, Katharine Susannah, *Coonardo*, Collins, North Ryde.

Montgomery, Hilda B 1908, *The empire of the East*, Methuen & Co, London.

Morris-Suzuki, Tessa 1998, *Re-inventing Japan: time, space, nation*, ME Sharp, Armonk and London.

Mouer, Ross and Yoshio Sugimoto 1986, *Images of Japanese society: a study in the structure of social reality*, KPI, London.

Murdoch, James 1890, *Don Juan's grandson in Japan, with notes for the globe-trotter's benefit*, Hakubunsha, Tokyo.

—— 1892a, *Ayame-San: a Japanese romance of the 23rd year of Meiji*, Kelly & Walsh, Yokohama

—— 1892b, *Tales of Australia and Japan*, EW Cole, Melbourne, also published as *From Australia and Japan*, Walter Scott, London.

—— 1910, *A history of Japan*, volume 1, Kegan Paul, Yokohama and London.

—— 1913, *A history of Japan*, volume 2, Kegan Paul, Yokohama and London.

—— 1919, *Australia must prepare: Japan, China, India: a comparison and some contrasts: an inaugural lecture delivered in the Union Hall on December 3, 1919*, Angus & Robertson, Sydney.

—— 1926, *A history of Japan*, volume 3, Kegan Paul, Yokohama and London.

Myers, David 1991, *Cornucopia country: satiric tales*, University of Central Queensland Publications, Rockhampton.

—— 1996, *Storms in a Japanese teacup: satiric tales*, Central Queensland University Press, Rockhampton.

Myers, David and Kotaku Ishido (eds) 1995, *Japanese society today: perspectives on tradition and change*, Central Queensland University Press, Rockhampton.

Nagase, Takashi 1990 'Epilogue' from *Cowra Nippon Gun Horyo Shuyojo* (Cowra Japanese Prisoners of War Camp) Aoki-Shoten, Tokyo.

Nagata, Yuriko 1996, *Unwanted aliens: Japanese internment in Australia*, University of Queensland Press, St Lucia.

Nairn, B and G Serle (eds), 1966 *Australian dictionary of biography volume 7: 1891–1939*, Melbourne University Press, Carlton.

Nakano, Ann 1985, *Bit parts*, Rigby, Adelaide.

Nelson, Hank 1985, *Prisoners of war: Australians under Nippon*, Australian Broadcasting Corporation, Sydney.

—— 1995, *Nihongun Horyo Shuyjo no Hibi: Osutoraria Heishitachi no Shogen* [*Prisoners of War—Australians under Nippon*], Cholikuma Shobo, Tokyo.

Nile, Richard (ed) 1994, *Australian civilisation*, Oxford University Press, Melbourne.

O'Conroy, T 1934, *The menace of Japan*, Hurst and Blackett, London.

Oe, Kenzaburo 1995, *Japan, the ambiguous, and myself: the Nobel Prize speech and other lectures*, Kodansha International, Tokyo.

Oliver, Pam 2004, *Allies, enemies and trading partners: records on Australia and the Japanese*, National Archives of Australia, Canberra.

Ono, 1997, *Pygmalion complex: genealogy of Pretty Woman*, originally published in Japanese as *Pygmalion complex: Pretty Woman no Keifu*, Arina Shobo, Tokyo.

Ooka, Shohei 1967, *Fires on the plain*, Charles E Tuttle Company, Tokyo.

Ouyang, Yu 1994, 'Representing the Other: the Chinese in Australian fiction 1888–1988', PhD thesis, La Trobe University.

—— 1995a, 'Australian invention of Chinese invasion: a century of paranoia, 1888–1988', *Australian Literary Studies* 17(1).

—— 1995b, 'The Chinese in the *Bulletin*'s eyes, 1888–1901', *Southerly* 55(2).

Parkin, Ray 1960, *Out of the smoke*, Angus & Robertson, Sydney and The Hogarth Press, London.

—— 1993 [1963], *Into the smother*, Penguin Books, Ringwood.

—— 1968, *The sword and the blossom*, Hogarth, London.

Paterson, AB 1902, 'The pearl diver', *Rio Grande's last race and other verses*, Angus & Robertson, London.

Pesman, Ros 1996, *Duty free :Australian women abroad*, Oxford University Press, Melbourne.

Pierce, Peter 1985, 'Perceptions of the enemy in Australian war literature', *Australian Literary Studies* 12(2).

—— 1995, *Australian melodramas: Thomas Keneally's fiction*, University of Queensland Press, St Lucia.

—— 1996, '*Is war very big? As big as New South Wales?*', Barry Andrews Lecture, School of English, University College, University of New South Wales, Canberra.

Poidvin, Leslie 1985, *Samurais and circumcisions*, self-published, Adelaide.

Poole, Philippa 1983, *Of love and war: the letter and diaries of Captain Adrian Curlewis and his family 1939–1945*, Century Publishing, London.

Porter Hal 1958, *A handful of pennies*, Angus & Robertson, Sydney.

—— 1962, 'House-girl', *A bachelor's children: short stories by Hal Porter*, Angus & Robertson, Sydney.

—— 1968, *The actors: an image of the new Japan*, Angus & Robertson, Sydney.

—— 1970, *Mr Butterfry and other tales of new Japan*, Angus & Robertson, Sydney.

—— 1971, 'A double because it's snowing', *Hal Porter: selected stories*, Angus & Robertson, Sydney.

Praed, Rosa 1899, *Madame Izàn: a tourist story*, D Appleton, New York.

Pratt, Ambrose 1907–08, 'The big five', *The Lone Hand*, 2 December 1907, 1 January 1908, 1 February 1908, 2 March 1908, 1 April 1908, 1 May 1908), 1 June 1908, 1 July 1908, 1 August 1908, 1 September 1908.

Prichard, Katharine Susannah 1941, *Moon of desire*, Jonathan Cape, London.

Probert, Sherriff and John Probert 2001, *Prisoner of two wars: an Australian soldier's story*, Wakefield Press, Kent Town.

Pulvers, Roger 1981a, *The death of Urashima Taro*, Angus & Robertson. Japanese translation, *Urashima Taro no Shi*, Shinchosha, Tokyo1981.

—— 1981b, *Yamashita*, Currency Press, Sydney.

—— 1994, *General Yamashita's treasure*, Angus & Robertson, Sydney. Originally published as *Three goals to Nhill*, Chikuma Shobo, Tokyo.

Radic, Thérèse 1992, *The Emperor regrets*, Currency Press, Sydney.

Reeson, Margaret 1993, *Whereabouts unknown*, Albatross Books, Sutherland.

Rivett, Rohan 1946, *Behind bamboo: an inside story*, Angus & Robertson, Sydney.

Robbins, Jane 2001, *Tokyo calling: Japanese overseas radio broadcasting 1937–1945*, European Press Academic Publishing, Firenze.

Romeril, John 1994 [1975], *The floating world*, Currency Press, Paddington.

—— 1997, *Love suicides*, Currency Press, Paddington.

Ronan, Tom 1958, *The pearling master*, Cassell, London.

Rutherford, Anna (ed) 1992, *From Commonwealth to post-colonial*, Dangaroo Press, Sydney.

Rutherford, Anna and James Wieland (eds) 1997, *War: Australia's creative response*, Allen & Unwin, St Leonards.

Ryan, Peter 1959, *Fear drive my feet*, Angus & Robertson, Sydney.

Sadler, AL 1935, 'The influence of Japanese culture and tradition on her foreign relations', in Clunies Ross, I (ed), *Australia and the Far East: diplomatic and trade relations*, Angus & Robertson, Sydney.

Said, Edward 1985 [1978], *Orientalism*, Routledge & Kegan Paul, London.

—— 1993, *Culture and imperialism*, Chatto and Windus Ltd, London.

Schaper Michael 1995, 'The Broome Race Riots of 1920', in Jan Gothard (ed), *Asian Orientations*, University of Western Australia, Nedlands.

Scott, Kim 1999, seminar, the Word Festival, Canberra, 19–22 March.

Seal, Graham 1990, *Traditions of prejudice: a report on the folklore of race and ethnicity in Australia*, Centre for Australian Studies, Curtin University of Technology, Perth.

Sekine, Masami 2006, 'Nichigo Koryu no 2.2 Seiki', *Wochi Kochi*, Japan Foundation and Yamakawa Shuppannsha, Tokyo.

Shaw, Caroline 1999, *Cat catcher*, Bantam Books, Sydney.

—— 2000, *Eye to eye*, Bantam Books, Sydney.

Sheridan, Greg (ed) 1995, *Living with dragons: Australia confronts its Asian destiny*, Allen & Unwin, St Leonards.

Shute, Nevil 1956, *A town like Alice*, The Book Club, London.

Silver, Lynette Ramsay 1998, *Sandakan: a conspiracy of silence*, second edition, Sally Milner Publishing, Burra Creek.

Sladen, Douglas BW 1892, *The Japs at home*, Collins, London.

—— 1904, *A Japanese marriage*, Anthony Treherne & Co, London.

—— 1939, *My long life: anecdotes and adventures*, Hitchinson, London.

Souter, Gavin 1989 [1972], *The idle hill of summer: an Australian childhood 1939–1945*, William Collins, Sydney.

Spender, Sir Percy 1969, *Exercises of diplomacy: the ANZUS Treaty and the Colombo Plan*, Sydney University Press, Sydney.

Spivak, Gayatri 1995, 'Three women's texts and a critique of imperialism' in Ashcroft, Bill, Gareth Griffiths, Helen Tiffin (eds), *The post-colonial studies reader*, Roudledge, London.

Statler, Oliver 1961, *Japanese Inn*, Secker & Warburg, London.

—— 1986 [1969], *Shimoda Story*, University of Hawaii Press, Honolulu.

—— 1983, *Japanese pilgrimage*, William Morrow and Company, New York.

Stephens, AG 1895, the *Bulletin*, 29 August.

Stewart, Harold 1960, *Net of fireflies: Japanese haiku and haiku paintings with verse translations and an essay*, Charles E Tuttle, Rutland.

—— 1969, *Chime of windbells: a year of Japanese haiku in English verse*, Paul Flesch & Company, Melbourne and Sydney.

—— 1981, *By the old wall of Kyoto: a year's cycle of landscape poems with prose commentaries*, Weatherhill, New York.

—— 1987, 'Harold Stewart: interviewed by Richard Kelly Tipping', *Westerly* 4.

Stewart, Ken (ed) 1996, *The 1890s: Australian literature and literary culture*, University Queensland Press, St Lucia.

Stow, Randolph 1984 [1965], *The merry-go-round in the sea*, Secker & Warburg, London.

Summons, Walter Irvine 1946, *Twice their prisoner*, Oxford University Press, Melbourne.

Tacey, David 1995, *Edge of the sacred: transformation of Australia*, Harper Collins, North Melbourne.

Tamura, Keiko 2001, *Michi's memories: the story of a Japanese war bride*, Research School of Pacific and Asian Studies, Australian National University, Canberra.

Tanaka, Yuki 1995, *Rape and war: the Japanese Experience*, Monash Asia Institute, Clayton.

—— 1996, *Hidden horrors: war crimes in World War II*, Westview Press, Colorado and London. First published as *Shirarezaru Senso Hanzai* [*Unknown war crimes: what Japanese forces did to Australians*], Japan, 1993.

Tolstoy, Leo 1961 [1904], 'Bethink yourselves!: concerning the Russo–Japanese War', *Recollections and essays*, translated and introduced by Aylmer Maude, Oxford University Press, London.

Turner, Graeme 1998, 'Film, Television and Literature', in Bruce Bennett & Jennifer Strauss (eds), *The Oxford Literary History of Australia*, Oxford University Press, Melbourne 1998).

Vader, John 1971, *Battle of Sydney*, New English Library, London.

Walker, David 1988, 'Invasion literature: the yellow wave: moulding the popular imagination', *Asian influence on Australian literature*, symposium proceedings, Library Society, State Library of New South Wales.

—— 1999, *Anxious nation: Australia and the rise of Asia 1850–1939*, University of Queensland Press, St Lucia.

Wallace-Crabbe, Chris and Peter Pierce (eds) 1994, *Clubbing of the gunfire: 101 Australian war poems*, Melbourne University Press, Carlton.

Webby, Elizabeth 1990, *Modern Australian plays*, revised edition, Cambridge University Press, Cambridge.

—— (ed) 2000, *The Cambridge companion to Australian literature*, Cambridge University Press, Cambridge.

West, Morris 1965, *The ambassador*, Heinemann, London.

White, Richard 1987, *Inventing Australia: images and identity 1688–1980*, George Allen & Unwin, Sydney.

Whitecross, Roy H 1951, *Slaves of the son of Heaven*, Dymocks, Sydney.

Whitworth, Robert P 1880, *Massina's popular guide to the Melbourne International Exhibition of 1880–1*, revised edition, AH Massina and Co, Melbourne.

Wilde, W, J Hooton and B Andrews (eds) 1994, *The Oxford companion to Australian literature*, second edition, Oxford University Press, South Melbourne.

Williams, Bernard 1993, *Ethics and the limits of philosophy*, third edition, Fontana Press, London.

Williams, Brian A 1990, *Blood oath*, Angus & Robertson, Sydney.

Williams, Raymond 1959, *Culture and society 1780–1950*, Chatto & Windus, London.

—— 1961, *The long revolution*, Chatto & Windus, London.

Willis, Ted 1980, *The naked sun*, Macmillan, London.

Wilson, Helen Helga 1970, 'A field of wheat', *A show of colours: a selection of prize-winning stories*, London Publishing Company, Perth.

Wood, J 1998, *The forgotten force: the British Commonwealth Occupation Force*, Allen & Unwin, St Leonards.

Yarwood, AT (ed) 1968, *Attitudes to non-European immigration*, Cassell, Melbourne.

Zach, Wolfgang and Heinz Kosok (eds) 1987, *Literary interrelations: Ireland, England and the world*, Gunter Narr Verlag Tubingen, Tubingen.